CREATING THE VIRTUAL STORE

Taking Your Web Site from Browsing to Buying

MAGDALENA YEŞIL

WILEY COMPUTER PUBLISHING

John Wiley & Sons, Inc.

New York ♦ Chichester ♦ Brisbane ♦ Toronto ♦ Singapore ♦ Weinheim

6 -17-99

*I dedicate this book to my husband Jim Wickett, who runs
the hosting service I have chosen for my heart.*

Executive Publisher: Katherine Schowalter
Senior Editor: Robert M. Elliott
Managing Editor: Angela Murphy
Text Design & Composition: North Market Street Graphics

Library of Congress Cataloging-in-Publication Data:
  Yesil, Magdalena.
      Creating the virtual store : taking your web site from browsing to
  buying / Magdalena Yesil.
          p.   cm.
      ISBN 0-471-16494-1 (pbk. : alk. paper)
      1. Retail trade—Computer networks.   2. World Wide Web
  (Information retrieval system).   3. Retail trade surveys—United
  States.   4. Consumer behavior—United States.   5. Internet
  marketing.   6. Teleshopping.   I. Title.
  HF5429.Y47   1996
  381'.1'0285467—dc20
                                                        96-32926

Printed in the United States of America
10 9 8 7 6 5 4 3 2 1

CONTENTS

Chapter 3   Designing the Shopping Experience   71

Chapter 6 Accepting Virtual Payments: Selecting Methods That Are Right For You   161

Chapter 7 Understanding Virtual Legality   195

Chapter 8 Preparing for the Future   221

PREFACE

Welcome to the virtual store! This preface tells you why this book was written and how to get the most out of it.

> **Topics presented in the preface:**
>
> ◆ Why I Wrote This Book
> ◆ Purpose of This Book
> ◆ Who Should Read This Book
> ◆ How to Read This Book

Why I Wrote This Book: Putting the Virtual Gold Rush in Perspective

I like frontiers. When I came to Stanford University for college, I fell in love with the West, which still had some of the spirit of the Gold Rush days. I discovered computers during my sophomore year. I knew from the start that computers would be the new frontier, the next Gold Rush. When I graduated in 1980, I became part of Silicon Valley and the PC revolution. I was responsible for getting local area networking chip sets designed into computers before anyone had really heard of the concept. The Ethernet was very successful and I learned the joys and rewards of taking part in the establishment of a frontier. Later, I joined the very first Unix desktop computer company, where I learned about the pains of living at the frontier, when computer dealers could not support such sophisticated operating systems, and our computers sat unsold on dealers' shelves. Then I dabbled in the multimedia, the interactive TV, and the Internet frontiers, and now I am part of a new frontier called *elec-*

tronic commerce, which promises to be the most exciting and also the most challenging.

During the 1849 Gold Rush, the key to ultimate gain was finding the gold veins. A lot of people who came to California during that period died poor. So being part of a frontier is not enough—the key to success is to figure out where the money will be made.

Although the Internet has existed in some form since the late 1970s, it was funded by the government through the National Science Foundation (NSF) and dedicated to research, education, and government endeavors. Thus, there is a lot of confusion about what can be done on the Internet and with on-line services today. Electronic commerce is still evolving, and, despite the hype about capitalizing on the mass market represented by 40 million potential customers on the Internet, many of those who thought they could cash in on this virtual gold rush have already been disappointed.

Just a few years ago, Appropriate Use Policy (AUP) rules made it illegal to use the Net for any commercial activity, including sending E-mail about the business aspects of research projects. But human nature took over and within the past three years channels have been created to conduct business over the Internet. In addition, the World Wide Web and Mosaic browser technology made the Internet a lot more usable and attractive, with graphics, pictures, photos, sound, and even video. Having a home page went from being cool to being essential, and top executives of the Fortune 500 had to print E-mail addresses on their business cards to stay current.

In the past three years, Internet companies have raised $1.2 billion from private and public sources. In 1996, financial deals reached way over ½ billion in the 1st quarter of the year. Overall, investors will have poured more than $2.1 billion into cyberspace companies in 67 separate financial deals as of mid-1996. Most of the financial activity has centered around software (34 percent), Internet service providers and on-line services (25 percent), as well as enabling services such as directories (21 percent), and content and activity (11 percent).*

This flurry of cyberactivity has made many feel anxious, like the easterners who were left behind in the 1849 Gold Rush that made the West.

---

* SOURCE: CyberAtlas Market Research.

As I travel the country, I am barraged by a single question: How do I cash in on this virtual world?

The Purpose of This Book

A lot of people today think that just because there are 40 million people on the Internet and because they have created a Web site, they will be able to sell things to those 40 million people and find prosperity. Nothing could be further from the truth. Having a Web site or a store on an on-line service is by no means synonymous with generating revenues in the virtual world. It is more realistic to think of Internet access as functioning like the telephone network—having a Web site is like having a phone number with a message machine on it. Just because there are millions of others connected to the same telephone network does not mean they all will call you; at the very least they will need to first find out your phone number. And even if they know your number, they will not call you unless they have a specific reason to do so. Finally, *just because they call you does not mean that you'll be able to sell them things and make a lot of money.*

The Internet has been characterized by many as the zero-billion-dollar business. Today, the market capitalization of the pure Internet companies is over $10 billion, ignoring the fact that the cumulative revenue of these companies is under $200 million. These high numbers have resulted in unrealistic expectations on the part of those who are new to the Internet and the on-line services. The purpose of this book is to help readers assess their business goals and the possibility of achieving them in the virtual world, to explain some easily misunderstood principles regarding the Internet, and to give readers a road map for successfully creating a virtual store.

Some of the most common myths that I hope to eliminate are listed here. (The chapters in which they are discussed are shown in parentheses.)

> *Myth 1.* With 40 million plus people, the Internet represents a mass consumer market today and will do so to an even greater extent tomorrow (Chapter 4, "Getting to Know Your Virtual Customers").

Myth 2.   As the Internet becomes the leveling field for marketing, brand names will no longer matter (Chapter 3, "Designing the Shopping Experience").

Myth 3.   The most important thing for electronic commerce is creating a high-traffic site (Chapter 3, "Designing the Shopping Experience").

Myth 4.   The Internet is the best advertising medium to come along since television (Chapter 5, "Advertising and Promoting Your Virtual Store").

Myth 5.   You should never ask for personal information on the Internet, or else you run the risk of being publicly chastised and flamed (Chapter 4, "Getting to Know Your Virtual Customers").

Myth 6.   You can create a virtual store overnight by running your catalog pages through a scanning device and putting them on the Internet (Chapter 3, "Designing the Shopping Experience").

Myth 7.   The Internet is a natural shopping environment, and eventually brick-and-mortar stores and malls will be replaced by virtual stores (Chapter 3, "Designing the Shopping Experience").

Myth 8.   You should have a virtual store only if your business customers come from a large geographic area (Chapter 3, "Designing the Shopping Experience").

Myth 9.   The most successful businesses in the virtual world will be large corporations (Chapter 5, "Advertising and Promoting Your Virtual Store").

Myth 10.   Your first objective in creating a virtual store is to build a community around it (Chapter 3, "Designing the Shopping Experience").

Myth 11.   You can have a million-dollar business on the Internet within the first year of operation (Chapter 2, "Planning the Virtual Store").

Myth 12.   You cannot establish trust in a virtual environment in which you cannot see and touch things (Chapter 3, "Designing the Shopping Experience").

Myth 13.   Laws that govern the real world do not apply to the virtual world (Chapter 7, "Understanding Virtual Legality").

and the biggest myth of all:

> *Myth 14.* The Internet is all hype, electronic commerce is a fad—it will all blow over like interactive TV did and the Internet will go the way of 500 television channels (Chapter 8, "Preparing for the Future").

Even though the Internet is a developing frontier, there are distinct earmarks of success in this virtual world. This book will take you behind the scenes at some of the virtual stores that have been successful. It will walk you, chapter by chapter, through the factors that make for success and help you establish a virtual store that could be used as a success story in subsequent printings of this book.

The purpose of this book is not to help readers understand how to connect to the Internet or to on-line services; it is not meant as a tutorial on the Internet or the World Wide Web, nor does it explain how to set up a Web site. These mechanics can be found in the multitude of books dedicated to such topics. This book focuses on the business issues of the virtual store, which include assessing its appropriateness for your business, setting realistic goals, understanding how to design an effective on-line shopping experience, developing relationships with your virtual customers, understanding the role of advertising and promotions in the virtual world, accepting payments over the Internet, and doing business internationally.

Who Should Read This Book

Anyone who is looking at the Internet as a business opportunity should read this book. That includes all corporate managers of large and medium-sized companies, business owners, and general managers of small to medium-sized companies. In addition, everyone who is involved with the Internet and on-line services would benefit from reading this book. It is written in layperson's terms and does not assume significant knowledge about the Internet—just some general exposure to and an understanding of what a Web site is, as well as some basic knowledge of computers.

This book is written for business people who view the Internet as a potential distribution channel for their goods or services, a place where they can generate new customers or significantly reduce their costs of doing business by taking advantage of the new virtual world. This book assumes that readers either have current Internet Web sites that are not commercial in nature or are reading other basic books on how to set up Web sites, and so do not need instruction in this area. This book is written to assist readers in establishing realistic goals for their virtual stores, guiding them through the specific steps needed to realize their goals.

Upon completing this book, readers will be able to analyze their businesses and decide what kinds of virtual stores make sense for them. They will then be able to design appropriate stores for their businesses, get to know their customers, create environments that fit the needs of these specific customers, market and promote their stores appropriately, accept payment on-line, and be ready to deal with the associated legal issues.

To date, most Internet sites have been collections of corporate and product literature, technical manuals, and a first stop for customer service and support. Though well suited for these functions, the Internet and, specifically, the World Wide Web environment hold great potential for generating revenue. Less than 10 percent of Internet sites today accept orders. This book intends to motivate the other 90 percent to take their sites commercial and aid them in the process, which is a lot more complex than meets the eye.

Creating the Virtual Store is a highly practical book. Even though subjects may be presented first at a theoretical level, each chapter goes on to explain how to successfully implement the theories. It is written in a conversational tone, utilizing real-life examples of merchants with whom readers are probably familiar and sharing with them the elements of success that these virtual stores have utilized.

The biggest benefit of this book will be to give readers a road map for getting the greatest advantage from their virtual stores. This is done by helping readers evaluate their own businesses and design the Internet commerce environments most suitable for them. It also identifies the common pitfalls in this process and shows readers ways around them.

This book is also appropriate for Webmasters in corporate America who either are operating Web sites today or are tasked with the job. Even though most of these individuals look at their responsibilities as technical, such as creating the HTML pages or the Java applications, the success of a site is seldom dependent on these technical issues. Webmasters will develop a strong sense of the business issues that differentiate successful sites from those that fail.

The Internet is, by definition, an international environment; therefore, this book is written with an international audience in mind. Regardless of whether you are located in Palo Alto, California, or Nice, France, the requirements for success in the virtual world are similar, except for certain banking and regulatory issues. Users of on-line services and the Internet are amazingly homogeneous, though they come to this medium from over 100 countries. In writing this book, I conducted interviews with users from North America, Europe, and Asia. The book also has a section on export laws, international money movement, and currency handling.

Anyone who is considering making money on the Internet selling goods, information, and services will benefit from reading this book.

How to Read This Book

If this is the first book you've consulted on doing business on the Internet, then you should read it from cover to cover. On the other hand, if you are looking for specific information on a topic, such as the Internet shopping experience or how to become a payment-accepting merchant on the Internet, then feel free to go directly to the appropriate chapter. Each chapter carries a packet of information and can stand on its own.

Essentially, there are five keys to making a virtual store successful:

1. Setting the right goals for your store
2. Understanding the shopping experience and creating an appropriate one on-line in which to offer your products and services
3. Getting to know your customers, thereby generating repeat business and adapting your store in response to their feedback
4. Advertising and promoting your store in the right venues, which leads to generating increased sales
5. Accepting payments in the virtual store

All this must be accomplished while maneuvering through the legal realities of the virtual world. This book dedicates a chapter to each of these topics.

Chapter 1: Introducing the Virtual Store

This chapter makes a case for electronic commerce by presenting findings from market research companies on current and future revenue that will be derived from electronic commerce on the Internet. It introduces the concept of the virtual store and the virtual customer and surveys the current demographics of the Internet.

This chapter discusses three types of virtual stores: those selling hard goods, information goods, and services. It provides profiles of several successful virtual stores of each type. The chapter concludes with a look at early pioneers of virtual stores and discusses some lessons we can learn from their experiences.

Chapter 2: Planning the Virtual Store

This chapter helps you, the virtual store owner, analyze the business you want to set up at your virtual store and evaluate the appropriateness of a virtual store for your specific case. It provides decision-making flowcharts to help you understand where the biggest potential for increased profitability lies for you in the virtual world. It walks you through the cost-reduction and revenue-generation opportunities that you will have through your virtual store. It also helps you develop realistic revenue goals if your desire is to sell on the Internet.

A series of road maps are provided for planning your virtual store. These will help you identify ways that you can use the Internet to increase profitability in a particular business. This chapter emphasizes the importance of following a sensible planning sequence in setting up your virtual store, and walks you through each major area step by step. Each decision diagram follows from the preceding one, so it is important that you read this chapter from start to finish instead of skipping around.

Chapter 3: Designing the Shopping Experience

This chapter stresses the development of trust as the basis for all commerce and discusses how you can create trust in the virtual world. It presents a detailed discussion on how and why people shop and categorizes the different shopping experiences and the appropriateness of each for the on-line environment. The intent is to help you understand what kind of shopping experience is appropriate for your virtual store and how you can create it.

The chapter also discusses how you can use your virtual store as a direct selling and infomercial site. It introduces the important topics of how to get shoppers to your store, some of the roadblocks to virtual shopping, and the presentation of the virtual invoice. The ultimate goal of this chapter is to help you turn browsers into shoppers on the Internet.

Chapter 4: Getting to Know Your Virtual Customers

This chapter tells you how to deliver better service by getting to know your customers on-line. It gives advice on learning more about your customers without upsetting the delicate balance of privacy. The chapter also introduces the different ways of tracking customer behavior and discusses in detail the subscription- and session-based tracking systems. It includes a glossary of terms.

Chapter 5: Advertising and Promoting Your Virtual Store

This chapter stresses what most virtual merchants forget: the need to advertise and promote their stores. According to market research conducted by several firms, this is the number one reason that on-line stores fail. It gives you an overview of the types of advertising and promotion that have worked on-line. You will find new and unusual ways to promote your store on the Internet, such as virtual couponing and using Usenet news groups to get the word out about your store.

But you can't do it all on-line. You will also get additional ideas for where and how to advertise your virtual store off-line. The chapter includes the advice of several advertising agencies that focus on on-line advertising as well as the perspectives of an on-line advertising placement company.

Chapter 6: Accepting Virtual Payments

What payment models exist on-line and are they safe? This chapter discusses the use of credit cards and electronic cash systems for on-line payment at the virtual store. It addresses the possibility of fraud and how to create a secure environment to foster your customers' trust. It also introduces, in layperson's terms, the concepts of encryption and public/private-key cryptography.

This chapter explains the recent VISA and MasterCard joint effort toward secure credit card capabilities on the Internet (Secure Electronic Transfer, or SET) and what it will mean to your business. This chapter also walks you through the process of becoming a merchant who accepts payments on-line. (Appendixes B–D supply more detailed information regarding specific virtual payment system providers.)

Chapter 7: Understanding Virtual Legality

This chapter discusses legal issues of which every virtual store owner needs to be aware to operate a store successfully. The Internet store is different from a physical store by virtue of the fact that it exists in an international environment from the first day it opens. Because of this, there is a lot of confusion regarding the laws and jurisdictions that bind it—some assume that the laws of the physical world don't apply in cyberspace. This confusion is further exaggerated by the fact that there is no single owner of the Internet. This chapter is intended to eliminate this assumption and give the store owner a thorough understanding of the legal structure.

In addition to the legal issues, this chapter discusses the social structure of the Internet, which is in great part how the Net governs itself. The chapter also discusses several key topics that will affect virtual store owners in the near future, although they may not be in full implementation today. Digital signatures, digital IDs, certificate authorities, and international currency conversion are important developments that soon will impact the virtual store owner.

Chapter 8: Preparing for the Future

What will the virtual store be like when it enters every home in the United States and many homes overseas? This chapter covers the evolution of the virtual store as technology moves forward over the next five to ten years—as the Internet becomes commonplace, as modems become faster, as people come to accept and trust the on-line shopping experience.

The first section of this chapter discusses the current state of technologies underlying the information superhighway and the status of interactive cable trials. It follows with a realistic discussion of these technologies and their impact on both the virtual store and the expectations of on-line customers. It also discusses the evolving business of the underlying industries, which include cable companies, Internet access suppliers, telephone companies, and the interexchange carriers (AT&T, MCI, Sprint) and their plans for the information superhighway.

Finally, there is a discussion of the social issues regarding the on-line environment and their implications for the virtual store owner, including topics such as parental guidance, rating of content, legislative limitations, and the social structure of the global village.

Each chapter contains boxed case studies of successful virtual stores. They illustrate the concepts described in the text and show how real people have put them to use.

Acknowledgments

This book would not have been possible without the work of many people, whom I would like to thank:

All those we interviewed and who gave so generously of their time and thoughts. This book would not have been possible without you.

All the market research firms and publications that contributed statistics, charts and figures, tables, and time lines. This book is much richer because of your contributions.

My editor, Bob Elliott, who sought me out of the crowd and approached me with the idea for this book. I am forever grateful to him for introducing me to the wonderful world of authorship.

My college friend, Leslie Lundquist, who reappeared in my life as my writing partner on this work. I am thankful to her for her creative insight, her ability to manage and organize complex tasks and her natural understanding of technology.

My trusted and always reliable assistant, Derek Gerrman, who worked numerous miracles during the writing of this book.

My friends, Deborah Claymon and Marc Fleishman, for their efforts and time.

There were several others in the background who had a great deal to do with my ability to write this book:

My father, Kevork Yesil, who gave me the taste for adventure and the gift of independence, which has enabled me to succeed as a pioneer in the rugged world of technology.

Dan Lynch, who invited me on his journey through the virtual world. I am forever grateful for his partnership and friendship.

My mother, Selma Yesil, who encouraged me to start writing at a very early age and has always provided stability in this turbulent world.

Chris Lynch, who saw the opportunity and pointed it out to me.

My son, Justin Wickett, for his incredible sense of adventure, who will keep pushing me to new frontiers, even when I am hesitant.

My son, Troy Wickett, who has an amazing aptitude for technology and, I know, someday will create new worlds for us to live in.

And finally, my husband, Jim Wickett, the real pioneer man, who is equally at home in the physical and virtual frontiers. His direction and ability to spot opportunities and pitfalls and survive have enabled me to navigate the turbulent waters of Silicon Valley start-ups. I also thank you for allowing me to spend endless nights and weekends writing this book.

CHAPTER ONE

INTRODUCING

THE VIRTUAL STORE

Putting up a Web site these days is like a tree falling in the forest.
—Steve Case, CEO of America Online

Topics presented in this chapter:

- The Case for On-line Commerce
- What Is a Virtual Store?
- Who Is the Virtual Customer?
- Different Types of Virtual Stores
- Early Pioneers

On-line commerce has arrived. This chapter presents evidence from a number of highly respected sources to show that the on-line market is real and growing. After you are convinced that this market is an exciting place to be, the chapter introduces you to the concept of the virtual store and gives you a portrait of a typical virtual store customer.

This chapter discusses three types of virtual stores: those selling hard goods, information goods, and services. It provides profiles of several successful virtual stores of each type. It also tells about some early pioneers of on-line shopping and the lessons many retailers have learned from their experiences.

After reading this chapter, you'll understand why almost every market analyst predicts a multi-billion-dollar on-line marketplace by the year 2000. You'll have some facts and figures at your fingertips from some well-respected market research firms to back up that viewpoint. Armed with an understanding of the virtual store and its customers, you will be ready to move on to Chapter 2, which walks you through the planning process.

The Case for On-line Commerce

On-line commerce is here to stay. Intuitively, many people feel that to be true; therefore, many market research firms have begun gathering information about this new medium. With clarity comes the courage to enter a new marketplace.

Currently, the actual commerce statistics are nominal. Reports indicate annual revenue figures somewhere between $140 million and $300 million. Most analysts project that electronic commerce may reach $3 billion to $7 billion by the year 2000, though bullish ones such as International Data Corporation (IDC) expect it to be around $150 billion. The statistics indicate that consumers are spending money on the Internet and will continue to do so as the barriers for entry begin to disappear.

Finding and charting accurate Internet statistics are difficult, because numbers generated by different reputable sources often are as different as night and day. Here are some specific Internet shopping figures that give a sense of the size of the market that is developing:

- ◆ Jupiter Communications, a media research firm, says that Web-based shopping amounted to $132 million in 1994.

For the same year:

- ◆ Forrester Research reports that on-line shopping generated $200 million worth of goods and services.

And for 1995:

- ◆ IDC was able to chart $300 million of transactions completed and paid for over the Web.

◆ Forrester Research says that Internet commerce totaled $350 million.

Regardless of the 1994 and 1995 statistics, The Yankee Group, a well-respected market research firm, projected that interactive consumer commerce would reach $300 million in 1996—which should be an easy feat, based on IDC's and Forrester's numbers! Furthermore, in February 1996, the two bankcard associations, MasterCard International and VISA International, announced agreement of standard secure credit card encryption protocols, called Secure Electronic Transfer (SET), and they have been working on the definition of these protocols ever since. (See Chapter 6 for further discussion.) The availability of SET for consumers and merchants on the Internet will be a major boost. Both parties will no longer have to worry about the security issue when it comes to payment with credit cards, as long as their payment service provider is using the SET protocols. Payment services, such as those from Cyber-Cash using SET, are just becoming available at the end of 1996.

In addition to the volume of commerce on the Internet, there's another contradiction that nevertheless points in a positive direction: Nielsen says that more than 2.5 million people have purchased products and services over the Web; however, both the Georgia Tech Valuation Study 4 (GVU4) and Nielsen surveys found Web-based shopping at the bottom of user lists. Imagine what these statistics might look like when Internet-based shopping is at the top of people's lists! In the grand scheme of things, those 2.5 million shoppers estimated by Nielsen aren't many compared to the number of Internet users overall—estimated at about 40 million. Still, this is a significant number, and it is growing rapidly.

Here's another viewpoint: IDC reports that, contrary to conventional wisdom that Internet shopping has yet to live up to its promise, approximately one out of three net surfers engages in shopping on-line. The results of a new IDC survey, "Cybershopping—The Truth Exposed," were released in the first week of May 1996. Says John Gantz, senior vice president of Personal Systems, "The data from this survey provides us with the most up-to-the-minute picture of the state of on-line commerce today. We hear a lot about how shopping on the Web is already declining, but these results indicate otherwise. On the whole, Internet commerce is doing better than can be expected, especially considering that it is still in the early adopter phase."

Over 750 people responded to the IDC survey with information about their shopping habits, including the number of hours spent on-line, dollars expended, and types of purchases made. Several interesting results emerged:

- One in three Web surfers shops during browsing sessions.
- Business shoppers spend more than $500 per month.
- Home shoppers spend more than $50 per month.
- Cybershoppers visit an average of eight storefronts per session.

IDC took the results of this survey and plugged them into its proprietary Internet Commerce Market Model, which is based on more than 40,000 interviews with homes and businesses in 15 countries each year. Using this model, IDC can forecast supply and demand for Web shopping in the near future.

A Yahoo/Jupiter-based sampling of 2,500 marketers reports that 71 percent of travel-related Web sites had some sales in 1996. During the month of March, 57 percent of consumer products sites had sales that month, and 43 percent of media and publishing sites had sales that month.

On-line Shopping Behavior

In 1996, an on-line shopping behavioral study was conducted by Bob Novick, with CyberPulse Research and Citicorp. The CyberPulse/Citicorp survey found two types of shoppers:

- Habitual browsers: people who look around at what is out there even when they aren't looking for something in particular
- Item-specific shoppers: people who shop mainly when they need a specific item

In these researchers' opinion, store browsing is an important precursor to buying. "Browsing," CyberPulse reports, "is a learning activity, where a person becomes aware of what is available, how much things cost, and which ones are appealing. Browsing is also a way of deciding where to shop. And people who browse and become expert about a particular category of products become referral sources for others who don't have the time or inclination to browse a particular category."

Q&A: Who's really shopping on the Internet today?

What Are People Buying On-line?

So far, customers who are buying on-line are a computer-happy group.

- The most popular products sold on the Internet in 1995 were computer hardware and software, followed by travel and event tickets.

Why Aren't More People Buying On-line?

Maybe the Internet hasn't reached the right people yet:

- One of the primary obstacles to on-line shopping success is women. Stereotypically responsible for 70 percent of nonvirtual retail shopping, they make up only 35 percent of total Internet usage.

How Many People Are Buying Products on the Internet Now?

According to a MasterCard survey conducted for the National Retail Federation in 1995:

- Eighty-four percent of the people currently surfing the Web believe they are somewhat likely to purchase items over the Internet this year.
- Twenty-seven percent have already bought something over the Internet.

MasterCard found that the most popular items purchased via the Web are computer software, information, entertainment, and computer hardware. The MasterCard survey further found that consumers are most interested in purchasing items with which they are familiar or for which they can define exactly what they want.

Continued

Americans are showing increased acceptance and interest in shopping on-line, according to new data released by FIND/SVP Worldwide Consulting & Research at the Web Marketplace Conference in Chicago, which released 1995 statistics. Although only 19 percent of Internet users in the United States have actually shopped on-line, a majority (59 percent) expressed interest in making on-line purchases, the report said, adding that willingness to spend on-line is prevalent among all age groups, from 18 to 50-plus (reported in *Ad Age,* April 12, 1996).

The CyberPulse study poses the question, "What does all this mean for on-line merchants?" Here are some of their suggestions:

- Provide a good place to browse. Make it interesting, compelling, entertaining in the way you present your products.
- Try to attract the people who like to browse your category. Link to other sites that can send you potential customers.
- Find ways to encourage them to share with others what they have learned about your products. Help your customers by creating chat groups and facilitating discussion.
- Word of mouth can be key to success. See if other sites are willing to post testimonials about your products.
- A relatively small number of shopping "experts" can have a large impact on your sales. Infomercials have shown us this on TV. Engage an expert in your field to host a chat group, or do a testimonial about your product.

The Future: An On-line Shopping Market Forecast

Based on the research that's being done, even if no one quite agrees on the numbers, everyone agrees that this market is real and growing. By the year 2000, it is expected to be several billion dollars in size. Here are more statistics from market research firms:

The Survey.Net July 1995 Internet Shopping Survey asked 989 Web users several questions. Here are the questions and the data resulting from the replies:

1. What Is the Primary Factor Which Influences Your Decision to Buy?

- ◆ 20%—N/A (never purchased anything on-line)
- ◆ 18%—No answer
- ◆ 16%—Price
- ◆ 12%—The convenience of shopping on-line
- ◆ 11%—The explanation of the item and its features
- ◆ 5%—The photo or the drawing of the item that was presented
- ◆ 4%—Ease of finding a specific item
- ◆ 3%—Payment method
- ◆ 3%—General quality of the Web site
- ◆ 8%—Other

Of the 55 percent of respondents who had actually purchased something on-line, price and the convenience of on-line shopping seem to be important aspects of their purchase decision. But also, based on these answers, the remaining purchasers definitely were influenced by the quality of the presentation of the products at the Internet site, including factors such as photos or drawings, explanations, ease of finding an item, and overall site quality. In Chapter 3, you'll learn more about what factors influence the way people shop—and how to move them from browsing to buying at your site.

Continued

2. What Is Your Reason for Not Ordering from the Internet?

- 56%—No answer
- 22%—Did not want to submit personal billing information over Internet
- 12%—Don't do a lot of shopping
- 7%—Not familiar with the company/store
- 1%—Need to deal with a real person
- 2%—Other

These answers suggest that people are still concerned about security when shopping on-line. Chapter 6 gives you some insight into helping your customers feel comfortable paying on-line. The need to deal with a real person, cited by 1 percent of respondents, is addressed in Chapter 3, which explains why people shop and what kind of shoppers most need the human touch.

3. How Did You Pay for This On-line Purchase (for the Majority of Your Purchases)?

- 25%—No answer
- 22%—Never purchased anything on-line
- 12%—Sent credit card information via secure form/method
- 11%—Phoned in credit card information
- 8%—Sent credit card information, but unsure if with secure form
- 7%—Sent info in unsecured form
- 4%—Mailed order
- 2%—E-mailed credit info
- 1%—First Virtual Account

Continued

- 0.3%—DigiCash
- 0.3%—CyberCash
- 7.4%—Other

It's clear from these answers that a lot of Internet users still haven't purchased anything on-line, and that security is important to those who do make purchases. It's also clear that credit card purchases remain the major payment method on-line. Of the 46.5 percent who made a purchase, a significant number (35.9 percent) were willing to trust the Internet with their credit card information without the certainty of secure transmission (that's 16.7 percent of the total number of respondents). No one reported negative experiences as a result of using the Internet in its native form.

Here are a few other interesting statistics from the Survey.Net information:

- 32.5%—Purchased from a stand-alone store
- 40.0%—Would make repeat purchases
- 62.8%—Have never had a problem with others using credit cards without approval

Based on the fact that 40 percent say they would make a repeat purchase and 62.8 percent have not had problems using credit cards on-line, it seems that people who are shopping on-line are having good experiences, once they take the plunge.

- Forrester Research expects on-line shopping to approach $5 billion by 1999 and $7 billion by the year 2000. Forrester claims that this is still a very small amount compared to the current $5 trillion in U.S. retail sales and $50 billion in catalog sales.
- The Yankee Group estimates $3.1 billion in "interactive consumer commerce" by 2000.

- Jupiter Communications says that $4.5 billion will be spent on the Web by 2000, plus another $2.4 billion via on-line services for a total of nearly $8 billion.
- IDC believes that by the year 2000 electronic commerce will hit $150 billion (including electronic cash transactions).
- Killen & Associates believes all E-money transfers on the Internet will reach $600 billion by 2000.

Based on these statistics, it seems clear that some major pulse takers out there see a big increase in on-line commerce over the next five years. Taking this as an assumption, you might want to learn more about the virtual store—what it is and how to set one up to accommodate or enhance your business. In that case, read on.

The World Wide Web has become popular with businesses because the potential on-line market is so huge. It has been estimated that over 40 million people visit the Web regularly. Therefore, theoretically, you can reach up to 40 million people with the information on your Web site. Realistically, however, having a Web site is like having an answering machine on your telephone. You can put a message there, and some people will hear it. Most will not. As this chapter's epigraph says: "Putting up a Web site these days is like a tree falling in the forest."

A major task in developing your virtual store will be *getting the word out* so that people will visit your store to see and buy your products. This book tells you how to do this successfully. By reading this book, you can learn to bring a significant number of those visitors to your Web site, your own virtual store, and offer them a pleasant shopping experience that's profitable for you.

What Is the Virtual Store?

The virtual store is a storefront in cyberspace, a place where customers can shop from their home computers and where merchants can offer merchandise and services for a fraction of the overhead required in a physical storefront. A virtual store exists on that portion of the Internet known as the World Wide Web. You get to a virtual store by entering its Web address—called a *universal resource locator* (URL)—into a Web browser such as the Netscape Navigator.

Once you arrive at the virtual store of your choice, you'll often see some information about the company behind the store, and you'll always see a product display. Often there are colorful graphic images to give you a better feeling for how a product looks. When you want to purchase a product, you can usually select it using a button.

You'll probably fill out a form right there on the screen with your payment information. However, some merchants don't transmit financial information on-line, preferring to let their customers use phone or E-mail to transmit credit card or electronic funds transfer (EFT) information. If you've ordered a product to be shipped to your house, it arrives in a matter of days. If you've selected some information-based good, such as an image or a news article, it arrives within seconds.

Not all of the Web sites you can reach from your browser are virtual stores, because not all Web sites are set up for the purpose of selling something. Many Web sites are informational; some are humorous; some are monuments to an individual ego.

Who Is the Virtual Customer?

Although women traditionally are perceived to be the shoppers of the world, on-line shoppers today are quite a different mix. The virtual customer is likely to be a relatively well-paid, well-educated male in his late twenties to midthirties:

◆ *Internet World*'s December 1995 subscriber study found male and female Internet participation to be 77 percent and 23 percent, respectively.

◆ The age of the average Internet user ranges from 32 (O'Reilly) to 34 (Nielsen).

◆ The FIND/SVP survey found that women are more likely to use the Internet to communicate with other people, while men are more likely to use it to look for information.

◆ SRI International (formerly the Stanford Research Institute) predicts that the Web population's average age will slowly decline. More college undergraduates and teenagers will become Internet users as its availability and ease of use increases.

On-line Shoppers Tend to Be Well Educated

According to Nielsen, 64 percent of on-line shoppers have college degrees, while 93 percent have some college education.

On-line Shoppers Tend to Be Affluent

Internet users tend to be upscale: Twenty-five percent report an annual household income over $80,000. Nielsen reports that 50 percent of Internet users hold professional/managerial jobs. (*Note:* O'Reilly and Nielsen chart the household income figures to be $60,000 and $80,000, respectively.)

On-line Shoppers Have Children

According to Jupiter Communications, nearly four million children under the age of 18 have Web access. With the advent of small digital coin payments and on-line video arcades, many on-line shoppers are likely to *be* children.

Where Do the On-line Shoppers Really Live?

To date, most on-line shoppers seem to live in the United States. About 80 percent of identifiable Internet users are from the United States, and 20 percent are from other countries, including 7 percent from Canada and 8 percent from Europe.

Within the United States, America Online reports that the following generate the most on-line traffic (in order):

- California (San Francisco, San Jose, Los Angeles, San Diego)
- Texas (Austin)
- Virginia
- Hartford
- Connecticut (New Haven)
- Washington D.C.
- Boston
- New York
- New Jersey
- Washington (Seattle/Tacoma)
- Oregon (Portland)

Germans with Internet access now number 2 million. Major on-line services include T-Online with 950,000 subscribers, CompuServe with 200,000 subscribers, and the newest arrival, AOL, with 40,000. In France, Minitel provides for 15 million regular Internet users in 6.5 million homes and offices.

However, these demographics are evolving. On-line shoppers are beginning to include more women, more seniors, and different socioeconomic groups. For more information about the virtual customer of tomorrow, see Chapter 8.

Different Types of Virtual Stores

This section presents a segmentation of virtual stores by industry category: hard goods, information-based goods, and services (see Figure 1.1). You'll find representative examples from publishing, computer gaming, and so forth. The examples in each section illustrate virtual stores that have been successful and well recognized in each area.

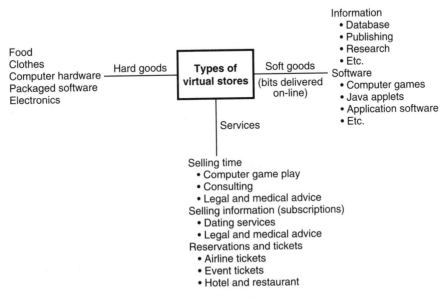

Figure 1.1   Different types of virtual stores.

Selling Hard Goods On-line

Selling durable goods, or hard goods, on-line is similar to operating a catalog sales business. The difference is that you'll receive orders and possibly also payments over the Internet. You'll want to offer your customers the same sense of security and maybe even the money-back guarantee that characterizes a reputable catalog sales company. Perhaps one of the most outstanding examples of a virtual store selling durable goods is the Internet Shopping Network (ISN).

Internet Shopping Network

The Internet Shopping Network has been operating on-line since April 1994 (see Figure 1.2). Cofounded by Randy Adams and Bill Rollinson, it was created for the sole purpose of on-line retailing. At that time, Netscape hadn't yet emerged, and Rollinson says, "Our friends thought we were absolutely out of our minds." Today, ISN generates in excess of $1 million per month in revenues.

Figure 1.2　ISN's virtual store site.

ISN actually was announced to the public on the same day as CommerceNet, the well-known consortium of companies supporting on-line commerce, so some of the publicity rubbed off. "We began getting customers right away," says Bill Rollinson. "At first we sold only computer hardware and software products, which fit the demographics pretty well. We sell other things now, but we keep coming back to our focus on computer products."

As a retailer, ISN sees that customers look for a narrow focus in an on-line store, but expect expertise in that area. For instance, Rollinson mentions a store called Hot, Hot, Hot, which successfully sells nothing but hot sauce to a worldwide audience over the Net. He points out that the store couldn't have done it without the Web.

Rollinson offers hope to smaller retailers, expressing his belief that "it's a misconception that big brands are the ones who will do well on the Internet. Certainly a brand can help in getting attention, but I believe you can *build* a brand on the Internet by building a good site. Sometimes having a big brand name works against you, because the skill set required for doing retailing on the Net is different. The way you do things is tailored to off-line merchandising. Some of the smaller-name CD audio stores are doing more sales on-line than some of the bigger name stores that also have stores off-line." He adds, "I think too much blame has been put on things like security for holding back the development of Internet commerce. I think the burden is on retailers like ourselves for coming up with enough unique goods and services to keep customers interested. I think the burden is on us."

For the on-line shopping medium to really take off, Rollinson feels that speed is still the biggest hurdle to overcome. "Anything we do to increase speed increases our sales." He continues, "Cable modems, integrated services digital networks (ISDN), or something we haven't even heard of yet that comes along to increase speed will help tremendously."

The other major hurdle in Rollinson's view is the ability to pay more easily. At the ISN site, shoppers fill out a form once with their credit card information and are issued PIN numbers. That system is working, but it inhibits spontaneity. "Things like CyberCash will make it a lot easier," he concludes.

ISN definitely is in this game for the long term. Bill Rollinson sums up his thoughts about doing business on-line this way, "Getting into this business and putting up a Web site is a lot like having a baby—not only do you have to put this thing through college, but it's probably going to come back and live with you for a while. You're in it for the long haul. I think you need to be committed to it, because like anything else, the more you put into it, the more you get out."

PriceCostco

PriceCostco is known for operating an international network of Price Club and Costco wholesale, membership-only warehouse distribution centers. The PriceCostco "working warehouses" system is designed to help small to medium-sized businesses reduce costs in purchasing for resale and for everyday business use. Individuals belonging to certain qualified groups are also allowed to purchase for their personal needs.

In the physical world, PriceCostco's warehouses present one of the country's largest product category selections to be found under a single roof. PriceCostco is known for carrying top-quality national and regional brands, 100 percent guaranteed, at prices consistently below traditional wholesale or retail operations.

PriceCostco's on-line site (see Figure 1.3) offers information about the company as a whole, which helps in building affinity with its customers. But there's more: The on-line site also includes a virtual store, which is the on-line version of the PriceCostco mail-order catalog. Soon, over 7,000 items will be available on-line at PriceCostco. It has succeeded in moving its working warehouses into cyberspace. PriceCostco also accepts CyberCash payments on-line.

The PriceCostco on-line catalog is particularly appealing to people shopping for gifts, since high-quality merchandise is available at reasonable cost. Add that to the convenience of shopping at home, and it's a recipe for success.

Throughout this book, you'll find profiles of many successful virtual stores. Table 1.1 contains a list of the virtual stores selling hard goods.

Selling Soft Goods On-line

Information-based goods are naturally suited to be sold in the Internet environment, because the entire transaction can be completed within the electronic medium. The goods can be ordered, payment can be collected, and goods can be delivered all by computer. Typically, information-

Figure 1.3 PriceCostco's on-line site.

based goods means some sort of published material, such as news articles or computer software. The Pathfinder site for Time Warner is an outstanding example of selling information-based goods on-line.

Pathfinder

Pathfinder is the Internet virtual store offered by Time Warner's New Media division (see Figure 1.4). It is one of the Internet's best-known and most popular content sites, which enjoys 30 million hits per week and has been operating since early 1995.

In May 1996, Time Warner's New Media division, CompuServe, and Open Market, a supplier of Internet server software for virtual merchants, announced a new subscription-based and individually cus-

TABLE 1.1   Virtual Stores Selling Durable Goods

Name	On-line Address	Type of Goods
1-800-FLOWERS	AOL keyword: Flowers	Flowers and gift items
2Market	AOL keyword: 2Market	Mall—collection of goods
Amazon Books	www.amazon.com	Books
Book Stacks Unlimited	www.books.com	Books
Children's Software Company	www.childsoft.com	Software
Gibson Guitars	www.gibson.com	Guitars and accessories
Godiva Chocolates	www.godiva.com	Chocolate
Golden Gate-Rebecca Raggs	www.best.com/~ggate/ 2rrags.cgi	Clothes
Hammacher Schlemmer	www.internet.net/H-S/ index.html	Handy gadgets
Music Boulevard	www.musicblvd.com	Music CDs
Nicole Miller	www.nicolemiller.com	Clothes
Omaha Steaks	www.internet.net/OSI	Food
PriceCostco	www.pricecostco.com	Household and business
Internet Shopping Network	www2.internet.net/ directories.html	Computers and peripherals
Tower Records	AOL keyword: Tower	Music CDs
Virtual Vineyards	www.virtualvin.com	Wine and gourmet food

tomizable information service from Pathfinder. This is a new step for Pathfinder, which to date has been a very successful generator of advertising revenues on the Internet, collecting close to a million dollars in revenue, based on its high traffic and good demographics.

When first conceived, Pathfinder said it would avoid the traditional subscription model so familiar to publishers. Internet advertising revenues have not grown as fast as many had predicted and Pathfinder plans on offering the subscription service to augment its advertising revenues. Pathfinder's new subscription service will have new content especially designed for the on-line environment, with frequent updates. Pathfinder will continue to generate licensing revenues from CompuServe.

This new subscription service is called Personal Edition and it uses Open Market's OM-Express technology to create personalized versions of Pathfinder for Web users and CompuServe subscribers. OM-Express is designed to let users designate Web sites they want to visit on a regular basis, then it automatically retrieves those Web pages and stores

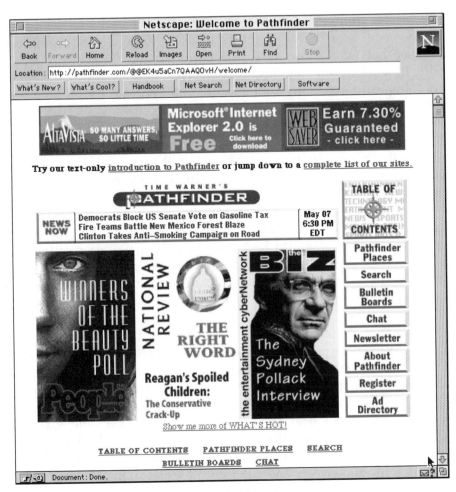

Figure 1.4 Time Warner's Pathfinder site.

them for off-line viewing. The new subscription-based Pathfinder service also relies on Open Market's OM-Transact system for handling on-line transactions and the OM-Express product for managing access and user identification features.

Pathfinder feels that two advertising and subscription services are very important as revenue sources to support quality content on the Internet. (See Chapter 4 for a detailed discussion on advertising- and subscription-based revenue generation.)

The lesson from Pathfinder for the virtual store owner is that, in designing your store, look at multiple ways to generate revenue and remember that, even if you have a very popular site (like Pathfinder's 30 million hits per week) that attracts advertisers and gives you substantial advertising revenues, it may not be sufficient to create a profitable store.

Microsoft

Software is similar to information goods in the sense that it can be delivered directly on-line, in real time. Microsoft, the world's largest software publisher, is moving forward with on-line distribution and becoming more aggressive in allowing its products to be distributed over the Internet. Prior to 1995, Microsoft was opposed to getting its popular software offerings distributed over the Net, fearing that its well-cultivated retail distribution channels would be angered by the new competition from the Internet. In 1995, Microsoft allowed the sales of its software packages at virtual software stores such CyberSource, the Internet Shopping Network, and Online Interactive as long as the virtual stores honored its retail pricing.

In the spring of 1996, Microsoft expanded the list of virtual resellers that were allowed to sell its products. Microsoft and a group of other software companies formed the Electronic Licensing and Security Initiative (ELSI) to act as a central clearinghouse for retailers that want to sell their software through the Internet. The current ELSI members are large corporations such as IBM, AT&T, BBN, LitleNet, and First Data Corporation. At the same time, Microsoft also released a set of guidelines that distributors and resellers are required to use when selling the company's products over the Internet. These standards, which stem from a six-month pilot project, make Microsoft's basic Office applications available immediately over the Internet through major resellers— not in shrink-wrapped form, but in downloadable form. For consumers who have fast-speed connections to the Internet, this system may prove to be the most popular way to obtain software—even large applications such as Microsoft Word. (It takes about two hours to download an application over a standard 14.4 Kbps computer modem.)

Freeware and shareware have been distributed over the Internet for a long time. But commercial software developers have not used the Internet aggressively as a distribution medium, mostly because of concerns regarding copyright protection and pirating, as well as from the fear of alienating the physical resellers channel. Microsoft's standards address those issues and include mechanisms that allow customer returns and verification of sales.

Most of Microsoft's revenues are derived from selling site licenses to large corporations, which would be the prime target for electronic distribution. Physical stores and shrink-wrapped Microsoft products are not going away any time soon, since most consumers will still need the manuals for their software and are not willing to spend two hours downloading a package. That could change, though, if the savings Microsoft passes on to the consumer are substantial.

Another real promise of on-line software sales is the ability to distribute niche products that would have no chance of finding space on the increasingly crowded shelves of retail stores. The virtual store has the ability to create unlimited shelf space, but position on that virtual shelf is still a consideration. Location in the virtual store is defined by how many pages deep a potential customer needs to go before seeing your products.

Table 1.2 contains a list of virtual stores, some profiled in this book, that sell information-based goods. You'll notice that many of them are publishers that traditionally work in print, such as local newspapers, and are finding an opportunity to lower their costs by delivering their products on-line.

Selling Services On-line

Selling services on-line seems to be an area where imagination and inventiveness go a long way. Essentially any service that can be sold in

TABLE 1.2 Virtual Stores Selling Information-Based Goods

Name	On-line Address	Type of Goods
The Electronic Newsstand	www.enews.com	News and information
Microsoft	www.microsoft.com/ products	Microsoft software applications
Pathfinder	www.pathfinder.com	On-line magazines
San Jose Mercury News	www.sjmercury.com	Local Silicon Valley newspaper
Software.Com	www.software.com	Software sales
The Wall Street Journal	www.wsj.com/ regUser.html	Interactive Personal edition of the Wall Street Journal

A Small Caveat for On-line Publishers

Dr. Alan Kay, well-known computer scientist and researcher, has pointed out that it can be more difficult to read on-line than on a printed page. In fact, studies seem to show that the better reader you are, the more difficult it is to read on-line.

The Moral: Be kind to eyes! Offer your customers an alternative for getting their on-line information into printed form, if possible.

the physical realm can also be sold on-line, sometimes with an interesting new twist. Table 1.3 lists services-related virtual stores, several of which are profiled in this book.

EarthLink

EarthLink Network is a nationwide Internet service provider specializing in quick, simple, and direct Internet access for individuals and businesses. It is becoming successful as a virtual store by providing people with inexpensive and foolproof access to the virtual world (see Figure 1.5).

TABLE 1.3   Virtual Stores Providing Services

Name	On-line Address	Type of Service
Alain Pinel	www.apr.com	Realty
Alamo Rental Car	www.freeways.com	Rental Car Reservations
American Airlines	www.flyaa.com	Airline information and tickets
Easy Sabre	AOL keyword: EASY SABRE	Airline reservations
EarthLink	www.earthlink.net	Internet access provider
FedEx	www.fedex.com	Package shipping—worldwide
Match.Com	www.match.com	Dating services
Motley Fool	AOL keyword: MOTLEY FOOL	Stock recommendations
Pizza Hut	pizzahut.com	Pizza delivery
Shrink-link	www.westnet.com/shrink	Psychological counseling
Waiters On Wheels	www.sunnyside.com/wow	Delivery from local restaurant
Wells Fargo Bank	www.wellsfargo.com	On-line banking

EarthLink was founded in the spring of 1994 by 23-year-old Sky Dayton, an entrepreneur with a background in technology and culture. After immersing himself in the Internet in 1993, Dayton immediately recognized its potential, but he was frustrated with how difficult it was to get on-line. With two employees and the idea that Internet access could be made easy for anyone, EarthLink sold its first Internet access account on July 1, 1994. The company has grown exponentially ever since. As of April 1996, EarthLink employed a full-time staff of over 300.

EarthLink's TotalAccess software dials a new subscriber into a registration server, automatically sets up an Internet access account, and configures the user's computer to navigate the Internet. Subscribers are on-line in as little as five minutes. EarthLink provides low-cost, flexible, and easy-to-use services throughout the United States, with good technical support when needed. Also, as Steven A. Dougherty, manager of Strategic Planning at EarthLink, points out, "We're a CyberCash merchant. That makes it easy to get customers set up. In fact, our whole registration process is automated, which is what makes it so fast. A lot of people setting up Web sites with us now want to use CyberCash."

Match.Com

Match.Com launched its site on the World Wide Web in April 1995 (see Figure 1.6). Its goal was to provide an on-line meeting place for people who are genuinely looking to meet other people. The creators of Match.Com researched off-line dating services, and they did a lot of thinking about how to differentiate themselves among the already existing 100+ on-line dating services available on the Web at that time. Some of their important goals were:

- To make it easy for people to browse the ads and meet others who fit their criteria
- To create a friendly environment
- To balance the number of subscribers by sex
- To create a safe communication environment through the use of anonymous E-mail

If word of mouth is any indicator, Match.Com has been highly successful in achieving its goals. Wendy Sue Noah, a Match.Com ambassador who has been with the company since before the Web site was up,

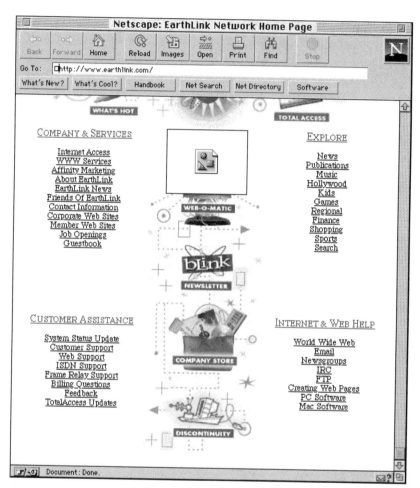

Figure 1.5   EarthLink's site.

puts it this way, "It works. We're bringing love to the planet. All over the world, people are thanking us for introducing them to their soulmates." Noah goes on to say, "It's a new genre of how people are going to meet in the 21st century. We're too busy to go to smoky bars. Match.Com provides an accessible, affordable way to meet."

For the first eight months of its existence, Match.Com was free. It grew very rapidly. Part of the strategy was to reach a critical mass quickly so

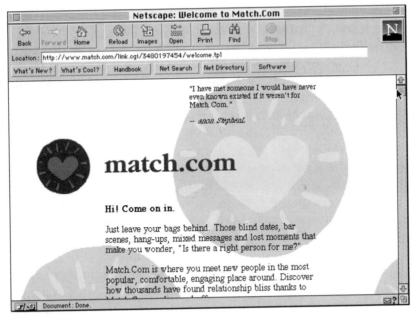

Figure 1.6   Match.Com: on-line dating services.

that there would be enough value for the customers. After February 1996, Match.Com became a subscription service.

As for advertising and promotion, Match.Com has used every means available. Early on, it created a presence by posting in Usenet groups, made sure to be in all the search directories, and tried sending proactive E-mail to mailing lists. It held off-line member events in the San Francisco Bay Area, which was the initial target area.

Match.Com also tested traditional direct mail as a means of advertising the service but found it expensive compared to direct e-mail, which, says Fran Maier, general manager, is becoming more acceptable with all the newbies on-line these days and less emphasis on "Netiquette." It seems to Maier that fewer and fewer people are objecting to what might formerly have been considered invasive E-mail.

Throughout its development, Match.Com has also focused on traditional print media. In its first year, most of its marketing budget was spent on building relationships with the press and getting the word out in print. Now Match.Com is doing some advertising on other Web sites, while still keeping a presence in the print media.

Match.Com accepts credit card and check payments, both on-line and off-line, for 1-, 3-, 6-, and 12-month subscriptions. It is also in the process of working out implementation issues for accepting digital cash. Right now, 80 percent of subscribers pay over the Internet by credit card.

The Match.Com revenue model is based on subscriptions, and the service attracts interest by offering a ten-day free trial with your profile online. Maier says, "Overall we're converting 20% of those who try our service into subscribers. And in our target group, which is people in their 30s and 40s, we're actually bringing people in at a 30% rate. A lot of people who come to the site are under 25, and they're not as likely to sign up for the service; they're still in college. In fact, 50% who try our service are under 30."

Not inclined to rest on its laurels, Match.Com plans to continue differentiating itself by offering more and better service to its membership and creating partnerships with other on-line groups. Says Maier, "We're constantly checking in with our users to see what they want." For instance, it's considering offering astrological chart services to members who have met and begun dating. The biggest effort currently is in building partnerships with on-line communities such as Women's Wire, Net-Noir, LatinoLink, and GNN.

American Airlines

American Airlines began offering deeply discounted fares to Internet users in May 1996 as a way to sell seats it would not have sold otherwise. Every Wednesday, travelers who have registered at the Web site receive E-mail containing a list of about 20 discounted air fares on domestic routes. The discounts are for weekend travel: All outgoing travel must begin on the following Saturday, with return travel on the following Monday or Tuesday. The fares are called NetSaver fares, and they are from 70 to 80 percent lower than the already discounted 21-day advance purchase fares, which also require staying over Saturday night. To purchase a NetSaver fare, customers call a special 800 number; credit card information is not transmitted directly over the Web site.[1]

American Airlines is using its Web site (see Figure 1.7) to generate revenue from resources that otherwise would go unused. Because it's

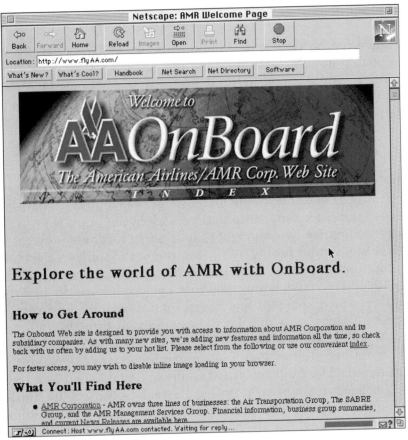

Figure 1.7   American Airlines' on-line site.

easy to send E-mail to thousands of prospective customers, the cost of offering this service on the Web is minimal. One supposes that if the program becomes successful, American will invest in creating a genuine virtual store through which customers can make actual purchases. In contrast, Southwest Airlines has a program whereby it does allow customers to purchase their tickets directly from the Web site. It will be interesting to see which site is most successful. One consultant for the travel industry criticized American for not letting users buy their tickets directly off the Web.[2]

Early Pioneers

A few brave and intrepid souls jumped onto the Web and found out a lot of information by which many of the rest of us have profited. Unfortunately, these virtual stores are no longer with us. This section describes some of the early attempts to create on-line shopping environments and hopefully enables us to benefit by their experience.

The First Meckler Mall

One of the early pioneers in the virtual mall world was Meckler Mall, run by Chris Locke. Locke spent most of 1993 putting together very impressive (for their time) graphics for an Internet mall. He was one of the early visionaries who thought that bringing businesses on the Internet under one virtual roof would mean increased traffic for each of the stores and therefore increase business. Meckler Mall was introduced in March 1994. The expectation was that companies would pay around $50,000 to occupy space in the virtual mall. Locke made several high-level presentations in which he likened himself to a shopping center developer selling virtual real estate. Though the first Meckler Mall created a lot of interest, less than five companies actually signed up.

What the Meckler Mall missed was already-established foot traffic. It was selling space in a virtual store, but the real location of the store—that is, the traffic it would get—was completely unproven. In our opinion, this was the biggest reason that the Meckler Mall eventually closed down.

Shortly afterward, Meckler bought Dave Taylor's I-Mall. Taylor had established a mailing message called Dave's Internet Mall. This was a long mail message that listed anyone who did any business on the Internet. Since this was in the pre-Web days, Taylor's list included E-mail sites, Gopher sites, and file transfer protocol (ftp) sites (these are different types of Internet servers similar to the WWW servers that we all know today).

Taylor's I-Mall listed over 1,000 businesses. People kept going to this list to search for things on the Internet. To enhance its usability, Dave subdivided and categorized his list, and after a short while, Taylor's list was comparable to Yahoo today. Thus, Meckler was successful with I-Mall because it already had established foot traffic of information and directories.

Building the density of visits on the Internet is the key to a virtual mall's success. Ultimately, advertisers and corporations are willing to pay for established traffic, but as we learned with the first Meckler Mall, they're not willing to pay for future promises.

Shopping 2000

In early 1994, a venture called Shopping 2000 was formed—the first genuine on-line shopping mall. It included several major retailers, such as Tower Records, Marshall Field, JCPenney, J. Crew, Spiegel, and other catalog stores. Shopping 2000 was built on the idea that a customer could browse through the products on-line, then place an order over the phone, using a credit card in a manner similar to placing a catalog order.

Shopping 2000 is still around today, offering shopping capabilities to consumers via CD-ROM. Shopping 2000 was a true pioneer, offering mall facilities to retailers; however, it learned some hard but valuable lessons regarding the Internet.

First, Shopping 2000 definitely was ahead of its time—in 1994, the Internet was not yet a household word. In addition Shopping 2000 had hoped to take advantage of the free advertising provided by the Internet; therefore, it never truly publicized its services using more traditional advertising methods. A fair amount of promotion was done on-line, such as in Usenet news groups, but that type of activity didn't seem to bring a lot of paying customers to the site.

Furthermore, there is a disjunction between looking at things on a screen and ordering them on the phone. It's not so much a problem of not being able to examine the merchandise thoroughly on-line as that, by the time you get on the phone, you've forgotten what you were looking at, can't remember all the stock numbers, and so forth. That puts a damper on impulse buying. More important, by the time customers got on the phone to place orders, they were not likely to go back and visit any of the other stores in the mall. Unlike trips to the physical mall, trips to Shopping 2000 tended to be one-store visits. Therefore, the catalogers gained no advantage by becoming part of a mall.

Why did Shopping 2000 fail?

- ◆ There were no advertising and promotion. At Thanksgiving in 1993, Shopping 2000 had more content related to shopping, including over 60 well-known consumer names, than any other site on the Internet. It was a true pioneer. Despite this, Shopping 2000 never promoted its site or spent any money on advertising, so very few people knew it was there. When Shopping 2000 was first created it was strictly an informational site; you could not place an order directly on-line. But that was no deterrent to consumers, who often called the 800 numbers listed and were happy to be able to do so much comparison shopping from their computers. The media gave Shopping 2000 some attention. CNN, the airline news magazines, and Bell Atlantic frequently featured Shopping 2000 as the shopping mall of the next century. But today Shopping 2000 has closed its virtual doors.

♦ There were no real public relations efforts. Shopping 2000 felt that the Internet defied the laws of advertising and the need for public relations because it was a new medium. It did not create a budget for advertising in consumer magazines or trade journals. The thinking was that if it is on the Internet, they will come. Shopping 2000 could have entered the business of selling ad space by increasing its visibility and making itself a dominant site on the Internet.

♦ There was a lack of customer support. The consumers who were coming to the Shopping 2000 site were desperate for communication. They were sending E-mails to the hosting service on a regular basis, making suggestions, giving opinions, and so on. There was no timely response to these loyal followers.

♦ The Internet was seen as an auxiliary business. The real focus of Content Ware, the Shopping 2000 parent company, was the CD-ROM it created for the shopping content. The Internet was an afterthought and not much was expected of it; therefore, no real resources were allocated to the Shopping 2000 Internet site.

One of the major concerns of the principals that created Shopping 2000 was that the virtual stores at their mall, such as Tower Records and Sara Lee, would eventually migrate and have an independent existence on the Internet. And this did happen. The only way Shopping 2000 could have avoided the migration would have been to create enough traffic at its site that virtual store owners would be compelled to either allow Shopping 2000 to host their stores or at least have a hot link from the Shopping 2000 site to their stand-alone locations on the Internet. All hosting services need to understand that unless they add significant value, the virtual stores they host will be motivated to create their own stand-alone stores. Ultimately, it really shouldn't matter where the store is created. Writing HTML pages is not a competitive advantage today and hasn't been for over two years. The only competitive advantage a hosting service has to offer is its ability to give the virtual store owner qualified traffic and maintenance of the servers.

Ultimately, the promise of Shopping 2000 proved hollow because, in that specific implementation, the mall concept could not add enough value. The larger companies pulled out and set up their own Web shops. Only smaller stores that could not afford to set up and maintain their own shops were left.

AMiX

The American Information Exchange (AMiX) was perhaps the first attempt to create an environment for selling services on-line. Described by *The Economist* as going far beyond existing information services (of its day, in 1992), AMiX provided an electronic marketplace for buying and selling business information and consulting services under open market conditions.

Using AMiX, vendors of consulting services such as technical writing could negotiate and come to agreements with others who had need of their services. AMiX included sophisticated software technology for making and monitoring agreements and deliverables, handling breaches of agreements, verifying reputations, tracking project deadlines, and just generally getting things done. In other words, AMiX created an easy-to-use, pragmatic environment in which trusted commerce could take place—an environment in which computers facilitated and automated many of the nagging details that dog every real-world transaction. AMiX technology also facilitated the payments side of selling information-based goods on-line, much like First Virtual's InfoHaus is successfully doing today.

Like Shopping 2000, AMiX was clearly ahead of its time. Former AMiX employees report that it often was difficult to convince content providers (who at that time were primarily vendors of freeware and shareware) that there were advantages to selling their wares on-line. It was perhaps more difficult to get people to trust that a contract negotiated on-line would stand up if disputed.

In spite of the difficulties of educating merchants about the advantages of on-line commerce in 1992, AMiX had a pilot population of over 400 users. It was ready to go full-scale, with all client software (DOS and Macintosh) and server software (SunOS) fully tested, when Autodesk underwent a major reorganization and terminated all funding for AMiX, along with several other information systems products. Fortunately, much of the marketplace infrastructure technology devised at AMiX lives on in a small company called Electric Communities, based in Cupertino, California (www.communities.com).

Closing Thoughts

On-line commerce is real and it's growing. You've seen examples of each of the three kinds of virtual stores and learned something about how they've become successful. Shopping in the digital world must offer a distinct added value to consumers if it is to succeed and coexist with shopping in the physical world. For this reason, branded and unique products, unlimited product inventory, pricing, delivery, customer service, shopping experience, and practicality all play important parts in Web shopping. Most important, however, the on-line shopping experience must be compelling and must ultimately simplify the lives of consumers.

The following chapters include profiles of many highly popular Web sites that have successfully implemented revenue models, such as Industry.Net, the Internet Shopping Network, and CD-NOW. These sites have helped sustain and build the industry. The book looks at different types of cost-cutting and revenue-generating models for Web sites. On the cost-cutting side, it discusses how to cut marketing and customer support costs via the Web site. On the revenue generation side it discusses advertising, subscriptions and memberships, and retail sales. The companies cited in this book discussed their current and future commerce-related revenue models, marketing/advertising strategies, sales figures, traffic numbers, and hardware and software platforms and applications.

CHAPTER TWO

PLANNING
THE VIRTUAL STORE

Topics presented in this chapter:

- Is the Internet for You?
- Is the Virtual Store for You?
- Setting Realistic Goals for Your Virtual Store
- Using the Virtual Store to Reduce Costs
- Using the Virtual Store to Generate Revenue
- Elements for Success at the Virtual Store
- Locating Your Virtual Store: Hosting Services, Malls, or Stand-alone Sites?

This chapter provides a series of road maps for planning your virtual store. These road maps will help you look at a particular business and identify ways that you can use the Internet to increase profitability or reduce costs.

There are many ways of creating and using a virtual store; this chapter walks you through the planning process for all major areas step by step. (Each decision diagram follows the previous one so it is important for you to read this chapter from start to finish instead of skipping around.) You'll find case studies about successful virtual stores that are either cutting costs or generating significant revenues on the Internet and have been doing so for a while. This chapter also discusses the decision of whether to locate the virtual store in a hosting or a stand-alone environment.

Figure 2.1 illustrates the overall planning process. The first step is to identify your type of business. The second step is to evaluate the Internet as a sales and distribution channel for your business. The third step, and a very important goal, is to set realistic expectations for your virtual store. The fourth step is to determine how you can use your virtual store to cut costs. The fifth step looks at how you can use your store to make sales. The sixth step focuses on choosing a location for your store. (These first six steps are covered in detail in this chapter.)

The seventh step, covered in Chapter 3, is to design the appropriate shopping experience for your potential customers. The eighth step, discussed in Chapter 4, explains how to get specific information about the demographics of your customers. The ninth step, discussed in Chapter 5, helps you design advertising and promotion programs for your store. The tenth step is to select the best methods for accepting payments at your store—this is discussed in Chapter 6.

In addition to these ten steps, ongoing efforts should be directed at two areas: staying current with both national and international laws that govern virtual stores and preparing for social and technical changes that can affect your virutal store. Chapters 7 and 8 are dedicated to these topics.

After reading this chapter, you will be able to evaluate your objectives, identify the type of virtual store that is appropriate for your particular business, know what steps you need to take to reach revenue or cost reduction goals, recognize the elements of success, and decide on the location for your virtual store. The rest of the book dedicates chapters to each of the essential elements of success and discusses them in detail.

Is the Internet for You?

There are various levels of investments and, in turn, rewards one can experience on the Internet. These are, in order of increasing investment (and hopefully rewards): 1) Using the Internet for communications; 2) Using the Internet for cost-cutting through a Web site; 3) Using the Internet for revenue generation through a virtual store.

Every business can benefit from using the Internet and on-line services. The ability to transfer files in electronic form from various offices or even within a building is one of the greatest benefits of the Internet. E-mail has changed the way a lot of us work, replacing voice mail and fax for certain types of communications.

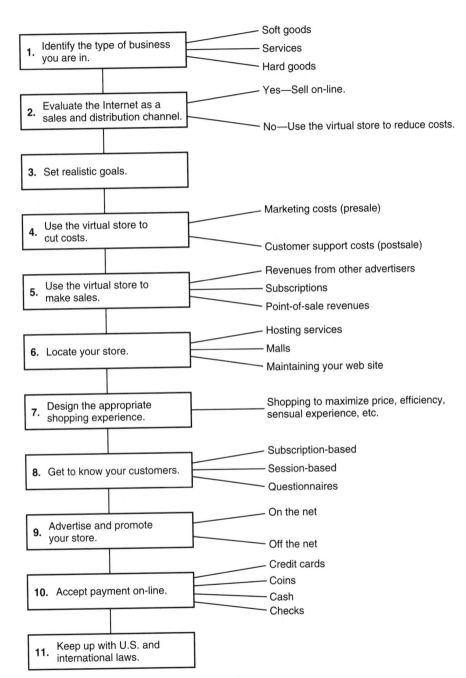

Figure 2.1 Planning the virtual store.

It is safe to assume that if your business takes advantage of telephones and fax machines today, it can benefit from the Internet. For example, sending an E-mail rather than a fax message allows the receiving party to add comments directly into the electronic version—the receiver might in turn send the edited version to a third party for further action. And if you find voice mail helpful today, you will find E-mail even more efficient—you can compose longer, crisper messages, edit them before sending them out, and attach files to your E-mails. Many corporations are also using the Internet as a private medium for communicating with their employees and select customers and vendors without creating a public presence or a virtual store—for example, as a cost-effective medium for electronic data interchange (EDI).

If your company is not on the Internet today, you're missing out on a communications revolution that's changing the world. Even if you only use the Internet to send E-mail, the benefits will far outweigh the cost of connecting to the Internet.

Is the Virtual Store for You?

Of course there's more to the Internet than E-mail and EDI. In the past year, many companies have established Web sites, mostly to promote their products to the world and to provide information to customers in the form of online catalogues and brochures. Others (like you) are looking to move to the next stage—directly selling products and services on-line.

How do you decide what kind of on-line presence is right for your business? As you'll see in a minute, not every company is able to generate significant new revenue by selling directly on-line. But an on-line presence can also be effective for reducing costs—for example, as a cheaper and more effective vehicle for marketing and customer support. Some companies create virtual stores designed to both generate new sales and reduce the costs of marketing, sales, and customer support; other companies choose to focus primarily on cost-reduction. (For simlicity, I use the term virtual store in this book to refer to any commercial on-line presence, regardless of whether its primary focus is generating revenue through direct sales or reducing sales costs.)

It should also be noted that some companies create a virtual store simply for its prestige value as an on-line "store display." (This is similar to the practice of certain European retailers who create store windows on prestigious streets of major cities, with miniscule shops behind them—the objective isn't to generate significant income, it's to promote an upscale image.)

Before investing in a virtual store, you need to clearly identify your objectives—what you hope to achieve by setting up an on-line presence. Whether it's to create a major new source of revenue, to cut marketing costs, or to promote a savvy online image, the key is to make sure your objectives are clear and your expectations realistic.

Publishers of software and information have the ability to deliver their products directly on the Internet; therefore, these goods are called *soft goods*. If your business focuses mainly on selling information and/or software, your virtual store has a great potential for generating revenue. Information and software are some of the easiest things to deliver on-line. Print publishers such as Knight-Ridder and Tribune Company, software publishers such as Microsoft and Adobe, CD-ROM publishers such as Rocket Science Games and Broderbund, and database publishers such as Dialog and Nexis-Lexis are all prime targets. The ability to deliver these goods on-line results in instant gratification for buyers, gives them the ability to obtain the most recent information, allows them to purchase things on a pay-per-view basis, and allows the publisher to sell things in smaller slices such as one photo or article at a time.

Selling soft goods through the virtual store also results in substantial cost savings, since the amounts paid out to the distribution channel and the retailer are eliminated. You can certainly use your virtual store strictly as a marketing communications and customer support tool if you do not want to accept sales.

If your business focuses mainly on selling services, then you should determine if there is a possibility of delivering your service on-line. If so, you also have the ability to increase revenue through your virtual store. If you are in one of the professional consulting businesses, you may have an opportunity to deliver your service through your virtual store. Several consulting houses, counselors, lawyers, and so on, sell their services on the Internet; these service providers usually charge clients on a per-question basis, but selling time in a chat environment is becoming a popular alternative.

If you are a service provider but are not ready to sell your services on-line, look at your virtual store as a cost-saving tool. In addition to using your virtual store as a yellow pages listing for the virtual world, you can significantly reduce the client support costs by communicating with your established clients who have Web access via the Internet.

If your business focuses mainly on selling hard goods, then you need to understand the selling process you go through today in the real world. If that selling process requires a significant amount of face-to-face, one-on-one selling, then do not expect significant sales to be derived from your virtual store. Rather, consider your virtual store as a cost reduction tool.

You should analyze your business in light of the following ten questions to determine the appropriateness of a virtual store for your business.

1. Are your marketing (presales) costs, such as advertising, promotions, direct mail, sales literature dissemination, presales inquiries, and qualification process, a high percentage of your overall costs? If so, you can use the virtual store as a cost reducer for your business.

2. Are your postsales costs in customer service, technical support, product updates, and so on, a high percentage of your costs? If so, you can use the virtual store as a cost reducer for your business.

3. Do you have a product or service that can be *uniquely* delivered on-line, such as up-to-date research or selling Internet access? If so, you can use the virtual store to generate significant new revenue.

4. Do you have a product or service that can be delivered on-line, such as software, information, articles, photographs, computer games, or arcade games that are sold by the hour? If so, you can use the virtual store to generate a significant percentage of your revenues.

5. If not, do you have customers who purchase products, such as office supplies, from you repetitively? If so, your virtual store can generate revenues using the subscription service.

6. Do you sell items that people buy out of habit in predictable intervals, such as birthday and anniversary gifts, groceries, or household supplies?

7. Do you sell items that save people time if purchased on-line, such as gifts that need to be wrapped and shipped?

8. Do you sell items that can be connected to an activity that can best be performed on-line—for example, items requiring research that can be done efficiently on-line prior to purchasing—although the delivery of the purchased item is not on-line?

9. Is your unique selling position that of the lowest-priced supplier of brand or commodity items? If so, the virtual store can generate a lot of sales for you.

10. Do you have a specific niche with a community following that is already on the Internet? An example of this is Star Trek merchandise. The niche-oriented nature of the Internet and small-town quality of its chat groups creates the ability to sell niche products cost effectively. But a word of caution: In the research done for this book, niche products did not excel in total revenue generated in the virtual stores. In Chapter 3, when we discuss the virtual buying experience, we will focus on this unique area of niche products.

Figure 2.2 can help you identify the most likely use of your virtual store for your particular type of business.

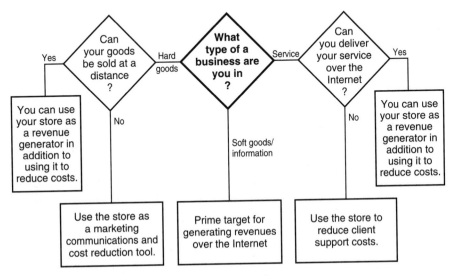

Figure 2.2   Is the virtual store for you?

MYTH: *You can have a million-dollar business on the Internet within the first year of operations.*

You must come to the Internet with realistic goals. Most start-ups in the real world spend their first year with no revenue and do not reach profitability until their third year of operation or even later. A start-up on the Internet is not any different from a start-up in the real world except that it competes for fewer dollars. If your business plan today calls for seven-figure revenue from your virtual store, go back and revise your expectations. A good rule of thumb is that the revenues generated from your virtual store will be in the tens of thousands of dollars within the first year.

Setting Realistic Goals for Your Virtual Store

When I was young, my father taught me the key to minimizing disappointments in life. It is very simple. You just have to know how to set realistic expectations.

The Internet and everyone associated with it are in great need of this advice. We are all flying high, chasing the sky. And with that comes disappointment. As discussed in Chapter 1, many early pioneers of electronic commerce ultimately failed to reach the goals they had set for themselves.

The biggest hits have been taken by those companies that have done away with their brick-and-mortar businesses to set up shop only on the Internet. The revenues have not materialized as fast as these businesses would have liked—browsers have not been converted into shoppers. According to several market research companies cited in Chapter 1, the total revenue generated from the sale of merchandise—on the Internet and on-line services—was under $300 million. To put things in perspective, that is about 15 minutes' worth of the transactions that MasterCard processes each day. Despite the fact that most people focus on using virtual stores as revenue generators, so far the greatest contribution to the bottom line of companies using the Internet has come from reduction in costs.

The decision tree in Figure 2.3 gives you a sense of the range of realistic goals for your virtual store. If you have no revenues today, do not expect to have your virtual store on the Inc. 500 list within the first few

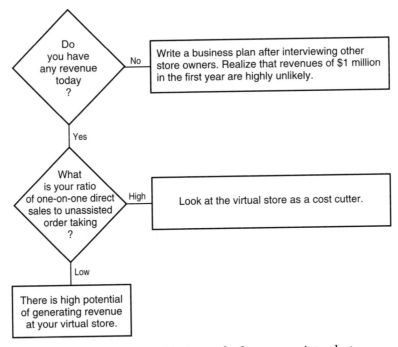

Figure 2.3   Setting realistic goals for your virtual store.

years. Very few virtual stores today have annual revenues of $1 million and above. In setting revenue goals for your store, the best you can do is to talk to others who are in similar businesses on the Internet and get a sense of how they are running their stores and how much revenue they are generating. Then, plan on spending at least twice as much as they do and generating minimal sales in the first year. Remember, most start-ups do not show revenue for a while, and the Internet does not change that.

In situations where one-on-one, face-to-face selling is important, you should not expect the virtual store to result in significant revenue for you, since it is not easy to duplicate the in-person selling situation in the on-line world. Nevertheless, you should continue to read about how you can reduce your costs through your virtual store. Although you will never eliminate certain real-world components of your stores, such as mailing brochures and customer service, you can reduce these significantly.

If your current selling environment involves mostly unassisted order taking, expect to generate sales through your virtual store. But remember, a million dollars in revenue is a high figure for today's virtual stores, so do not set your heart on six-figure revenue until you have operated a store for a few years.

To summarize, there are fewer than 50 virtual stores on the Internet today that generate more than $1 million in revenue on-line. These companies have made significant investments in their virtual stores, and they spend significant money advertising and promoting them. So if your focus is revenue generation through your virtual store, keep this fact in mind and do not expect to be a million-dollar business in the first year of operation. There are also companies, such as Microsoft, that save over $10 million in customer support costs per year through utilizing the on-line world.

The next two sections of this book walk you through both the cost-saving and revenue-generating aspects of the on-line store, with representative success stories.

Using the Virtual Store to Reduce Costs

As shown in Figure 2.4, most virtual stores that are set up to reduce costs provide presales product information and/or postsales customer support. Costs can be reduced for several reasons: for example, with a virtual store, product information is displayed on-line so that printing and mailing can be eliminated or substantially reduced.

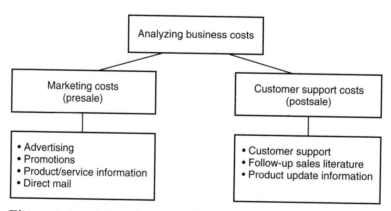

Figure 2.4 Using the virtual store to reduce costs.

TIP   *A cost reduction–oriented virtual store can provide on-line advertising, a product showcase, or a channel for customer support.*

Reducing Presale Costs

If your presale costs are a large percentage of your overall costs, here are some ways to put your virtual store to work by reducing these costs:

- *Advertising.*   You can view your virtual store as a big billboard on the information superhighway. Of course, this works only if there is significant traffic that passes your virtual billboard. You can ensure a desired volume of traffic by advertising your Web site address in magazines, at other Web sites, in your printed literature, and through other advertising venues such as real-life billboards and links from other high-traffic sites to yours.

- *Direct mail and sales literature.*   Providing product information and sales literature at your virtual store reduces the expense of shipping presales literature with overnight mail. When printing, handling, and shipping costs are combined, an average information packet today costs a corporation around $15. Making the same information available on-line eliminates this cost for the segment of your potential customers with Web access. As Web access becomes more popular, this cost saving will increase in magnitude. So once you have a virtual store equipped with your presales information, instruct your telephone operators to ask if callers have Web access and, if so, direct them to your store to download the information. Your telephone operator can still ask for the name and mailing address of the caller, if you find that information valuable. Eventually, as your target customers get to know about your virtual store, they will go there directly.

- *Telephone and on-line sales support.*   You can reduce your sales support cost significantly by using your virtual store. It is customary for companies to post their frequently asked questions (FAQs) and then direct potential customers to their Web sites. Potential customers can also be offered a dynamic list of questions to profile their needs to see if they can be met by the products offered. This prequalification process can save significant sales support costs and reduce the selling cycle.

◆ *Testimonials.*   Nothing sells like testimonials. Yet they are usually expensive to disseminate via advertising. Your virtual store offers you the ability to do *narrowcasting.* Whereas broadcasting sends the same message to a large audience, narrowcasting sends customized messages to small, segmented audiences. Testimonials are most effective if the receiver of the message can relate to the person sending the message. Because the Internet, by definition, is an interactive medium, the virtual store owner, through a sequence of questions, can qualify the store visitor and direct the appropriate testimonial to the potential buyer.

◆ *Links to complementary virtual stores.*   Work with related companies to get your presales information out to qualified prospects. For example, EasySabre, an airline reservations site, may want to include information about Alamo Rental Cars with a link to the Alamo site.

Reducing Postsale Costs

If your postsale costs are high, dragging down your profitability, you can put your virtual store to good use in the following ways:

◆ *Provide customer support through your virtual store—for example, by providing a FAQs page.*   Companies with Web sites have discovered that their customers use the site and the information in it as an alternative to calling on the customer hotlines. Therefore, it is now common for corporations to add lists of frequently asked questions and their answers to their Web sites. In addition to reducing the number of incoming customer support calls, these FAQs provide customers with graphics to explain difficult concepts.

Alain Pinel Realty: Providing Great Marketing Information at Low Cost

Alain Pinel is a realty agency established on the concepts: "Make it Unique, Do It Better, and Make a Difference." From the outset, the company has focused on presenting an image of uniqueness and quality. Of their six years in business, more than three years have included a business presence on the Internet.

Alain Pinel has five offices and over 300 agents. The agency anticipates sales volume on the order of $1.7 billion for 1996. Suzun Abbott, director of operations, currently estimates that between 10 percent and 20 percent of those sales are a direct result of Alain Pinel's presence on the Internet (see Figure 2.5).

Abbott says, "Real estate benefits a lot from the Internet. It works with people's natural curiosity. When they drive through a neighborhood and see a sign, they wonder: 'How many bedrooms does that house have? What is the square footage? What's the price?' With Alain Pinel, they can get on the Web and find out.

"The real estate industry is an information industry. At Alain Pinel, the minute a house is listed, that information is distributed by email to over 300 agents. In this market, our agents can sometimes make a sale before other agents even know there's a listing."

Since Alain Pinel Realty is located in Silicon Valley, many prospective customers have access to the Web at their places of employment. Thus, sellers know their houses are getting exposure among well-qualified buyers—largely employees of high-tech companies such as Silicon Graphics and Intel.

At an Alain Pinel office, a computer—either a NeXT or an Intel—sits on every agent's desk. Agents pay a technology fee to help defray the costs of maintaining a computer and a beeper. Every Alain Pinel agent automatically gets an E-mail account, along with a photograph and biography on the company's Web page. All of the agent's listings appear in a group. The agents believe that the technology fee they pay is worthwhile, because it consistently gets them listings.

Continued

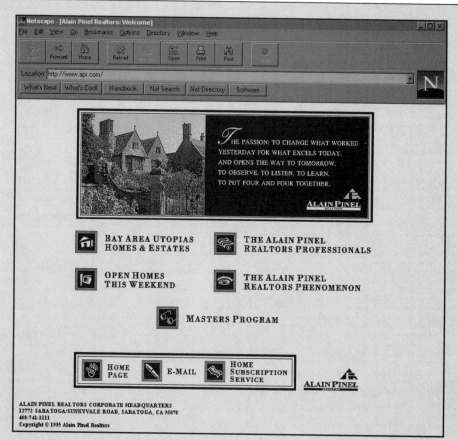

Figure 2.5   Alain Pinel's Web site.

About five years ago, Alain Pinel spent four months to develop custom, object-oriented real estate applications for the NeXT machine. The agency's internal network environment is compatible with NeXT and Intel platforms. Now, it's evolving steadily toward a Windows-based environment and porting some of the

Continued

customized real estate software to Windows, thus gaining the flexibility and cost benefits of off-the-shelf word processing, spreadsheets, and other general office applications.

Alain Pinel operates its own Web server and employs a full-time Webmaster. Much of the material on its Web site is updated automatically each day from an in-house database that includes MLS listings; thus, Webmaster Colin doubles as the company's system administrator and troubleshooter. The Alain Pinel Web site currently uses a T1 line and an Intel platform running LINUX, which is a public-domain version of the Unix operating system. The T1 line seems fine, but for better server performance, the agency is planning to migrate to a Sun Sparc station running Solaris and grow into multiple servers and increased bandwidth as needed.

As part of its long-term Internet strategy, Alain Pinel is working to become a worldwide, full-service, one-stop-shopping provider for real estate sales in the Silicon Valley area. For instance, the agency currently offers a direct ISDN-line connection to a mortgage broker with access to 1,100 loans. It offers home insurance and title insurance, too. Carole Rodoni, president of Alain Pinel, has the philosophy that, in a world where time is everything, the company should make buying a home as easy as possible for the customer. Eventually, it may be possible for Alain Pinel Realty to accept digital down payments over the Internet and consummate deals right then and there.

As for advertising, Alain Pinel is hot-linked to the search engine sites and other hot links are in the works. The agency advertises in *Home and Lands* on-line, but it attributes most of its success to the fact that every agent's business card and every brochure contains Alain Pinel's Web site address as well as an E-mail address. The agency also does regular direct mailings in the Silicon Valley area.

In summary, Alain Pinel Realty uses the Internet to provide superior marketing information in the presale phase at no more cost than other real estate agencies.

♦ *Provide customer support through E-mail and display the address prominently at your site.* For customer support cases involving a unique question that cannot be answered via the FAQs, encourage your customers to first contact you via E-mail, which encourages customers to compose questions clearly and allows the support representative the opportunity to find the right answer. Handling a customer question over E-mail could be as much as 50 percent less costly than a telephone call.

♦ *Integrate your telephone and Internet-based support teams.* These need to be unified for both to be effective. New questions coming in by phone should be added to the FAQs, and customers who often call with trivial questions should be directed to the virtual store.

♦ *Provide for backward integration into the customer support databases.* Both telephone and E-mail inquiries need to be integrated into the company's customer support databases. It is never too early to start a relational database for customer support, since Internet users are highly interactive and will come to your store with many questions.

Realistically, your business can probably find ways to use all of these cost-reducing suggestions in your virtual store.

Using the Internet as an Intranet to Reduce Costs

Just because your virtual store is on the Internet, do not assume that it has to be open to the whole world. Several companies have realized that they can use the Internet more as an *intranet,* or a private network. Private networks connect companies to a select number of others, usually to the suppliers, distributors, retailers, and corporate customers. Until recently, companies that wanted to take advantage of such networks to keep their partners up to date on capacity, availability, pricing, and delivery information had to purchase expensive dedicated telecommunications links and set up and maintain private networks. The major cost and maintenance involved with private networks made them an option only for a limited number of corporations.

FedEx: Excellent Postsales Customer Support; Tremendous Natural Advantages

When Fred Smith founded FedEx 23 years ago, he stressed two things: speed and reliability. As translated by a worldwide corporation, these two things mean *good information,* in as close to real time as possible. It's only natural that a company like FedEx would move on-line, where information is the name of the game (see Figure 2.6). A $10-billion global company, FedEx has managed to put its core competency onto the Internet. At FedEx sites, customers can track their own packages anywhere in the world. As a result of two distinct development efforts, FedEx has been available on AOL since October 1994 and on the Internet since November of that same year.

"It cost us $100,000 to get started in November of 1994," says Robert Hamilton, manager of Electronic Commerce Marketing. "We don't know exactly how much we've saved, but we're convinced just on anecdotal evidence that we crossed over the break-even point in the third month." First, FedEx has realized tremendous savings in the cost of agent interactions with its customers. Second, the company has realized cost savings in the area of telecommunications—it's expensive to pay for 800 numbers. Third, the increase in new volume as a result of the new, better service it provides is immeasurable.

"Customers are moving business over from the competitors," Hamilton says. "I can't tell you how many calls and messages I've seen from existing customers saying, 'We've decided to move all our shipping over to FedEx,' especially those customers who ship on a global basis." Finally, there's no easy way to measure the intangible benefits of instant customer gratification that the Web site provides.

FedEx faced a number of significant technical challenges in opening its virtual store. As Hamilton puts it, "It's quite an exercise to go through a company as densely structured with databases and so forth as Federal Express and begin to open it up for customers. Our systems are tightly controlled and exquisitely redundant; they depend upon data cascading in a certain order from one system to

Continued

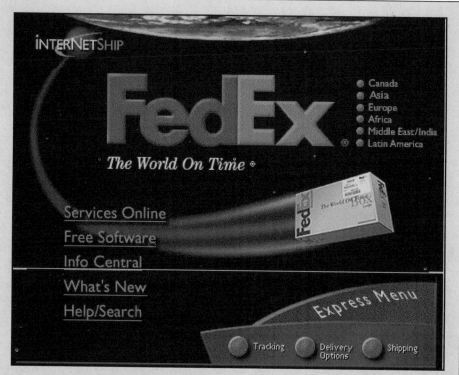

Figure 2.6   FedEx's Web site.

another. That's essential in order to control the tight timeframes we have for delivery. To open that system up for customers to make their own transactions is like changing the tires on a car as they drive at 60 mph down the road." But now, in an information-centered world, the freshest information is always there. "It's still whipsawed us quite a bit and we've had some growing pains. We're learning how to scale resources up as needed."

However, FedEx also comes to the party with some expertise in helping customers handle information. "Eleven years ago, we started a program called PowerShip with some of our larger-volume cus-

Continued

tomers," says Hamilton. "We just put a computer on their back dock. The customer filled out screens, and the shipping labels printed out on dedicated printers. This was a tremendous help to our customers shipping hundreds of packages a day. It was just a win-win situation all the way around." He continues, "As the price of PCs went down, we were able to provide PowerShip cost-effectively to smaller- and smaller-volume customers, down to as few as three packages a day. Now we have about 90,000 of these PowerShip PC systems in operation. We ship about 2.5 million packages a night, and over 60 percent of them are processed on PowerShip. We were doing electronic commerce before there was a term for it.

"Our tracking software for the PC is just the PowerShip application made stand-alone. We made the shift to a software-based shipping system for customers about one year ago [1995], introduced with ads at the Superbowl. When our customers saw this software, the answer was thunderingly, overwhelmingly, *yes*. The next incarnation of that software obviously was the public networks. Now you can download it at the Web site. We have about 300,000 software customers, but we had been doing this for years."

FedEx also has a built-in win for accepting payment. Shippers set up a FedEx account, and that account number validates the user as an authentic FedEx shipper, without inputting credit card information each time. At some point, FedEx intends to include credit card services so that people can make one-time shipments and they're considering electronic cash at some point. "That's down the road for us," says Hamilton, "The governing factor is the readiness of our customers for that. We're not looking for critical acclaim, but for box-office success, if you know what I mean. It's not just having people experience razzle-dazzle at the site."

FedEx hasn't done a lot of advertising. It's added the URL of its Web site to all marketing collateral worldwide and done some print ads and a few ads on the Web. "The standard things," says Hamilton. FedEx views advertising as part of the developmental budget for the Web site; there's no separate Web advertising campaign as such.

Continued

Hamilton explains why FedEx is serious about the Internet, "At FedEx, capacity comes in big chunks like airplanes and forklifts. Unless you have good information, you don't know where to go lease equipment at peak times or where to buy equipment in areas of historical growth. Our ability to deliver great information and great service to our customers comes out of our ability to have this business *at all*."

In conclusion, Hamilton adds that the Internet "represents a conviction for us, not just a hobby. We're now doing research among our customers, asking people to comment directly. We're looking for low-hanging fruit and to deliver it in the order our customers want." In July 1996, FedEx released interNetShip[SM], the first automated shipping transaction available on the Internet.

The Internet provides the same advantages of connecting with high-speed links without the undertaking of network maintenance and the high price tags. If your company can benefit from having fast links to its partners, consider using the Internet as your private business network.

In May 1996, Netscape Communications and Hewlett-Packard announced that they were joining forces to bring to corporations the capability of using the Internet as a private network. Netscape is the premier supplier of the user interface software for the Internet called *browsers*.

Using the Virtual Store to Generate Revenue

Virtual stores built to generate revenue are intended to create a significant amount of revenue through the on-line storefront (see Figure 2.7). Three specific ways in which firms currently generate revenue on the Web have been identified:

- ◆ Advertising
- ◆ Subscription/membership
- ◆ Point of sale

A Case Study of Using the Internet as an Intranet

A large international freight forwarder, with offices, customers, and suppliers worldwide, uses the Internet to facilitate communication with its partners, thereby using the Internet as an Intranet, or a large private network, for its operations.

The company's Web site contains up-to-the minute information regarding procedures, customs regulations, pricing, duties, shipper contact information, and so forth, which is made available only to its partners through the Web site. How does the company keep this information private?

- The Web site name is not publicized and does not start with *www*.
- The domain name (address) is not easily guessed, even with a computer program that randomly generates names.
- Access to the site is controlled through an ID/access code.
- The company uses firewall technology.

Even with all this security, the company does not keep sensitive information at this site. The purpose of the security precautions is to limit access to business partners and minimize unnecessary traffic, not the need to keep sensitive data.

Through the use of the Internet, this company can reduce operating costs and become more competitive by providing real-time information to its customers and partners.

Advertising Revenue

The most common and proven business revenue model for the Web at present is advertising sales. Forrester Research reports that $37 million to 45 million was spent in on-line advertising in 1995—and the majority of revenue from all this advertising was generated in the final quarter of the year. A business model base that points to advertising as the primary source of revenue gives a firm a tentatively solid base for creating a business on the Web.

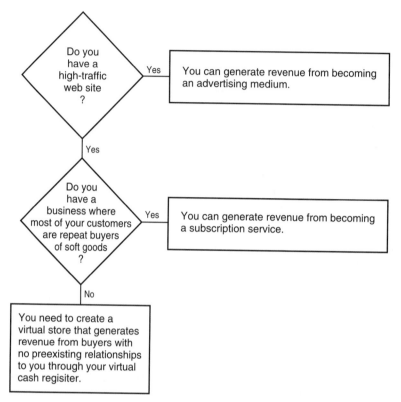

Figure 2.7   Using the virtual store to generate revenue.

Average advertising click-through figures are rather low, however, ranging from 0.36 percent to 1.4 percent. These nominal figures are due largely to the marketing and promotional strategies of the advertisers.

Revenue Based on Subscriptions and Memberships

Revenue models for creating Web businesses based on subscriptions and memberships have generally proven unsuccessful for several reasons:

- ◆ Web surfers must navigate a Web site and acquire and remember a password. This is a barrier to generating revenue; it is time consuming and can be annoying to potential customers.
- ◆ Web sites have traditionally not had success converting subscribers or members into purchasing customers.

- Users do not want to pay for flat-fee subscription services unless they clearly understand the value proposition upfront.
- Web surfers like to be part of a community of interest, but they also like to control the information about themselves that they present to selected Web sites. Becoming a subscriber or a member is objectionable to a large percentage of surfers because it means accepting a loss of anonymity and control.

Sites that have offered paid or free subscription/membership-based services have largely proven unsuccessful. However, as sites begin to attract a regular flow of traffic and a loyal following, subscription/membership-based revenue models may metamorphically return soon.

Point-of-Sale Revenues

While experts agree that electronic commerce, including product sales, banking, and money transfer, will soon explode, many Web-based businesses are planning and selling products and services now. And as a result, their business plans and revenue models are including commerce as an integral part of their successful business chemistry. The barriers to successful and easy electronic commerce have not been easy to break for the application developers, merchants, and consumers.

Many of the top traffic- and commerce-oriented Web sites cited here plan to sell physical and digital products and information through a variety of transaction payment/processing services.

The main goal of a revenue-generating virtual store is to close sales on-line. In contrast to the cost-reduction virtual store, this kind of store does not consider information valuable in its own right. Information is important only when it relates to closing sales.

TIP *If you already operate a store in the physical world, you can integrate your on-line sales process with your current process. Take advantage of your "3-D" brand leverage by:*
- *Setting up cross-promotions*
- *Using the virtual store for special purposes, such as closing out discounted inventory*
- *Using the virtual store for introducing and testing new product acceptance without upsetting the dynamics in the physical store*

Good examples of revenue-generation on-line stores include 1-800-FLOWERS, Amazon Books, and Virtual Vineyards. These stores are profiled elsewhere in this book.

Most companies can take advantage of both these models to some degree: That is, a company can reduce costs and generate revenue at the same time through a virtual store.

Elements of Success at the Virtual Store

In summary, the five keys to a successful virtual store are:

1. Setting the right goals for your store
2. Understanding the buyers' shopping experience and creating an appropriate environment for offering your products and services on-line
3. Getting to know your customers, thereby generating repeat business and adapting your store in response to their feedback
4. Advertising and promoting your store in the right venues, which leads to increased sales
5. Accepting payments in the virtual store

One needs to do all this while maneuvering through the legal realities of the virtual world. Subsequent chapters of this book cover these topics individually.

Merchants must offer their customers compelling reasons to shop, and most important, they must simplify the lives of shoppers. Consumers are familiar with the shopping paradigms and payment services available in the physical world. Effectively transferring these paradigms to the digital world will enable shoppers to utilize the same behavioral patterns. A large percentage of merchants agree that they must:

- Obtain specific audience demographic information about the target market
- Provide an incentive to visitors for behaving as the merchant wishes

Tower Records: New Revenues and Lower Costs

Tower Records was born in a family-owned drugstore in Sacramento, California, during the 1940s, and it has come a long way since then. Mike Farrace is vice president of Publications and Electronic Marketing for MTS, Inc., a privately owned, billion-dollar multinational company.

Tower has been selling on-line since June 1995 (Figure 2.8). In December 1995, Tower did $200,000 worth of business on AOL, which is a small percentage for the company, but it's new revenue, and it's growing. The company's primary presence so far has been on AOL, but at this writing it is days away from opening a site on the World Wide Web. How do the two compare?

Farrace says, "To make an analogy with physical reality, the on-line services are like beachfront property. They are more real. You have a user base that, while it churns, you have a community, a mindset. For a retailer like us, that's a good thing. It benefits someone that has a brand." In contrast, he adds, "The Internet is like the ocean. You can always launch your boat on the ocean, but you have to work and save to get that beachfront property. When you pay attention to all the features—like customer service—you can create something of value. You also have a partner when you're starting out, which is really helpful. I love the commercial services, I love AOL, they're a good partner. Hopefully we'll be a permanent resident of on-line services—we're adding CompuServe soon—yet our goal is to be ubiquitous." Farrace continues, "We like the Internet because it has a bit of a 60s sensibility, as does Tower Records. We have a brand history back to the 60s. And like the Internet, we're trying to evolve in a healthy way."

To bring customers to its new Web site, Tower has the advantage of placing advertisements in six company-owned magazines, with a combined circulation of over 725,000 worldwide, including the United States, Taiwan, Japan, and Mexico. Tower will be running its new URL under its logo in print ads, putting up posters in the

Continued

Figure 2.8 Tower Records' Web site.

retail stores, and tagging some radio and TV spots. The company has even created a deal with Netcom. In short, Farrace adds, "We're open to anything that doesn't cost a lot." On-line, Tower intends to buy banners on some of the search engine sites and create reciprocating hot links.

To keep costs even lower, Tower has rounded up a partnership with Apple Computer, which provided some AIX server machines for the Web site. Farrace feels that it may be cheaper for Tower to advertise on-line in the long run: "Although building a Web site is expensive and with the on-line services there are connectivity charges and commissions to pay, long term there seems to be a need for fewer personnel and less overhead in the on-line world."

Continued

On AOL, Tower accepts credit cards only: MasterCard, American Express, VISA, and Discover. The Web site will also be set up to accept credit card payments over the phone, for customers who have security concerns. The company is taking a look at electronic cash payments such as CyberCash, but since the business has slim margins, "close to those of grocery stores," says Farrace, "we're watching that. A penny to make a CyberCash wallet available doesn't sound like much, but we're focusing now on the basics, making sure the shopping cart works properly and things like that."

In the long term, Farrace says that Tower is looking to the Internet as a means of reducing costs for its 800 numbers and showing itself better to its customers: "We can show our vintage pictures and make our policies clearer than in the retail stores, where our image can get a little frantic sometimes." The on-line domain has already provided a better means of customer support. "We've already had lots of input from our customers on AOL—love letters, hate letters, that sort of thing. We love that."

CD sales seem to be especially suited to the Internet, and Tower's sales trend is proof of that. Perhaps its biggest remaining challenge is creating good on-line music samples, because it's been shown in retail stores that customers buy more CDs when they can listen first. For shopping on the Internet, most people's equipment can't produce sound of high enough quality. Also, the music licensing firms BMI and ASCAP are in the process of deciding whether to charge Tower for playing samples on-line, a cost which would be difficult to defray.

Tower is looking for any opportunity to get an edge in the highly competitive record business and believes that on-line sales may give them that edge. Farrace summarizes, "The record business is challenged now. Record clubs get over 15% of the sales because they can offer favorable prices. Stores like Best and Circuit City actually use records as loss leaders. This creates a lot of pressure, and there's also traditional competition. For instance, HMV and Virgin are opening stores here in the States. We're looking to cut costs, increase revenues, or both."

1-800-FLOWERS

1-800-FLOWERS is one of the best known and most successful on-line retailers today. It began its interactive initiative in 1992, and when its fiscal year ends in June 1996, it is projected to gross approximately $25 million (or 10% of company sales) from on-line transactions. 1-800-FLOWERS has more than 15 electronic commerce partners and maintains sites on America Online, CompuServe, several niche on-line services, the World Wide Web, and several other interactive platforms.

The 1-800-FLOWERS "store" on the Web went live in April 1995, after a process of careful development and testing that began in August 1994. Presently, the single largest order generator is America Online, and the bulk of the company's overall on-line sales come from the commercial on-line services. "However," adds Donna Iucolano, Director of the Company's Interactive Services Division, "the Web site is doing extremely well and has shown the largest percentage growth year to date of all our interactive efforts."

1-800-FLOWERS accepts payment over the telephone by credit card and check or money order, and cash in its physical retail stores across the Country. On-line payments are accepted by credit card at the present time, but the Company is exploring the possibility of incorporating electronic cash alternatives shortly.

At this writing, the Web site does not have hotlinks to other sites. A link strategy is, however, being developed for synergistic and complimentary sites. Several gardening and botanical sites as well as a few gift sites offer links to 1-800-FLOWERS. "And, they were all nice enough to send us E-mail and request our permission before making the link live," adds Iucolano.

As for the Company's future on-line? "We are well beyond the test phase!" says Iucolano. "We are a retail company committed to providing access to our customers anywhere and anytime—by telephone, brick and mortar retail, and on-line or interactive ser-

Continued

vice," she added. "What began as an idea and a research and development activity in the early 1990s has become one of the fastest growing divisions of the company. I believe business will continue to get better for us as more and more people come on-line and decide to participate. The Internet is fast becoming the standard—as the on-line services embrace it and abandon or open up their proprietary platforms, we will be able to point to our Web site from them. This will save retailers money as their interactive development and maintenance can become streamlined, and . . . more importantly, it will save customers money as the cost of doing business on-line will be reduced and the savings passed along," Iucolano said.

Iucolano points out that the commercial on-line services have offered a well-organized array of content and, more importantly, easy access, but "the Internet is the future . . . and the on-line services will face real competition from companies offering an in-the-box Internet solution at an unlimited, inexpensive, flat fee pricing structure."

According to Iucolano, the on-line services have a "love-hate relationship with the Internet." "On the one hand, they are holding on to their proprietary and closed platforms for as long as possible, yet they have simultaneously made major investments in Internet-related companies that provide access, content, and software."

In summary, Iucolano concludes with what she believes has made 1-800-FLOWERS such an effective on-line retailer: "We have approached the on-line world from a complete retail perspective. People often ask me what it's like being a virtual florist. My response is usually that I don't know! 1-800-FLOWERS is not a virtual florist . . . we are a real world florist with more than 20 years experience. This is extremely important for consumers because no one can deny the strength, power, legitimacy, and security of a recognized brand such as ours. Not that virtual brands have no place . . . because they do, but it will be harder to

Continued

achieve the success of a Virtual Vineyards or Amazon Books," she added.

Iucolano continues, "The biggest mistake companies make when deciding to go on-line is believing that if they build a Web site, people will come to it. A retailer would never invest hundreds of thousands of dollars to build a 'brick and mortar' store without stocking it, staffing it, managing it, promoting it, etc. . . . so why believe it can be done on-line? If it's holiday time, the 'store' needs to reflect it. And, the day after Christmas, the decorations and holiday products must be removed and replaced with new ones. The most important thing to remember is that what works at retail . . . works at retail! Whether you're engaging in commerce via traditional means or on-line, take advantage of proven retail (and direct) marketing strategies such as first order incentives, discounts, contests and sweepstakes, grand opening promotions, etc. And, when you offer them on-line . . . don't be afraid to tweak to take full advantage of what the new medium has to offer!"

- ◆ Offer a cash-based payment system
- ◆ Effectively offer and market high-quality products and services
- ◆ Provide informative and responsive customer service
- ◆ Generate repeat business
- ◆ Have an identity by name and brand
- ◆ Make it easy to purchase products
- ◆ Provide a good place to browse
- ◆ Find ways to encourage customers to share with others what they learn about the products

Despite low electronic commerce figures from products and services of between $100 million and 200 million, electronic commerce and Web shopping are, as some experts claim, "beginning to kick into high-gear," as Web users become connected and consumer-oriented.

Locating Your Virtual Store: Hosting Services, Malls, or Stand-alone Sites?

In the real world, you have heard the saying that location is everything. In the virtual world, where geography disappears, does location lose its relevance completely? Not really. Location is still relevant, not only in absolute terms (meaning where your server is located), but also in relative terms (that is, who you are next to). The discussion here will focus first on the absolute, or physical, definition of location. The goal of this chapter is to help you decide whether you should keep the server where your virtual store is housed at your facilities and maintained by one of your employees or use a company that specializes in maintaining Web servers, usually referred to as *hosting services*. Figure 2.9 walks you through this decision process.

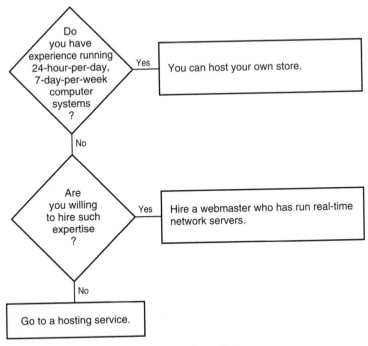

Figure 2.9 Locating your virtual store.

Setting up Your Own Web Site

Many good books have already been written about setting up a Web site, so we will not go into detail on the process here. (See the Recommended Reading listing at the end of the book for more information.) If you are planning on setting up and maintaining your virtual store, make sure that you have the internal resources to keep the light on 24 hours a day, 7 days a week. On the Internet, your customers expect your store to always be open and will be frustrated if their attempts to reach your store are turned down.

TIP   *There will be many cases in which your Web server is up and operating yet your customers cannot connect to it. This is caused by the heavy traffic loads on the Net or a down mode between your server and the consumer.*

Hosting Services

Hosting services are the easiest way for a new business on the Internet to set up shop. One can choose a series of services from the long list of menu items offered. Hosting services differ in size and style. Some offer simply the technical pieces, such as the Web server and the Internet connectivity. Others offer creative services in designing the Web site, marketing services in running promotional programs, and consultative services on issues such as transaction systems. The most important step in choosing a hosting service is to do thorough reference checking with the service's current customers, and check their performance in the specific areas you are interested in.

There are several bigger hosting services that are available to the virtual store owner, which refer to themselves by a variety of names such as malls, shopping services, and so on. MCI Mall, GNN Forum (America Online), and AT&T all offer hosting services. On-line services such as AOL and CompuServe also offer hosting in their own branded service networks. There are several smaller, regional services that operate virtual store Web servers for fewer than ten sites.

Microsoft and IBM announced in June of 1996 their entry to the hosting services business. Both companies plan on offering merchandizing, transaction and payment technologies, making it very easy for a merchant to have a turn-key virtual store.

TIP *Over 50 percent of the top sites on the Internet are hosted by hosting services. Do not think that you have to create your virtual store in house. Some of the highest traffic sites, such as Playboy, are operated by hosting services.*

The best thing about hosting services is that they can help you get going quickly and take the technical headaches off your shoulders, enabling you to concentrate on the issues that you really should be focused on, such as the shopping experience at your site and advertising and merchandising.

What do hosting services offer? Most offer the capability of creating a Web site for you, from your designs and instructions, in the HTML language. Some are beginning to add further animation capabilities by using technologies such as Java and Sharkwave. Some hosting services can also supply graphic design capabilities. Our advice is to use the graphic design firm that you currently use in your real-world business in order to maintain consistency with your other materials. Use the hosting service–supplied graphic designer for input on what works in the virtual world. Small graphics will usually not work in the virtual world since the resolution is not high enough.

Most hosting services also offer the ability to incorporate customer-tracking software into your virtual site. They may use the packages offered today (see Chapter 4) or design customized tools especially for your needs. In addition, hosting services can help a virtual store owner accept payments by installation of the software available from companies such as CyberCash and First Virtual.

The most common benefit of using a hosting service is that it saves the cost of ongoing Web server maintenance, which is a 24-hour-a-day, 7-day-a-week job that usually entails hiring a full-time Webmaster at $3000 to $5000 per month. Thus, in comparing the cost of buying a server machine to the cost of using a hosting server, be aware that maintenance of the server will be the biggest ongoing expense—and you can't afford to skimp on maintenance, because if your server is down, potential customers may form a negative impression of your business.

TIP   *Robert Olson, proprietor of Virtual Vineyards states, "A server has to be snappy." Virtual Vineyards has a high speed data (T1) line, because Mr. Olson feels that the user shouldn't have to sit around waiting for the site to respond.*

Malls

Most people on the Internet do not differentiate between hosting services and malls. Technically, there is a difference. You can be part of a mall even if the mall operator does not host your Web server, just by having a link to the mall, that gives the appearance that you are "physically" there.

Malls on the Internet provide the same value to virtual shop owners that is provided by malls in the real world—that is, bringing a certain amount of traffic to the store and giving value to an individual store by housing it under one roof with similar types of stores. You may have noticed in the real world that malls have personalities of their own and attract stores of a certain kind. Discount malls usually have a mass retailer such as Kmart or Wal-Mart as the anchor tenant, with a lot of small specialty discount stores. High-end malls usually have Nordstrom or Neiman Marcus as an anchor, with upscale boutiques. Internet malls are not yet so specialized as to differentiate by type of shopper, but this is expected to happen soon.

TIP   *The biggest benefit that the Internet adds to the mall concept is that, regardless of where the virtual stores are located (the physical servers), the store can have the appearance of being in the mall by being hot-linked to it. This enables stores to be in more than one virtual mall without opening branch stores.*

The Internet is a natural place for malls to grow and flourish. Plan on familiarizing yourself with malls that can provide you the right demographic traffic, and establish links to them soon.

IBM's World Avenue service is an example of a turnkey hosting service/mall, which also gets referred to as a shopping service in some of the trade literature.

Launched in fall of 1996 with twenty brand name merchants, such as the Express unit of the Limited, the Hudson's Bay Company and others, IBM operates a "full-service" hosting service that will offer merchandising, transaction and payment capabilities to its merchants.

World Avenue runs on Netscape's Merchant servers (see Appendix E for detailed discussion). In addition to hosting the virtual stores for its merchants, World Avenue will provide its merchants sales data that can be manipulated through search tools. A World Avenue merchant has the ability to get information on market conditions, purchase volumes and site usage patterns.

Initially merchants will be able to accept SET (Secure Electronic Transaction) compatible credit card payments. Eventually, World Avenue merchants will be able to provide personalized views of their merchandise to shoppers, if the shoppers are willing to provide them with specific information.

All this comes at a price to the virtual store owner. Pricing varies by merchandise, categories and the number of items included. World Avenue will charge a start-up fee of around $30,000, a 5 percent commission on sales and a monthly maintenance charge of around $2,500.

Another big entrant to the world of hosting services and malls is Microsoft. With its purchase of e-shop, Inc. of San Mateo, Microsoft now offers the eShop Plaza mall service to major retailers such as Spiegel, Tower Records, Avon, the Good Guys and 1-800 Flowers. The eShop Plaza is expected to move to the Microsoft Network (MSN) for MSN's relaunch in the fall of 1996.

E-Shop Plaza will run on Microsoft's Merchant servers when it is ported to the MSN which also includes secure credit card transaction capability based on SET, the protocols developed jointly by VISA & Mastercard.[1]

Closing Thoughts

Planning your virtual store is one of the most important steps toward ensuring success. The planning process starts with understanding what

Hosting Service: Internet Distribution Services

IDS, located in Palo Alto, California, is one of the earliest Web development houses, dating back to 1993. Its current customers include Clorox, *Palo Alto Weekly,* the San Jose Sharks, Informix, and Trimble Navigation (see Figure 2.10).

IDS currently manages 12 Web servers that are on 24 hours a day, 7 days a week. This is done by automated monitoring. Marc Fleischmann, president of IDS says, "It is trivial to consume 100% of an individual's time baby-sitting only one Web server. The real challenge is to serve multiple servers without being a full-time systems operator".

How is Fleischmann able to do this? Each one of his 12 machines "wakes up" every five minutes and asks the following self-diagnostic questions:

1. Am I up and operating?
2. Am I fully connected to the Internet?
3. Do I have enough disk space?
4. Do I see all the other machines?

In this fashion, in addition to checking its own operations, each machine is able to check on the other 11 servers.

Fleischmann has these checks staggered so that every minute, two or more machines are in check mode. When one server cannot "see" another, it pages Fleischmann to tell him which machine is down. If the machine is actually down, he gets additional pages from the other servers. Very often, the server that was identified as down comes up on its own because its connection to the Net will be reestablished. It is common for Internet servers to lose their Internet connectivity for a few seconds. When they come up, Fleischmann is paged again, notifying him that everything is okay. On the Internet, acceptable downtime for a server is less than 0.01 percent. Fleischmann's 12 machines have had about two hours of downtime in 2½

Continued

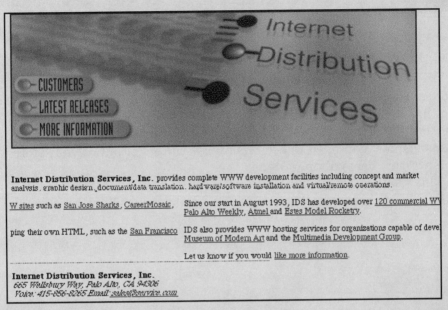

Figure 2.10   Internet Distribution Service's Web site.

years. One minute of outage once a week is acceptable and should be expected. Fleischmann uses remote diagnostics when a machine does not come up right away. He often is able to bring the server up remotely but sometimes, in situations when the server is out of hard-disk memory, human intervention is necessary.

Fleischmann's idea of service can be characterized as a virtual listing service. The reason it is called *virtual* is that not all the machines are at one site. Lots of support is necessary in a hosting service, in addition to making sure that the machine is up on a regular basis. The support ranges from simple creation of HTML pages to virtual store layout, graphic design, consumer-tracking capabilities, and accepting payment. On the servers that are physically located at IDS's customer site, a local IDS employee needs to be available. This local IDS person has to know how to run a Unix machine but does not need to have any Internet or Web expertise.

Continued

> There are several bigger hosting services that are available to the virtual store owner: MCI Mall, GNN, and AT&T all offer hosting services.

your business is today and assessing its potential in the virtual world. Setting realistic goals is also key to your success. Keeping in mind that most of the stores on the Internet today are used as cost cutters and not sales venues, you need to establish what you want out of your store for the first few years of operations.

This chapter has also introduced you to hosting sites and malls and helped you choose the option appropriate for your situation.

CHAPTER THREE

DESIGNING THE SHOPPING EXPERIENCE

Topics presented in this chapter:

- ◆ Trust: The Most Essential Element of Commerce
- ◆ Creating the Irresistible Shopping Environment
- ◆ Moving from Browsing to Buying
- ◆ The Shopping Experience
- ◆ Presenting the Electronic Invoice
- ◆ Getting the Shoppers to Your Virtual Store

Once you've decided that a virtual store makes sense for your business, you'll want to create a shopping environment that's as attractive as possible to your customers. The focus of this chapter is on the customer's experience in your store. It discusses all the psychological elements of designing a virtual store.

After you've read this chapter, you'll understand a lot more about the psychology of shopping and about how that knowledge can be applied to your virtual store. You'll see why trust is the most important aspect of commerce, and you'll understand how the presence or absence of trust influences a decision to buy on-line.

You'll learn five reasons why people shop and, thereby, how to make your store exciting to as many of the type of shoppers that you are trying to attract as possible. You'll learn how to turn browsers into buyers, and

71

you'll learn how to keep your customers from canceling their transactions when they're presented with an electronic invoice at the end of an otherwise successful shopping experience.

Trust: The Most Essential Element of Commerce

Trust is the most important element of commerce. During a commercial transaction, if the buyer and seller do not trust each other, the cost of the transaction is escalated, because of the need for trusted third parties, such as escrow agents or certified payment instruments.

Human beings establish trust by having knowledge about each other (see Figure 3.1). In a transaction, such knowledge is obtained, thus trust is attained, when the transacting parties reveal information about themselves. In our real world today, we have various levels of trust in transactions, depending on the amount of information that is revealed by the buyer to the seller, and vice versa.

In small towns, where most people know each other, both buyer and seller have a fair amount of knowledge about who the other person is. In that environment, merchants often allow their customers to defer payment by signing for merchandise, thus extending credit at no additional charge until a more convenient time for payment, usually at the end of a month. This type of exchange still goes on in the smaller communities in the heart of modern Silicon Valley, where clerks at Robert's Grocery in Woodside and Drager's in Menlo Park know over 80 percent of their customers by

Figure 3.1   Establishing trust.

name, allow them to sign for their purchases, and without any discussion give credit for complaints. In the small-town situation, dispute resolution is not governed by laws as much as by acceptable social norms. Both buyer and seller have as an important goal the desire to maintain and uphold their reputations. Within that value system, it is perfectly acceptable for people to just sign for the merchandise, instead of using a credit card.

Away from high-trust environments, where a reasonable degree of familiarity exists between buyer and seller, in larger communities, such as cities, transactions change nature. In these environments, trust is established in different ways. A merchant trusts the buyer in accepting payment through an intermediary—usually a bank and/or a check guarantee company when the buyer writes a check, a card association such as VISA/MasterCard/AmEx when the buyer uses a credit card, or the government when the buyer uses cash or coins. In the case of credit cards, the fee that the merchant pays to this third-party trust intermediary depends on whether the buyer physically walked into the store. Transactions using cards, which rate a higher trust level because the merchant gets to see both a human being and the physical card, are approximately 50 basis points less expensive than transactions without cards, in which the card number is presented over the telephone.

In these environments, the buyer's trust in merchants often is established through brand names. A buyer's propensity to trust a seller is directly related to the brand image the merchant has been able to establish. Brand identity usually is established through very expensive advertising, promotion, and brand awareness–building programs in the community, such as sponsorships.

MYTH: *You cannot establish trust in a virtual environment where you cannot see and touch products.*

There are many ways of establishing trust. Tactile contact is one of them, but on a daily basis in our lives we deal with trusted entities in situations where we're not seeing and touching things. A good example involves a savings account. We trust that $5,000 is safe in the bank, even though we have no tactile assurance of this. Through the use of trusted entities—through allowing your consumers to get to know you—you can establish trust at your virtual store.

How to Establish Trust in a Virtual World

The same need for trust between buyer and seller exists in the virtual world. The same people conduct the commerce, only now they sit behind computers. Merchants still need assurances that the buyer's payments are good and the buyers need assurances that the merchandise and services they are buying are of the quality expected—and if not, they need an assured way of getting their money back.

To date, one of the attractive features of the virtual world has been that its participants can completely hide their identities and take on new ones. This feature has been a very positive influence for chat groups, in which people gain the ability to discuss subjects they would normally shy away from, with the complete security of being anonymous. However, what has been a boon to chat groups and forums in the virtual world has been a bust for commerce.

Until now, the virtual world was too easy for buyers and sellers to enter and exit without serious consequences. Participants could change or disappear overnight, or misrepresent their identities. All of these capabilities are detrimental to establishing trust, the basis of commerce.

Consumers have shied away from spending a lot of money at virtual stores, at least partly out of fear that a merchant might take their money and run without delivering the promised wares. They have not had the comfort of brand names they recognize—or if they do recognize names, they have not been assured that these are authentic sellers rather than impostors. Similarly, virtual merchants have been frustrated by the inability to get to know who their customers are and establish relationships with them for repeat sales, which are the basis of creating a successful store in the real world. On the other hand, merchants have been scared of insulting their customers' desires for anonymity or of being "flamed" (harshly criticized or chastised) in front of 40 million people on the Internet.

This book suggests that the virtual world is not isolated from the rest of the real world. Those hits to the Web sites represent actual human beings with human needs that the virtual merchants have to recognize. New ways must be found of fostering trust so that those needs can be met by on-line purchases. Trust must be earned and maintained by building brand identities and delivering high-quality goods and services.

Shopping is not a uniform experience that always results in a sale. In fact, it is a diverse collection of experiences, each with a totally different goal. Having a Web site does not mean you have a virtual store, and having a lot of visitors does not mean you will have a lot of sales. This book helps you analyze your business, assess the appropriateness of a virtual store, design a compelling experience, and sets realistic expectations for yourself as a virtual store owner.

Creating the Irresistible Shopping Environment

Why do people shop? Psychologists who seek to understand shopping psychology try to answer this question and others, such as: How do people make the decision to buy? How, when, and why do they move from looking to buying? Is this process different on-line than in the physical world?

Amy Kim, an on-line designer who studies shopping behavior as well as technology, answered this question and several others. The next several sections reflect Kim's excellent analyses of on-line shopping and the virtual store experience.

MYTH: *You can create a virtual store overnight by running your catalog pages through a scanning device and putting them on the Internet.*

Looking at the Internet as the on-line analogue of mail-order catalogs is a big mistake. Direct-mail catalogs have a lot of advantages over the Internet. They arrive in your mailbox and you can scan through them while you are in bed before going to sleep. With an Internet catalog, the consumer has to actively turn on a computer, activate communications software, make sure that the communications link is established, activate the browser software, and type in the domain name of the catalog. So just putting a print catalog on-line is not sufficient because, ultimately, consumers tend to use what is easy and fast, and the on-line store will not have a chance. For an on-line catalog to be successful, it has to offer features and capabilities that are not available with print media. A futuristic example might be: You are at an on-line catalog looking for a cotton sweater; you find one that you like but it comes in 13 colors. You have your own photo stored on hard disk and you can electronically overlay the sweater in different colors on your photograph to see which one you like the best. This virtual dressing room cannot be had with a print catalog.

First of all, people shop to obtain the things they need, such as food, clothing, shelter, and entertainment. People have different criteria by which they shop, and they have different shopping styles for obtaining the necessities and niceties of life. Psychologists can identify five types of shopping experience: for entertainment, for companionship, for efficiency, for price, and for features.

Shopping for Entertainment

Shopping for entertainment is likely to result in a search for a sensual experience—soft music, well-dressed people, pretty flowers—whatever it takes to create an image of beauty and pleasure. When shopping for entertainment, a lot of time is spent browsing and not much time is spent buying.

Shoppers for entertainment are likely to visit high-end sites such as Tower Records on-line or obviously sensual sites such as Playboy. They'll want to hear the songs and see the videos and pictures.

In the physical world, retailers appeal to shoppers who are shopping for entertainment by creating positive moods. If your store seeks shoppers who are looking for entertainment, use some of the same techniques.

You might think that it is difficult or expensive to create a virtual store that appeals primarily to people who shop for entertainment, but it can be highly creative and rewarding to offer some appeal to the senses at your store. In fact, most of the Internet Web sites—mostly unknowingly—try to be entertaining by becoming "cool." For instance, good graphic design can go a long way toward creating visual appeal, especially if you avoid the temptation of adding too many large graphics files to download, because they take a long time at 14.4 kilobits per second (Kbps).

Shopping for Companionship

People shop for companionship in the physical world because they enjoy the social interaction involved. For instance, an older woman whose children have left home might go shopping with friends or she might go alone just to savor the interactions with the salespeople.

In the on-line world, you'll most readily find the equivalent of shopping for companionship in the chat groups. In a chat group, people gather for interactive conversations using typed messages or sometimes presenting themselves as animated on-line characters called *avatars.*

In the physical world, shopping for companionship is enhanced by the use of 800 numbers. By calling an 800 number, a customer can ask questions, get suggestions, and generally have a real interaction with a living, breathing salesperson at the other end of the line.

At your virtual store, you might appeal to shoppers for companionship by offering a forum or E-mail exchange about your products or services. For example, a Land Rover store on-line might offer customers an opportunity to send in stories about their adventures in Land Rovers so that other customers can read and respond. Gibson Guitars offers a forum in which customers can exchange information—everything from general tips about guitar playing to specific Gibson guitar models played on particular album tracks.

Forums, chat groups, and moderated Usenet group discussions are wonderful and inexpensive ways to promote social interaction and companionship for potential customers. If this is the profile for your potential buyer, think of your virtual store as a comfortable virtual café, where your customers drop in regularly, chat with others, and spend significant time at your site. Such environments lend themselves to strong customer loyalty and repeat sales.

Shopping for Efficiency: When Time Is at a Premium

People usually shop for efficiency when they're buying the necessities of life or routine items. For instance, people who use the Peapod on-line service to order groceries (for delivery) want to get the grocery shopping done as quickly as possible. They don't want to feel or smell the tomatoes prior to buying; they just want some tomatoes in the house! It's interesting to note that, when shopping for efficiency, price usually is not an issue. The Peapod shopper is quite happy to pay the shopping fee to get groceries delivered.

Other types of shoppers who are likely to look for efficiency in their on-line shopping include:

- ◆ *Gift shoppers.* When buying a gift, a shopper often wants simply to get a nice item quickly, at a reasonable price. Many of the more successful virtual stores offer gift items.

- ◆ *Home-based businesses.* Small business owners need many of the same items that large businesses need. However, small business owners may not have the benefit of a purchasing department to spend the time researching and procuring products. These people appreciate the efficiency of shopping on-line.

MYTH: *You should have a virtual store only if your business customers come from a large geographic area.*
   A virtual store can be very effective even in a geographically small community. A restaurant in Palo Alto posts its menu and allows its customers to order on-line for pickups. Waiters on Wheels also allows on-line ordering of food, and they deliver in usually fairly small geographic areas.

Shopping for Price: When There's Plenty of Time but Not Much Money

You'll know you're shopping for price when you just want the cheapest version or brand you can get of a particular product. Interestingly enough, right now there is not much of a price differential between shopping on-line and shopping in the physical world. Why? Manufacturers are protecting their physical world distribution channels. Because the cost of goods and cost of distribution may be much lower on-line, over time you can expect to see large differences in prices of on-line versus physical world distribution channels. Eventually, physical stores will charge for a higher level of service and not just for the product itself.

MYTH: *As the Internet levels the field for marketing, brand names will no longer matter.*
   It is difficult to establish a sense of what the products are on the Internet since you cannot see and feel them; therefore, brand names will play an even *more* important role than they do in the real world. A consumer is going to be a lot more willing to buy a 32-inch television set made by Sony than a similar product from an unknown manufacturer. The friendly salespeople who are often the vehicle used to sell unknown brands do not exist on the Internet, so distinction among brands becomes paramount.

Shopping for Specific Features: Getting Information about a Product to Be Sure It Will Meet the Need

Many times shoppers are interested in finding products that have a particular combination of features to meet their needs. A customer might want a plain-paper fax machine with a three-mailbox voice-mail system *and* a cordless handset. That customer will look far and wide to find just the right product. Sometimes price is a factor in the purchase, and sometimes it's not too important. Your virtual store can appeal to these customers by providing detailed information about the features of your products or services. You could go one step further and offer comparisons of your product with other products on the market, with point-by-point listings of features.

A good example of a Web site that appeals to feature shoppers is www.edmunds.com. It's a site devoted to cars, new and used. It compares and rates cars according to several criteria, such as safety and whether they're fun to drive. It also provides a brief written evaluation of each car. Shoppers who visit edmunds.com will get a good perspective on the objective and subjective features of the car they're considering.

Many Shoppers, Many Styles

In fact, the same person may shop in each of these ways at various times, depending on mood and other factors. How can you help more types of shoppers to find satisfaction at your virtual store? Here are a few suggestions:

- For those focused on efficiency, offer the option to eliminate fancy graphics that take a lot of time to download.
- For those focused on a sensual shopping experience, (optional) sound, animation, video, and graphics can enhance your site.
- For features shoppers, offer a bulletized list that summarizes the features of your product or service.
- To appeal to companionship-oriented shoppers, make sure there's a way to communicate with someone at your site. Try putting an E-mail address at the bottom of each page, where a customer can be assured of getting a quick response. In fact, you may wish to staff your virtual store with someone whose job it is to respond to customer E-mail.

- ◆ Also for companionship-oriented shoppers, offer forums, chat groups, and Usenet news-group discussions. Try to moderate these or at least participate in them actively. They will be a very valuable source of information about your customers.
- ◆ For those focused on price, be sure to pass along to the customer any cost savings you may have. For instance, keep shipping costs as low as possible if your store ships merchandise to the customer.

Let's look at an example: A merchant such as Virtual Vineyards appeals to a number of different types of shoppers already. To those who shop for companionship, the personal touch of receiving a letter from the sommelier to recommend a selection of wines has appeal. To those who shop as a sensual experience, the pictures of wine and the background profiles of winemakers add richness. To those who shop for best price, the monthly specials have appeal. To those who shop for features, the ability to select from broad categories of wine is attractive (red versus white, chardonnay versus cabernet, and so forth). To those who shop for efficiency, the snappy T1 connection at Virtual Vineyards is a boon.

The Appropriateness of the Virtual Community

The chat groups and forums of the on-line world have received a lot of attention in the last several years. They are the second most common usage of the on-line service on the Internet, after E-mail. Communities created in this virtual world can be very strong in shaping consumer opinion and behavior. It is not right, though, to approach your virtual store with a goal to create a community if you do not have such a community today in the real world. Certain businesses, such as Gibson Guitars and the ice hockey team San Jose Sharks, have natural communities around them. They can take advantage of the technology that the virtual world offers to promote these communities. Other businesses do not.

For example, Levi's, the clothing company, is busy developing free computer games for its Internet site where children can play and hang out. Why would Levi's spend money to create such a place in the virtual world when it would not consider funding a playground in the physical world? And why is Levi's making computer games when it is in the clothing business?

If your business has never had a natural community or a following, then it may not be appropriate to set out into your virtual store with the goal of starting one. (There are some products that do not have a natural community and a community would not be sustainable even if it were possible to create one.) Instead, embrace a community that naturally exists in the virtual world. Support it, work with it, add value to it, and through this adoption process you will receive the rewards of belonging to a community. There are several towns that are in the process of developing or already have virtual communities on the Internet. This would be a good place to start.

Returning to our example, Levi's would be better off embracing a natural community centering around education on the Internet or a computer game manufacturer's home site, such as Rocket Science Games, rather than starting from scratch with its own.

One caveat: In Chapter 1, we learned that today's on-line shoppers are quite computer savvy. How can a virtual store create more appeal for the majority of shoppers? With so much emphasis on being cool, you can be certain that this isn't enough to create lasting appeal for your customers. Don't get caught up in cool. It may get people to visit your site, but it probably won't convince them to buy. What makes people buy is convincing them that they want what you have.

Barriers to On-line Shopping?

Right now, just logging on to a computer to go shopping is a big barrier. Most ordinary, nontechnical folks won't even get past that one. But many providers of infrastructure services, such as phone and cable companies, are working to overcome this hurdle (see Chapter 8). Says Amy Kim, "Simplicity is the key for people."

How can you make shopping as simple as possible? One way to overcome the barrier of logging on is by attracting customers *who are already logged on.* That's where Web banners come in, and why they're so important—your customers may be at another site, ready to pop over and shop at the drop of a hot link. For instance, a shopper might be at the Netscape site, downloading some software, when he or she sees a Ticketron Web banner. Suddenly, the thought of that upcoming concert is too much to resist . . . and Ticketron has a customer.

Compare on-line shopping to the way things work in the physical world: Research shows that people usually order from mail-order cata-

CMD/Studio Archetype

Clement Mok designs (CMd), newly renamed Studio Archetype, has created some of the best-known sites on-line to date, including the Photodisc site, QVC (on both the Microsoft Network and the Web), HarperCollins Publishing, 20th Century Fox, and 24 Hours in Cyberspace. They view themselves as "information and identity architects" for their clients.

At this writing, the company's work is split just about fifty-fifty between traditional print design, such as branding, identity, and packaging, and interactive design, such as Web sites, on-line services and ATM Interfaces. But they point out there is a lot of crossover—clients who wanted one type of design are asking for the other, and vice versa.

Studio Archetype sees their own Web site (www.studioarchetype. com) as a place to discuss things, to show examples—not as a marketing tool. Because the company is so successful that they turn away up to 50 percent of clients seeking to work with them, they don't need to do a lot of advertising nor use their Web site to promote themselves. Their site has hotlinks to sites they've created, just so customers can see their work in action (see Figure 3.2).

When asked if Studio Archetype has any principles of Web design to recommend, Eric Wilson, one of the firm's two Executive Producers, replies on behalf of Clement Mok, Mark Crumpacker, and Amanda North, the company's three principals:

> We see ourselves as guardians of the user experience. We want users to experience a product we have designed with a sense of ease and security. It's hard to come up with hard and fast rules to guarantee this result. For instance, one common question is: Should we always provide a way to step out of a transactional flow? Some people think yes, absolutely, thinking the customer might want to step out to order another product; others are leery, thinking the customer might simply not come back.

Continued

Figure 3.2 Studio Archetype's Web site.

Continued

Another common question is: Given the technology back-end system we are using, how can we make the experience easiest for the customer? For example, we know it is not user friendly to make a customer re-key information they have already input if they leave an order screen and then return to it, but can the system accommodate this and still remain secure? Two other solid rules of thumb are not to offer too many navigational choices and always make sure the user can go back from whence they came.

Ultimately, our approach is different for each client. We do not impose any cookie cutter strategy on a client because their vision may be completely different from ours. At the same time, we have strategic suggestions and we share them based both on their specific business goals and on what we have learned in the past. One issue is how much knowledge we can share from project to project and still maintain client confidentiality. Client confidentiality always comes first.

The bottom line is that all of our projects are team efforts, both within our studio and with our client. There is always a huge amount of mutual learning.

As for the long term, Wilson states, "We would love to be in the business of creating modules that could be easily replicated and then customized for a specific client, but we're not there yet. There simply aren't enough standards yet."

logs within 48 hours if they're going to order at all. Why? The immediacy of having the catalog physically present is a reminder to make a purchase. It encourages buying, because it's *there*. In contrast, the computer is not always on. A customer must proactively decide to shop on-line and turn on the computer to do so; or the person must be on-line for another reason when deciding to browse. This is one reason that it's so important for merchants to have a strategy for bringing customers to their sites: Give people any good reason to go to your site, and while they're there, they may decide to buy.

Certain additional barriers exist, which the market itself will help overcome. Right now, even without the barrier of logging on, on-line shopping actually is more difficult than, for example, ordering from a catalog because it takes more time. Also, shipping costs for items ordered on-line seem to be slightly higher than those for catalog items, averaging $7.50 to $8.50 compared to a prorated shipping fee or the shipping-included policy of catalog stores such as L.L. Bean.

Another weakness of the on-line shopping experience is requiring the consumer to enter a lot of personal information. Many shoppers balk at this portion of the on-line transaction, either because they hate to type or, more likely, because it seems slightly risky to send so much personal information off into the unknown. For tips on effective ways to present an invoice on-line, see "Presenting the Electronic Invoice" later in this chapter.

Uniqueness

Another important thing a virtual store can offer is uniqueness. In fact, one highly recommended technique for creating a successful on-line business is to provide goods or services not available elsewhere. For instance, your virtual store might offer:

- One-of-a-kind items (such as vintage guitars, auction items)
- Unreleased material (such as music clips or video outtakes)
- Customized items (such as monogrammed shirts or autographed books)
- Personalized services (such as Amazon Book's access to obscure book titles)

The more you can offer goods and services like these, the more incentive people have to overcome the hurdles of logging on and getting to your merchandise. If you have a brand identity off-line and want your customers to move on-line, you can use your virtual store to offer additional goods or services that are not available offline.

Lifestyle Creation

There are some ways in which on-line shopping will never replace the actual, physical experience of shopping. For instance, several on-line malls have failed because they did not incorporate the aspect of lifestyle creation that people expect from their experience with physical malls.

QVC

QVC approached Studio Archetype to design the QVC on-line shopping site (see Figure 3.3). The overall goals of the project were: (1) to create a presence with shopping functionality and (2) to create a fun, distinctive appearance. Centric Development, of Seattle, did the technical portion of the work.

If you visit the site, you'll see that it has five "magazine" areas, as follows:

Figure 3.3   QVC's Web site, designed by Studio Archetype.

Continued

- Corporate
- What's new
- Backstage
- Assistance
- Shopping application

The shopping application area is divided into subcategories, such as kitchen or home office. Within each subcategory, a range of product types is offered. Once you find the item of choice, you can fill out an order form to purchase it.

Some of the challenges faced in developing the site for QVC are not unique to on-line shopping. Studio Archetype looked at QVC's business models and helped envision what the Web could do for its business. It needed to make sure that tens of thousands of products would be available—"everything all the time."

The on-line business model is somewhat different from the identity QVC developed for television. That model is time-based: An item appears on-screen and then it's gone. The host explains the product, which helps sell it. For developing the on-line site, Studio Archetype used demographic research to come up with an identity completely different from the TV identity.

QVC created new database systems to accommodate this new model before the system ever went on-line. An unexpected benefit was that, since the operators had access to the new database systems, they could cross-sell many items. The new on-line business model created more selling opportunities, even on the phone.

The QVC site is available on Microsoft Network (MSN) at this writing, but should be available soon directly on the Internet.

Even a good catalog sells lifestyle, not things. A well-planned catalog is a collection of items that support a lifestyle concept. Catalogs such as those from L.L. Bean, The Sharper Image, or Lillian Vernon instantly bring a lifestyle image to mind for customers. If it's an image they like, they tend to buy.

A lesson to draw from these observations is *take time to plan your presentation.* Select your merchandise with care. If your virtual store is a hodgepodge, it's not likely to be remembered. When you create a lifestyle, people interested in that lifestyle will instantly associate it with your store. When the need arises, they remember, "Oh, that's where I go to get this kind of gadget. . . ."

MYTH: *The Internet is a natural shopping environment and will eventually replace physical stores and malls with virtual stores.*

There are many experiences that one cannot have in a networked environment. Many people view shopping as an activity that takes them physically out of the house, provides companionship, and allows them to look at beautiful things. Though you can offer companionship and beautiful things in a virtual store, the sheer experience of getting dressed up and leaving the house on an outing cannot be replaced.

Moving from Browsing to Buying

Why do some people surf and browse, but not buy? The next several sections explore some possibilities for how to persuade browsers to become buyers, by comparing the Internet to three of the more traditional *direct marketing* techniques: infomercials, direct mail, and telemarketing.

MYTH: *The most important aspect of electronic commerce is creating a high-traffic site on the Internet.*

Creating a high-traffic site is very important for visibility and marketing image, but it does not necessarily mean you will be able to sell things there. Having a high-traffic site attracts advertising dollars, but it doesn't naturally translate into an environment where browsers get converted to buyers. For that, the virtual store owner needs to actively design a buying environment. More important than creating a high-traffic site, then, is creating a site that's comfortable and convenient for people to use so that they will stay long enough to make a purchase and come back again.

Infomercials and On-line Shopping

Perhaps one of the better models for how to build trust on-line without an existing brand name is found in what's commonly called *infomercials*. An infomercial is an extended commercial, lasting from 15 minutes to a half hour, which tells about a product in more detail than a conventional commercial can. Typically, an infomercial is hosted by a celebrity, who lends credibility to the product and it usually contains an animated segment demonstrating how the product works. The vendor usually offers an 800 phone number for credit card purchases and a 30-day money-back guarantee. Some vendors go so far as to say they won't charge your credit card for 30 days while you decide whether you're getting value from the product.

The infomercial doesn't just present information—it presents information that provides *decision support* for customers. A crucial part of on-line sales is helping customers get the information they need to make buy decisions, when you can't be there to interact with them personally.

Techniques frequently used in infomercials include:

- ◆ Celebrities who talk to us, often from their own homes, to provide a sense of trust and a feeling of person-to-person contact
- ◆ Testimonials or comments from other customers
- ◆ Product information that is compellingly presented, with the implication that this product will improve your life
- ◆ A persistent soft sell that takes place through the entire presentation (which makes the customer feel more invested than after a 30-second commercial)
- ◆ Language that makes customers feel secure
- ◆ Money-back guarantees
- ◆ Easy purchasing using credit cards and 800 numbers

All of these techniques can be adapted for use in your virtual store.

Multimedia, the capability to present sound, video, text, graphics, and photo images in an integrated way, offers new and exciting opportunities to create on-line infomercials at your site. The Java programming language, a big sensation among software developers for the Web, allows a lot more flexibility in what we can present on our Web sites. HTML is useful, especially when extended with CGI (Common Gateway

Interface, used in the interaction between a Web site and a database) scripts and other technical tricks, but Java can go a long way toward making Web sites seem truly interactive.

Keep in mind that, in the long run, the best way to get people to move from browsing to buying is to win their trust. Whatever you can do to create trust is a step in the right direction. For instance, building your brand identity on-line is one way to foster trust, because it enhances name recognition for your products and services.

Direct Mail and On-line Shopping

Direct marketing is defined by the Direct Marketing Association as "an interactive system of marketing which uses one or more advertising media to effect a measurable response and/or transaction at any location." Thus, the Internet certainly qualifies as a direct marketing medium.

When converting customers from browsing to buying, remember that on-line marketing is a lot like direct-mail marketing. Even if you're not going so far as to create an on-line infomercial, you can take advantage of the fact that, like direct mail, the Internet is customizable. You can target the presentation of your products and services to very specific audiences, either on your Web site or through mailings to subscribers. And the Internet is quicker than direct mail: You can literally create a new presentation and have it on-line the same day.

By creating a variety of presentations, you can deliver your message very quickly and targeted for different audiences. (Be aware that inappropriately targeted E-mail is regarded as a major intrusion on the Internet.) Use this customizing ability to convince your customers that you have the products and services they need. Direct your presentation precisely to their desires and concerns. Listen to their feedback, strive constantly to improve the ways in which you meet their needs, *and let them know about what you've done.* Your on-line presence provides a quick and inexpensive way to get the word out about improved products and services.

Telemarketing and On-line Shopping

Telemarketing refers to the familiar process of making one-on-one sales calls over the telephone. Internet marketing is like telemarketing because both can be customized to address the needs of a particular customer and both are interactive in the sense that the customer can provide immediate feedback about the message. Furthermore, both transactions can be completed right then and there. There's no need to dial a phone number or mail a check.

In the physical world, some customers don't respond well to the telemarketing approach, because they feel it's an invasion of privacy. Fortunately, people logged onto the Internet aren't likely to regard marketing messages as aggravating intrusions into the dinner hour—they're already using the computer. Be bold about putting yourself in front of them!

Internet marketing is an improvement on traditional telemarketing because, instead of a one-to-one connection, you're actually creating a one-to-many connection. Other than the performance of your server machine, there's nothing to limit the number of customers who can be visiting your virtual store simultaneously.

The Buy Decision

Once trust is established and you've targeted your customers carefully, perhaps the most important factor in encouraging your customers to make the buy decision is giving them a compelling reason to buy right then, not tomorrow or next week. Specials and promotions can help a lot in this regard. For instance, you could set up a special with wording like this:

> *Buy a CD-ROM today and get a free CD-ROM for your child. Offer good this weekend only.*

There's a good offer combined with a compelling reason to buy right away, not next time.

The moment of the buy decision is, of course, the crucial one in the shopping process. There's a mystique associated with what entices a particular customer to buy. What we do know is that customers tend to put off buying until they begin to feel a certain urgency, a sense that time is running out. There are some creative, nonintrusive ways you can influence people to buy *now,* not later. Following are some very specific techniques you can use to help convince your customers to buy:

- *Take advantage of holidays.* Easter, Hanukkah, Mother's Day, Cinco de Mayo all can provide good selling ideas. In addition, you may offer your established customers promotions for their re-occurring special days such as anniversaries and birthdays.

- *Use ongoing promotions.* Contests create excitement. Promotional offers, such as offering a gift with every purchase, are often used in cosmetics. These special offers, of course, are limited in quantity or duration.

- *Create scarcity.* Set up specials that expire or advertise limited quantities of special merchandise available on a first-come, first-served basis.

- *Provide special pricing incentives.* Car dealers do this a lot: "The '97s are coming, we're moving out the '96 models now at special prices. . . ."

In general, use your creativity to come up with every possible reason for putting a new "buy now, not later" message out to your customers.

Coming back to that mystique surrounding the buy decision, what really convinces customers to buy on the Internet rather than off-line in ways that are more familiar to them? It seems that two major psychological factors come into play.

First, the on-line customer has an opportunity for direct contact with your company. You can use your virtual store to build a closer relationship with your customers than is possible in any other medium—closer than anything except one-on-one sales transactions. By building this closeness, you make your customers feel more in control of the purchase process, as well as acknowledge their feedback about your store. You can also use the relationship to find out a lot more about what your customers really want and need than you can with any other medium.

Second, the virtual store offers instant gratification for you and your customer. It's rewarding to make a complete transaction so quickly. It's a feeling of empowerment for the customer. It has been said that the Internet provides up to a tenfold increase in time savings for customers, and if so, it is likely to become popular because it crosses Peter Drucker's tenfold threshhold for adoption of a new technology.[1]

Thus, the virtual store offers the possibility of creating a more satisfying shopping experience for customers at your virtual store. The next section looks at how to make the on-line shopping experience compelling.

The Shopping Experience

What is the ultimate measure of the quality of your virtual store? The customer's experience when shopping there. The better the shopping experience, the more likely the customer is to buy your product or service, this time *and* next time. As we saw in Chapter 1, Internet surveys indicate that the actual presentation of information is influential in persuading a customer to buy. This section looks at how to present a more satisfying experience to your customers, moment by moment, by focusing on the store itself.

How can you create a successful shopping experience? Think about the kind of shopping experience you want your customers to have, from start to finish (see Figure 3.4). Develop scenarios: Think about where each click will lead customers and what will happen if they take an unexpected path through your site. Think about how you will get them back if they follow hot links away from your site. Following are some questions you might ask yourself as you envision your virtual store.

◆ *How much reliance on graphics should my store have? In general, are graphics good or bad?*   As everyone who's done much Web surfing knows, graphics are slow to download, but they look nice. It's realistic to plan your graphical images to download crisply at 14.4 Kbps, which is the most common modem speed today. It's unrealistic to create graphical images that rely on having a T1 connection so they can download before the cows come home.

From the viewpoint of a sensual-experience shopper, graphics add a lot to the presentation of your products and services. From the viewpoint of an efficiency shopper, they can take up valuable seconds. Think about the customers to whom your products or services are most likely to apply and design your graphical presentations accordingly. To give a fictitious example, if your site is called "Budget Liquors On-line" you may want to plan on simpler graphics than would a store called "Exotic Lingerie On-line."

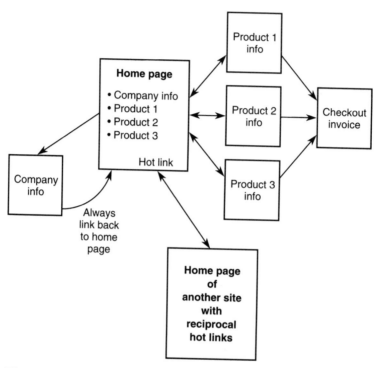

Figure 3.4   Create scenarios about the customer's shopping experience.

◆ *How should my virtual store be laid out? How many sublevels should it have?*   Your store should be designed to present your information in an orderly way. Overview or background information should appear on different pages from more detailed or more frequently updated information such as prices.

By the way, don't even think about getting into the virtual store business unless you're planning to update your site regularly. One of the most important reasons customers are getting on-line is to get the most up-to-the-minute information. Once a week is a good rule of thumb for how often to update your site, especially special promotion and pricing information.

◆ *At which level should the customer see the goods? Should I open with some verbiage about the company or immediately focus my cus-*

tomer on the goods themselves? It's often a good idea to give some information about your company before opening a catalog of products. On the other hand, you won't want to make your customer click through layers of pages before seeing the product. Consider which aspect would be easier to trust: your company or your product?

For example, Gibson Guitars has created an effective on-line presence. Gibson has a cult following, so the store designer chose to present the company image first. The product is secondary, and customers traverse several levels before they can actually buy any merchandise.

- *From the moment the customer connects to the store site until the purchase is complete, what happens?* As a rule of thumb, your customer should be led from more general information to more specific information (if desired), and to the "checkout counter" within three or four screens. Take time to think through each moment of the shopper's experience. What happens if I click here—or here? Draw up scenarios (called *storyboards*) that illustrate what the customer will see on each screen. Timing is a factor here. How long will it take an average customer to reach each screen and move on? Test and retest to determine what actually works before you take your site live.

- *How long does each phase of the process take?* In general, it shouldn't take any longer for your customer to make the purchase on-line than it would to call an 800 number. The shopping process should ideally be as quick and pleasant as possible. Even someone who is shopping for entertainment is likely to appreciate a crisp and straightforward shopping experience. For instance, avoid any need for shoppers to enter a lot of information. If they must enter data, capture it and make sure they never have to enter anything twice.

- *How many minutes into the store will the customer make the buy decision?* You'll want to move your customers toward making a decision to buy as quickly as possible. Customers will buy when they see you have the product(s) they want and if you've gained a sufficient measure of their trust. These two criteria have to be satisfied extremely quickly in the on-line world—the average 25-year-old male who is paying $3 per

Gibson Guitars: An Overnight On-line Success Story?

Gibson Guitars (see Figure 3.5) has been making guitars for 100 years. At this writing, the company has been on-line for about one month. But what a month! In that time, monthly revenues have soared from approximately $1500 to approximately $15,000—a tenfold increase. Gibson is not making guitars any faster, however; most of that increase has been in associated merchandise, such as strings and T-shirts.

Henry Juskewicz, CEO and chairman of Gibson, attributes the success to the realization of two important goals:

◆ Be true to the customer base: Give them the information they're asking for.

◆ Be true to dealers: Ninety-nine percent of the time, a purchase can be made through an authorized Gibson dealer, and the site is not in conflict with the dealer network.

Being on-line gives Gibson the ability to provide better customer service and to serve customers in areas where no Gibson dealers exist. Juskewicz says, "We don't see it as a major outlet for goods, we see it as a service for people who can't get to dealers. We honor our commitment to our Gibson dealers. Part of our site is a dealer reference, where you can find a dealer near you. Also, a second way we honor our commitment to our dealers is that we sell at full retail. There's no discount on-line." He continues, "We have an active forum on the Net and on CompuServe. We answer questions, and we let people talk to each other about guitar-related problems. Our company historian is on-line—we're very responsive."

Since Gibson is already a household name in guitars, it's not spending a lot of effort on building a brand through on-line advertising or E-mail campaigns of any kind. Juskewicz says, "At this point we're tagging our Web page in our other ads, just harnessing the ads we're already doing. We do have some plans for next year to do an ad campaign in periodicals."

Continued

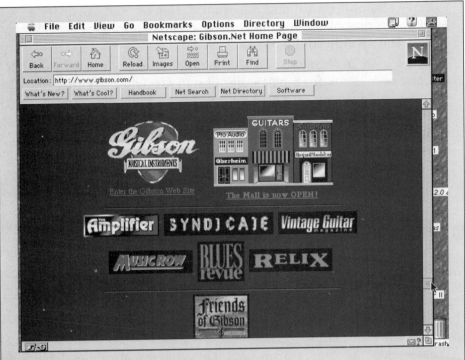

Figure 3.5 Gibson Guitars' Web site.

To attract customers to its site, Gibson focuses on providing a lot of content. According to Juskewicz, "We can give you an estimate of how much a vintage Gibson is worth. We have the *Music City News, Mix* magazine, and other publications as well." Gibson is also hot-linked to some other sites with whom it cooperates.

hour for connect time isn't going to remain at a site that doesn't accomplish these things more or less immediately.

◆ *This decision process may vary according to a customer's background: Do on-line novices differ in their behavior from on-line experts? Do males differ from females? Does age play a role?* There's no evidence to suggest that newcomers make a buy decision differently than experienced Internet users; however, newbies are especially likely to appreciate a virtual store that's straightforward and easy to use. Gender and age criteria likewise do not seem to make any greater difference on-line than they would in the physical world.

◆ *To go after a particular crowd, what should your considerations be?* Look for a particular crowd elsewhere—either on-line in a news group or off-line—and learn what concerns and attracts them. Offer products and services that fit their needs, and let them know you're available. Get on mailing lists that your customers are likely to read and join discussion groups to find out what they're concerned about.

Presenting the Electronic Invoice

Unlike purchases in a physical store, almost 40 percent of on-line customers quit the transaction at the time the invoice is presented, according to the market research firm, Management Forum. Few people quit at that point in a physical store. Needless to say, this is a critical moment in an on-line transaction.

What makes customers drop out? They have a strong resistance to entering a lot of personal information on the screen, and most electronic invoices today have too many fields (see Figure 3.6). One way to get around this problem is to have an electronic wallet, such as the Cyber-Cash wallet, which already contains the needed information. Thus, at the point of sale, the typing is kept to a minimum.

Alternatively, you could ask your customers to register in advance. First Virtual requires a customer PIN number. To complete a sale, the customer need only type in the PIN number, and all the relevant information, such as name, address, and credit card number, are automatically transferred to the vendor. This method also works well for subscription services.

Similarly, at FedEx, every customer has an account number. That same number works when tracking packages on-line or when shipping them through the FedEx on-line site. There's no need to transfer credit card information or even electronic cash over the network. FedEx just sends the usual account bill to each customer at the end of the month.

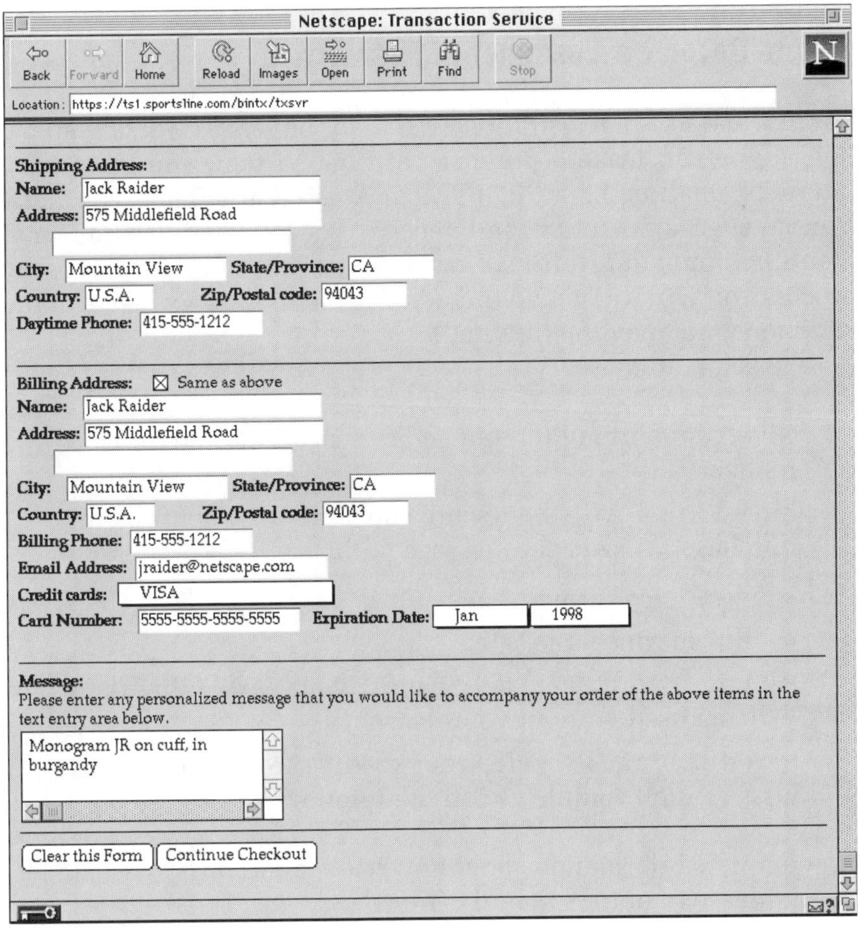

Figure 3.6   An electronic invoice.

Getting Shoppers There

It's generally true that you have to advertise somehow to let people know about your store, both in the physical world and in the virtual world. The Internet is causing quite a stir in advertising, because the old methods don't work on-line. In the first wave of Internet advertising campaigns, agencies hadn't yet comprehended the need for interactivity, the customer's insistence on participation, the instantaneous click-

How to Become a Customer at First Virtual

First Virtual uses a registration system for buyers as well as sellers. Before you can make a purchase at First Virtual, you must have Internet E-mail and a valid VISA or MasterCard. Then you must complete an application and receive your VirtualPIN (personal identification) number from First Virtual. (*Important:* As part of the process you will register your credit card with First Virtual over the telephone, not over the Internet.)

To make a purchase:

1. Give your VirtualPIN to a seller instead of a credit card number.
2. First Virtual will then send you E-mail to confirm the purchase. Answer the message with:

   - "yes" to confirm the sale.
   - "no" to cancel the sale.
   - "fraud" to immediately cancel your VirtualPIN (it is being used without your consent!).

3. If you confirm the sale, your credit card is charged by First Virtual, completely off the Internet.

For complete information about how to become a First Virtual merchant, please refer to Appendix C.

How to Become an Electronic Wallet Holder

There are several companies that offer consumers convenient electronic wallets for carrying their credit cards, checkbooks, and digital IDs on-line. These wallets can be used to securely make payments with any one of these methods. Wallets are branded by many different on-line services and payment service providers,

Continued

Figure 3.7   The CyberCash wallet.

such as CyberCash (see Figure 3.7), CompuServe, Checkfree, and AOL's GNN.

These wallets are free of charge and completely interoperable with each other. A consumer can download them from any of the Web sites or software packages of the companies named above or from merchants' virtual stores that accept payments secured by these electronic wallets. These wallets are available for PC and Mac platforms and can be downloaded in under ten minutes.

Once you have your electronic wallet on your desktop, you activate it by entering your credit card number or your checking account number. This is the only time you will need to enter your credit card number. If you intend to use electronic coins and checks, you may also enter your checking account number.

During this activation period, which you as a consumer go through only once, you generate a set of public/private key pairs,

Continued

which from there on are used to encrypt your payment information, such as your credit card number. (For a more detailed discussion of this technology, see Chapter 6.)

To make a purchase:

1. After you choose the items you want to buy, see if the merchant accepts an electronic wallet. If so, click on the pay button and your wallet opens up for you to choose a credit card or coins.

2. Choose your payment type—for example, VISA card or electronic coin—and click on the pay button.

3. You will receive a confirmation in under ten seconds if your credit card was valid and a request for another card if it was not.

off that customers give to traditional information-oriented advertisements on the Internet. Newer Internet ads are more interactive, involving such things as interactive games and downloadable software.

Where should your advertising focus lie? This section examines hot-linking, discussion groups, news groups, and the like, as methods for reaching potential customers. As a general rule, there's just no substitute for getting onto the Web and learning how people really use the Internet; it's the best way to discover what your customers really want and need.

Many times we've heard the hype: Use the Internet; reach 25 million customers! But the truth is, you don't want to reach all those customers. You want to reach only a small subset—those who are interested in what you have to sell. The only question remaining is how to find your customers among the hordes. Here are a few suggestions.

Hot-linking

As a way to reach customers who are already on-line, hot-linking is perhaps the most effective advertising tool available. Customers may be visiting other sites, but a hot link to your virtual store can pique their interest. That's why it's a good idea to form partnerships with businesses whose products and services are complementary to your own. Exchange hot links. Many customers who visit one site will be likely to visit both. For instance, a virtual store selling computer hardware may wish to link to a software seller, and vice versa.

Most virtual store owners profiled in this book purchased hot links on the major search engine sites, at a minimum, during the first year of their presence on-line. They seem to agree that hot links on such heavily traveled sites are a must for getting started.

On-line Discussion Groups

Participating in on-line discussion groups, sometimes called *on-line forums,* is a good way to develop the respect and trust of your customer base. In posting to a discussion group, your goal should be to provide helpful and valuable information, not to blatantly advertise for your virtual store. Remember that every time you mention your virtual store you run the risk of having your message interpreted as an advertisement, so keep it low key. A common practice is to read the postings of the group for a week or two before joining in. That way, you have a feel for the flow of opinions among the participants. There's less risk of creating a major gaffe.

Discussion groups often are sponsored by magazines on-line, such as *PC Week* and *Wired.* They also exist on the major on-line services. Forums are designed to focus on one topic, so make sure all your postings are relevant. If you mention your product or service, explain right up front why it is relevant to the topic of discussion. If your announcement is an out-and-out advertisement, be sure to include "Ad:" in your subject field.

News Groups and Mailing Lists

Some news groups are structured to accept advertising, and they are free. For instance, any news group whose name begins with biz.marketplace will accept advertisements related to the topic—for example, biz.marketplace.computers.mac.

More than 100 classified ad news groups exist as well. Some are worldwide in scope; others are locale-based. For instance, fj.forsale is specific to Japan. All of these news groups have one of these words in their names: *forsale, marketplace, classified, auction,* or *swap.* Be sure that the news groups you are targeting accept advertisements from businesses as well as individuals, because some do not. You can get this information by reading the group's FAQ list.

There are mailing lists of people who want to receive advertising, especially lists of people who want ads about certain types of products. For more information, you can send E-mail to inside@tyrell.net, to reach a company called Inside Connections.

TIP   *To help get customers to your virtual store, choose a Web address (URL) that's as close to your company name as possible. Always include the URL in your printed advertisements and be sure it appears on all your other marketing collateral as well, including business cards. As a rule of thumb, wherever you'd put an 800 number, you should put your company's URL.*

For more complete discussion about attracting customers to your virtual store, see Chapter 5.

Closing Thoughts

Trust is essential for all commerce. To gain trust on-line, it takes more than a Web site with a two-page summary of who you are and what you do. Why should anyone believe you? On-line, the customer never sees your face and has no other physical-world cues to rely on about trustworthiness, such as the part of town in which your business is located or the feeling of quality apparent in your office furnishings.

Once you've established trust, the quality of the shopping experience becomes important. To enhance the shopping experience, it certainly helps to infuse your Web site with quality and seasonally appropriate decoration. But more than that, solicit third-party testimonials from happy customers—let others tell them who you are and what you do. Give the customer accurate information, support the buy decision, and always place the customer's experience foremost in your mind. Make your site easy to use. Make it one that stands out in their minds, even when they're not shopping.

To advertise your site, the best thing to do is get on-line and participate. Go where your customers would go, listen to their wants and
needs. Offer your products and services where appropriate, using hot
links, news groups, and on-line forums as ways to reach people who are
already on-line.

CHAPTER FOUR

Getting to Know Your Virtual Customers

Topics presented in this chapter:

- Getting Information about Your Users
- Session-based Tracking
- Subscription-based Tracking
- Asking Your Users for Information—Privacy Issues

Consumer information is an important tool. It can form the basis for promotional programs. It can help your market research: to define future products, or even to define your next storefront to be more pleasing to your desired customer base.

The key to getting consumer information is to get it without violating respect for the consumer: It's a fine line. You want the information, but you want to ask for it in a way that is palatable to the consumer. This chapter helps you explore ways to gather the information you need, without ruffling any feathers.

When you have read this chapter, you will understand the different ways you can gather information about the patrons of your virtual store. You will be able to conduct surveys, communicate with your customers via E-mail, and create a highly documented site to attract advertisers and generate advertising revenues.

Getting Information about Your Users

The Internet is a radically different place for shopping and browsing. Consumers and merchants must be prepared to adapt to this new and dynamic medium. They must establish a comfort zone for all types of visitors, users, and consumers.

Certainly, the anonymity of the Net is as appealing to people as the relative anonymity of walking through a shopping mall or retail store, where no one asks for your ID or personal information in order to walk around. Of course, if a consumer decides to do business with one of the stores, information about that consumer is transmitted. I don't recall stores in the physical world blocking their doors until a potential customer fills out a form. A site that asks up front for registration info—or worse, payment—without giving the customer at least a sample of the benefits of registering won't get much of a response.

In this environment, customer-tracking systems and applications play an important role in gathering necessary information about visitors from Internet sites. Businesses using subscription/membership services and tracking systems can begin to piece together the psychographics of their visitors, thereby enabling themselves to deliver products and information directly to the user—relative to that user's interests and at competitive prices.

The two cardinal rules of getting consumer information are:

◆ Do not abuse this information.
◆ Give the customer something in return.

For instance, most of the time in the real world, merchants know who we are, but this information is not abused. Today, credit card companies have a lot of information about what we buy and where we travel, but they are very careful to keep this information confidential.

The Individual Nature of Internet Consumers versus the Mass Market

The Internet should *not* be thought of as a mass market. Mass markets assume the existence of a homogeneous buying population. The Internet of today is anything but homogeneous. It is filled with individualists who are proud of their uniqueness and promote their eccentricity to the extreme. Mass markets often assume a uniform type of behavior. Charles Schwab, in California, has done a great job of taking discount brokerage from a specific niche into a mass-market product, but on the Internet it is not the Charles Schwabs that are getting the attention and the traffic. It is sites like the Motley Fools. Internet consumers are more willing to create individual relationships with oddball personality types such as those represented by the Motley Fools than by going to an established brokerage house.

In mass markets, the communication between buyer and seller is kept at a minimum. The Internet should not be thought of as a mass market, but as a collection of small towns. The Internet lends itself to the creation of communities because it is a very easy medium in which to communicate using E-mail, chat groups, forums, and so on. People can exchange knowledge and information in ways that are impossible in a mass market.

The Internet is more like a collection of small niche markets, each of which might appeal to a unique population, such as Land Rover lovers, followers of African music, or macrobiotic cooking devotees. But when you put all these niche markets under one virtual roof, you have yourself an enormous shopping mall.

In an environment that is not a mass market, it is even more important to get to know the customers. The Internet offers the ability to target one's message to the unique tastes of each niche. The ultimate ways in which merchants position their products and services to appeal to these different customer groups will differ widely. For example, if you are selling leather bags, the styles you show Land Rover fanatics might resemble African safari bags, whereas you might display backpacks for the macrobiotic food followers and bags with West African designs for African music lovers.

Because the Internet is not a mass market but a collection of small, unique markets, it is especially important for you to identify the correct demographic and psychographic characteristics of your potential customers. There is no better way of doing this than asking your visitors to fill out a short form telling you about themselves. You will be surprised how much they will be willing to share with you, if you are willing to give them something worthwhile in return.

MYTH: *Never ask for personal information on the Internet or you run the risk of being publicly chastised.*

The issue is not *what* you ask for, but *why* you ask for it. Asking for information is completely acceptable if you are willing to give something in return. People on the Internet are willing to divulge a lot of demographic and psychographic information about themselves—and sometimes even their identities—as long as it is done in a way acceptable to the Internet consumer, who is generally intelligent and resistant to being told what to do.

The biggest violation of "digitally correct behavior" on the Internet is to send unsolicited, pushy, irritating, and intelligence-insulting promotional material to others. As long as your customers do not expect this from you, they will be willing to trust you with a lot of information about themselves.

In early 1993, the Internet was still governed by the Appropriate Use Policy (AUP) regulations, which restricted commercial traffic on the Internet. At the time, I was running Management Forum, a firm that specialized in providing management consulting to online services, interactive content companies, Internet access providers, and telecommunications firms. Many of my clients wanted to know more about Internet use and the associated demographics. The Internet Society at that time published information regarding servers on the Internet, but there was no information on who was behind those servers.

Management Forum conducted the very first survey on the Internet, which questioned users regarding identity, Internet habits, mode of access to the Internet, and so on. The research study was conducted with the aid of universities and large corporations. This was an E-mail study, and filling it out was strictly voluntary. As a reward for the time involved, the survey entered participants in a drawing for several giveaways.

Management Forum got over 3,000 responses. Most respondents were pleased to be part of the survey because they themselves were curious about the outcome. The results were published in various trade journals in late 1993 and early 1994 and resulted in over 100 companies contacting us for additional work. This demonstrates that the Internet is the perfect medium to gather information, because of its two-way communication capability through E-mail.

San Jose Sharks

The San Jose Sharks use their Web site to communicate with their fans, who are scattered all around the world. Their nonlocal fans get a feeling of closeness and involvement by having access to the Sharks Web site. The site promotes a strong following and a sense of community to the geographically dispersed. It does this while greatly reducing marketing communications costs.

The San Jose Sharks do not sell any tickets through their site. Season tickets are sold out long in advance and they sell specific event tickets only on the morning of the day of the event. They do not sell these at their Web site because they do not want to unfairly advantage those who have Internet access and thus incur the wrath of the rest of their fans. Like many virtual store owners, the Sharks are sensitive to the issue of fairness to their traditional distribution channels.

The San Jose Sharks store offers all the team statistics, as well as specific player information, Sharks press releases, and other information that the fans follow. Recently, when the Sharks did not have a winning season, they responded to their disappointed fans by holding an on-line chat session, during which their general manager answered questions, thus alleviating some of the pain of a bad season.

The Sharks will be adding a merchandise catalog in the Fall of 1996.

Chat groups, forums, and Usenet news groups are also great—but often overlooked—ways of collecting information about the identity of your users. Anyone can start a news group discussion concentrating on a specific topic. *Lurking,* though a negative term, is often done in news group discussions when one is not actively participating but rather monitoring others' comments. This is an excellent way to gather information about your potential customers. You can even direct discussions by starting a moderated news group yourself.

Customer-Tracking Systems

In addition to actively asking your prospects and customers for information, there are tracking systems available on the Internet today. There are two main methods of obtaining information by consumer tracking—that is, by following your consumers electronically as they visit your virtual store. These are *session-based tracking* and *subscription-based tracking*. The following sections describe each method in detail.

Using Session-Based Tracking

One customer's visit to an Internet Web site, from start to finish (login to logout), is considered a *session*. During a session, a visitor connects to a Web site, travels around the site, performs some actions, and then leaves. (A session is not the same as a *hit*. Many hits occur within a session as a result of page requests and image downloads.) All these events are recorded, or tracked as they occur, by that host's server. Thus, the concept of session-based tracking. (For more definitions of terms, see the "Web TrackingTerms" sidebar in this chapter.)

Session-based tracking opens and closes a customer relationship in real time. No information about the customer is kept on the system beyond the duration of his or her visit to the site. Session-based tracking is useful because it encourages spontaneity while providing anonymity for customers. Examples of sites that presently use session-based tracking are Open Market and Time Warner's Pathfinder.

The session-based tracking model makes sense, especially for Web-delivered goods. If the goods are delivered over the Internet, absolutely no information may be retained with the possible exception of an E-mail address for downloading. On the other hand, if hard goods are purchased using the session-based tracking model, at least a shipping address may need to remain on file.

The Shopping Cart

Session-based tracking works by creating a shopping cart for the consumer, which lasts for the duration of the shopping experience. When the consumer pays, the prices of the contents are totaled for that session. Then, as in a physical store, the customer presents the payment instrument, settles, and the transaction is done.

Web Tracking Terms

AdClick rate: AdClicks as a percentage of AdViews, or the number of clicks by end users on an in-line ad as a percentage of the number of times that ad was downloaded by end users.

AdClicks: The number of "clicks" by end users on an in-line ad within a specific period of time.

AdViews: The number of times that an in-line ad (commonly referred to as a *banner*) was downloaded (and presumably seen) by end users within a specific period of time. The actual number of times the ad was seen by end users may be higher due to caching.

bandwidth: The number of bytes used in transmitting content. Intersé market focus doesn't include TCP/IP overhead or the actual browser requests within its bandwidth counts because these values are not logged.

cookie: The capability of some Web browsers to allow Web servers to store information about user visits to the Web site on the hard disk in the user's PC or workstation. Because it can be used to identify repeat visitors, the cookie allows on-the-fly customization of a Web site to feature items the user showed an interest in during previous visits. The cookie also allows a Web server to track the sequence of a session on a Web site, including how long a user spent on each Web page. While a boon to marketing on the Web, the cookie raises some privacy issues because it removes some of the traditional anonymity associated with viewing Web sites and uses a small portion of the user's hard disk.

geography: The continent, country, region, state, city, and zip code are based on an organization's Internet domain registration. Each Internet domain is associated with only one zip code; all users from an Internet address used in multiple loca-

Continued

tions are considered to be at one location, such as all IBM employees are considered to be from New York.

hit: An entry in the log file of a Web server. A hit is generated by every request made to a Web server. It has no predictable relation to users, visitors, or pages. The number of hits per page depends on the amount of graphics files the page has. Every graphical element (image, icon, button) is a separate file. For example, a home page with five buttons and four graphics would generate ten hits.

media objects: Files, other than HTML, that are used for sound, video, high-end graphics. Examples include GIFs, JPEGs, video, audio, PDF, and HotJava Applets.

organization: A commercial, academic, nonprofit, government, or military entity that connects users to the Internet, identified by an entity's Internet domains. This holds true only for the United States.

page: An HTML document that may contain text, images, and other in-line elements. It may be static or dynamically generated. It may be a stand-alone HTML document or one that is contained within a frame.

qualified hits: Hits to a Web server that deliver information to a user. Qualified hits exclude error messages (e.g., "URL Not Found" or "Permission Denied"), redirects, and requests by computer programs (as opposed to end users).

request: A hit that successfully retrieves content. Requests do not include image requests and errors. Requests counts are conservative because browser software and many Internet gateways intercept some requests before they reach the server, and these cached requests are never logged.

unique users: Anyone who visits a Web site at least once is recognized as a unique user. If your extended log files contain persistent cookie data, the software uses this data to recognize

Continued

unique users. If no cookie data is available, the software uses a registered username to recognize users. If no registration information is available, as a last resort, the software uses users' Internet hostnames. Many organizations use Internet gateways, which mask the real Internet hostnames, so user counts may be conservative for those users determined through their Internet hostnames.

visit: A series of consecutive file requests made by one user at a given site. If such a user makes no requests from that site during a predetermined (and discretionary) period of time, her/his next hit would constitute the beginning of a new visit. The industry standard time-out interval is 30 minutes for all sites, for purposes of comparability.

visit duration: The time between the first and last request of a visit. This time doesn't include how long users viewed the last request of a visit.

SOURCES: I/Pro Corp. and Intersé Inc., 1996.

O'Reilly, BroadVision, and OMI are leaders in shopping cart technology at this writing. Certainly this technology has already improved from its previous implementations, when for example, a customer couldn't remove items from the cart once they were selected. That feature caused a lot of consternation and loss of sales, since the only way to remove an item from the cart was to quit the session and start over again.

TIP   *Understand where your customers come from.*

All customer-tracking services use the domain registration database that is kept at InterNIC, affectionately referred to as the NIC. The InterNIC is a cooperative effort by the National Science Foundation, Network Solutions Inc., and AT&T. The NIC in InterNIC stands for Network Information Center and they can be found at www.rs.internic.net. The geographic distribution that this database uses is the corporate address of the host; therefore, everyone who visits your site from CompuServe is marked as living in Ohio, those visiting from AOL are marked as living in Virginia, anyone from Sun Microsystems is marked as from California, and all employees of IBM are marked as from New York. This is obviously inaccurate and, therefore, as a virtual store owner, you should not rely heavily on geographic distribution information about your customers. The best way to receive geographic distribution information is to allow your potential customers to directly identify what state they're from.

There is another problem with automated tracking systems. Unless an intelligent human being manually converts the domain name to a corporation, there will be a lot of confusion about consumer origin. A good example is the domain name ford.com, which could be Ford Motor Company, Ford Aerospace, or Joe Ford's Delicious Foods. So, unless there is a directory of domain names to registered addresses, it is impossible to tell strictly from the domain name what company that domain name belongs to.

The best way to get information about your consumers is to *ask them* to tell you who they are. It is surprising to many virtual store owners that their customers or visitors are frequently willing to fill out demographic surveys. As long as you are not forcing them to register, you can get very valuable information, such as geographic location, interests, and habits, by just asking visitors to fill out a form. If you are willing to give away some goods or offer a prize drawing, the propensity to fill out those forms will increase. The key to increasing the response rate is to ask for demographic and psychographic information, not individual information such as name and address. People want to remain anonymous on the Internet unless there is a strong reason to identify themselves.

HotWired, the on-line site of the popular magazine, *Wired,* required its visitors to register to access its content. Most visitors forgot the password shortly after they left the site, so HotWired found itself in a situation where the same person registered under different visitor names each time he or she came to the site.

The San Jose Sharks promotion is an example of collecting demographic data. The Sharks ran a 30-day promotion featuring a "question of the day," which, if responded to, entered the visitor into a drawing for San Jose Sharks memorabilia. To answer the question of the day, the visitor had to give some demographic information about him/herself, such zip code and areas of interest. The Sharks also put in a field where visitors could *choose* to give their names, but this was not required. The response to this promotion was phenomenal. Sharks fans from all over the world sent answers, trying to get the T-shirt that was prize of the day. This illustrates that, if you have a site that has a following, running a promotion to collect user data does not have to be expensive.

Career Mosaic

Career Mosaic was an early pioneer, like Shopping 2000. It wanted to be the place that people looked for jobs in the high-technology business. Career Mosaic owners, Bernard Hodis Advertising, understood early that the site had to be promoted and the URL had to be on billboards, in print media ads, on buses, and so on. The focus early on was not to make money but to create a high-traffic site that was focused on job opportunities. This served Career Mosaic very well. Today Career Mosaic has over 200 employers that list their jobs, for a fee, from all over the United States and Canada. It has become one of the places to go if you are looking for a job around the Internet.

Customer-Tracking Technologies

One tracking technology that enables a site to acquire user demographics is the I/Pro I/Code system, a universal registration system. Quite a bit of information can be obtained about users without asking them to register or provide any information. All they need to do is enter their codes at sites that have installed the software.

The traditional and proper way to learn about users is to ask them and offer incentives. For example, the I/Code system works as a universal registration system that lets users provide their information once, then makes it available to as many other sites as the users want. I/PRO's system lets sites track what users do, so that users' characteristics and usage patterns can be combined and analyzed. I/PRO also lets you give incentives to users for disclosing their personal information.

Many sites need to understand individual users' personal and demographic characteristics, and products like I/Code can help them. In fact, if a host enables itself with a fitting combination of I/Pro services

(I/Count, I/Code, I/Audit, and JAVA Count), or similar services, it will be able to construct visitors' psychographical profiles.

I/Pro is one of several Web tracking products presently available. Four companies currently offer Web traffic analysis systems:

- *Internet Profiles (I/Pro).*   Founded in 1994, I/Pro is generally considered the leader in Web tracking systems. It tracks 25 of the top 30 traffic-heavy Web sites.

- *Intersé Corporation.*   Intersé Corporation has developed an above-average, useful Web tracking system.

- *The Cortex Group.*   The Cortex Group offers a new advertising and general traffic-tracking application.

- *Digital Planet.*   Digital Planet offers a new Web site traffic-tracking solution perfect for storefronts and content- and advertising-based services.

Using Subscription-Based Tracking

Subscription-based tracking currently is an accepted method of obtaining customer information in the off-line world of commerce. For instance, if you subscribe to a magazine, the publisher can learn a lot about you, including names of other publications to which you subscribe.

Translating subscription-based tracking to the virtual store means that the customer fills out an information form on-line and opens an account before making purchases in the store. All the payments go to one central processing center, no matter which merchant the customer buys from.

Examples of sites that use subscription-based tracking are First Virtual and the Internet Shopping Network. The good news about subscription-based tracking is that it encourages a friendly, mall-type environment, in which shopkeepers can present a rich variety of objects, with many more opportunities to buy. Over time, with the use of technology, the array of objects can be customized to match the shoppers' tastes. Since information about each customer is preserved even after the shopping session is over, agents can search anytime for products and services to meet the customers' needs.

The missions and plans of businesses setting up shop on the Web are widely divergent. In accordance with their individual niches and channels for revenue, many are incorporating different forms of subscription and membership services. Based on their success, sites are continuing to refine and evolve them according to the needs of consumers and their plans.

Two Types of Subscription-Based Sites

Subscription and membership services fall into two primary categories:

- *Paid*—includes required and nonrequired subscriptions.
- *Nonpaid*—includes required and nonrequired subscriptions.

Since the introduction of the Web, sites have offered both paid and nonpaid subscription and membership services to visitors. Presently, many sites offer services that are dynamic combinations of both paid and unpaid. Based on success, businesses are evolving their membership and subscription plans to suit their visitors, thereby hoping to attract and sustain a solid user base.

Paid and nonpaid services all generally have required personal information about the subscriber or member. Requiring registration to customize and personalize the shopping experience is justifiable: It can have a positive impact on a company's on-line sales, market awareness, and overall success.

Personal Information Enhances Opportunities for Success Those sites that offer products for sale and hope to generate revenue on the Web seek to translate the shopping paradigms of the physical world into the digital world. In this way, product offerings and services, as well as the marketing strategies that surround them, are more likely to be accepted. As a medium, the Internet enables services to gather information about their markets. Services seek as much information about their visitors as possible, because the end result is that they are better able to serve their users.

Merchants and shopping environments must create a perception of value and credibility before asking for personal information from visitors. A visitor needs to perceive a value within the service, content, and product offering, which increases the likelihood that he or she will provide a service with personal information and remember the password. Some services require registration as they develop technical shortcuts to create personalized environments. Many stores are small- to medium-sized businesses—mom-and-pop stores—that find it difficult to market themselves in a competitive world, much less to offer free gifts or purchase incentives.

Companies that offer products and services for sale must keep in mind that the success of a virtual store on the Web is largely dependent on how well it can tackle the barriers it encounters. Because consumers are using a computer as device or medium of choice in electronic commerce, the comforting elements of the handshake and human voice simply aren't there. As the physical world has demonstrated, stores must cater to their prospects, establish a rapport, and build trust. For most unknown entities on the Web, credibility and a solid reputation are musts for achieving success.

How Will My Information Be Used? Some on-line registration requests may not be getting many visitors to comply simply because users/consumers have no way of knowing with any certainty what the information will be used for and who, besides the gatherer of the information, will have access to it. Typical questions Web surfers ask Web sites are:

- Who, besides the Web site, will ever see my information?
- Will my information be packaged and sold or rented as part of a mailing list?
- Will my information produce reams of real junk mail or junk E-mail?
- Is there an option for me to choose specifically how my information will be used? For this transaction only?
- Can I trust you to guard my privacy and keep this information confidential?
- What can I *really* do about it if you lie?
- What am I getting in return?
- Is it worth it to me to give you the information? (or the corollary) What's in it for you?

Paid Subscription Sites

For many reasons, most virtual stores that employ paid membership models require registration. One outstanding technical reason is that these services attempt to create a customized user environment and a relationship. Thus, when visitors access and travel, view content, and make purchases within the site, they can be closely tracked. A customized or *narrowcasted* environment is extremely helpful in creating a one-to-one marketing and sales approach.

Narrowcasting   Technologies such as Netscape's cookies are beginning to bridge the gap between understanding the user and targeting narrowcasted, or personalized, information from the service to the user. The cookies technology enables a host or a publisher to retrieve and store information from the visitor's browser. The cookie itself transmits a line(s) of object-based code that can provide information about the visitor and recent history of his/her travels and experiences (see "Magic Cookies," sidebar). Future trips to a service transmit code values that send narrowcasted information back to the visitor, establishing an interest-based experience.

Overall, cookies have become an important part of the creation of shopping cart technologies within Web stores. For instance, the Cyber-Source Corporation has developed a cookie-based technology that configures its Web site (http://www.software.net/) to the platform of the visitor (Macintosh or Windows).

As the Web moves toward customized, narrowcasted, and incentivized visits for consumers, with or without registration, consumer shopping will become more impulsive. Requiring registration to create shopping carts on the Web is, to a certain extent, understandable, but it certainly is not necessary for basic levels of visitor information. For instance, it is possible to keep track of some visitors' actions without requiring them to log on using a password or code. Session-based Web tracking systems do precisely this.

While the basic Web tracking systems cannot track a vast amount of personal information about users, the information generated by these systems assists in the development of the visitor's psychographic profile—those elements (demographics, interests, usage statistics) that establish a complete picture of the visitor. It is a user's psychographics that sites seek.

Another important need for member registration services is to retain some knowledge about customers within the host site while they are shopping and until they return. This can be advantageous to both the visitor and the service. While logging on to shop, a member can be authenticated and acknowledged. Again, registration is still not required for customizing a single visit or for completing a purchase. Some sites prefer not to risk scaring away customers with registration, and they ask for user feedback and personal information when customers leave the shopping experience. This model corresponds with common practice in real-world shops (a paradigm transport).

If a service/site/store is going to require registration, it must:

- Make the visitor feel comfortable.
- Give the prospect a compelling reason to register.
- Use the information collected to add value to the shopping experience.

Unpaid Subscription Sites

Internet businesses attract customers in a variety of ways. A popular method for attracting a user base is free or nonpaid subscription services. The nonpaid services have been somewhat more successful than paid services; however, they, too, have limitations and barriers to success. Free membership subscriptions and services are continually being modified, as merchants are desperate to attract as many visitors as possible and cater to their interests.

These types of services usually ask visitors to set up an account, with the benefits of user authentication, club rewards and discounts, and new service updates. If the company is well known, the offering compelling, and the program reasonable, the consumer will likely partake. Setting up the account is generally not an easy task for consumers, and some do not set them up willingly (pending the incentives to do so). Consumers often run into snags along the way. For example, when I visited the Amazon Books Web site, (www.amazon.com) I had to set up an account to make a purchase of any size. Next, I had to choose between a "secure" and a "nonsecure server." As a security-conscious shopper, I chose the secure server, and as with the setup at Virtual Vineyards, I could not make contact and was told that my connection was refused. Not wishing to sort through the details, I made the choice to cancel—and a sale was lost. My book purchase at Amazon was impulsive.

The bad news about subscription-based tracking is that it detracts from the customer's ability to make spontaneous purchases. Further-

ESPNet.Sportszone Membership Services

Most Web sites at varying levels have integrated subscription and membership programs into their service offerings. ESPNet Sportszone employs a low-cost subscriber program into its plan and is successfully generating revenue. For the merchant, the benefits include user authentication, demographics, and revenue. Conversely, for the consumer, benefits include the latest and best sporting news, interaction with sports superstars, and a low-cost program.

While many services have failed with their programs, ESPNet has succeeded. It is considered by some to be the hottest and most up-to-date sports environment on the Internet. Paying subscribers have access to exclusive chat room sessions and interviews with popular sports figures. By enabling Web surfers interested in sports to interact with the on-line guest(s), it offers services that visitors value while solidifying the brand name. Quite a bit of effort is chiseled into the construction of the service as content—sports scores and information are edited and added to the service immediately.

ESPNet markets its services and attracts new members using the same sales and marketing paradigms that consumers and people in general are familiar with in the physical world. Lessening the barriers to consumer acceptance and providing the right incentives has worked. The special offers to subscribers rotate frequently; however, the price for the service usually stays consistent. By doing so, users continue to perceive the service as credible and worthwhile, due in part to brand identity. ESPNet generates revenue and builds a loyal customer base. The free trial offer is also attractive.

A recent on-site promotion on ESPNet promised a ticket to the best sports site on the net, including latest scores, statistics, and breaking sports news daily. Subscribers got even more: rich multimedia, dynamic graphics, in-depth analysis, and detailed statistics, for $4.95 a month (the first 30 days free) or $39.95 a year. For sports fans, this is a hot ticket.

more, customers sometimes resist giving out the personal information needed to set up an account, since many of them value the on-line environment specifically because it offers anonymity.

The subscription-based tracking model makes sense, especially for the purchase of hard goods on-line, since delivery information must be given so that the purchases may be shipped. By definition, selling hard goods does not ensure anonymity (but the payor is not always the recipient of the goods), so the more traditional retail model for obtaining information about your customers can be applied.

Asking Users for Information—Privacy Issues

Major concerns have been raised about privacy on-line. For instance, America Online once received some unfavorable publicity for selling its subscriber lists and has promised never to do so again. Similarly, Netscape has promised to disable the cookie software that could be utilized to keep track of information about its users over time.

A privacy issue arises with the popularity of Java for creating Web applets. Java's security architecture is easily disabled, and when running a Java applet, you're constantly connected to a host server. It might make sense to take a look at the privacy provisions of any Java applets you plan to run.

The one tradition on the Internet that must be respected more than any other is regard for an individual's privacy. Internet users point to loads of junk mail that fill their real-world mailboxes and swear that they will never let that happen in the virtual world. Therefore, if you are collecting information about users directly or via a software mechanism such as cookies, be wary of selling this information to others. Using it discreetly for your own purposes is fine, but selling it to others, resulting in unwanted direct mail, will anger your users.

There is a lot of generic information about users on the Internet today. Therefore, before you set out to do your own research project, spend some time visiting Web sites or market research firms to see what information is already available. CyberAtlas, published by Interstellar, a San Francisco–based management consulting and research firm that specializes in the Internet, is an example. Did you know that:

Magic Cookies

The addition of a simple, persistent, client-side 'state,' or recognition device, significantly extends the capabilities of Web-based client/server applications.

—Netscape

"Magic" cookies are a mechanism by which host servers can store and retrieve information to and from a client's browser. The cookie, developed by Netscape and MCI, is useful for Web hosts who wish to provide a "stateful" or "customized" experience for their visitors, because by using a cookie, a host can tag a visitor at the end of a session with information for a future visit. This situation occurs when a server returns an HTTP object (including HTML pages), which can include a description of previously visited URLs and other general traffic information. The action of encoding information into the cookie of a user is referred to as *user hard drive storage*. This type of server access, storage, and caching typically has been forbidden. Users must survey and know the sites, just as the sites wish to survey and know the visitor. The information stored and accessed in a cookie is purely behavioral information.

- ◆ The average Web surfer has 36 bookmarks?
- ◆ The current visits-to-hits ratio is 13 percent?
- ◆ Twenty-three percent of all Web surfers have authored at least one HTML document?
- ◆ Adobe has sold more than 100,000 copies of PageMill?

These are just a few highlights of the more than 1,000 factoids you'll find on CyberAtlas—The Internet Research Guide (http://www .cyberatlas.com).

Closing Thoughts

Knowing your customers is very important, in both the real and virtual worlds. You may not have a chance to actually see the prospects that come to your virtual store, but you can get to know them just the same. There are three points you should remember:

◆ Never be too shy to ask for information, as long as you make it voluntary and give the respondents something in return. Make sure what you give them is of value and relevant to the specific business you are in.

◆ There are tools available today on the Internet to help you track and qualify the traffic. (Appendix A includes detailed information regarding these software products.) Use them or have your Webmaster develop one for you, but do not operate a virtual store without tracking software.

◆ Most important is privacy. It is easy to collect a lot of information about your customers and be tempted to sell it to advertisers and others targeting them. This is a very common practice and has resulted in junk mail pollution. Internet users, many of whom are libertarians and fierce individualists who want to be treated with dignity, despise junk mail. They love their "pollution-free" community and will flame those who abuse the privileges.

CHAPTER FIVE

Advertising and Promoting Your Virtual Store

Topics presented in this chapter:

- The Diversity of the On-line Market
- Advertising on the Internet
- Web Banners—Are They Worth It?
- Traditional Advertising for Web Goods
- Advertising Agencies in the Interactive World
- Hot Links—Back to Trading Baseball Cards
- Promotion on the Internet
- Four Functions Your Virtual Store Must Perform
- Tips on Effective Use of Internet Advertising
- Getting Your Message across Clearly on the Web

One of the main questions addressed in this chapter is: Why advertise? Answer: It's important to get the word out about your business! Advertising and promotion ultimately lead to sales. They are methods that have been used successfully by consumer goods manufacturers, yet in the world of technology providers, they are seldom understood or used in a successful way. And since much of the Internet is still made up of technologists, most virtual merchants do not take advantage of what advertising and promotions can provide for them.

This chapter includes several interviews with advertising agencies that work in the world of on-line commerce. These professionals offer tips and suggestions for setting up a compelling virtual store and letting people know about it.

After reading this chapter, you'll understand why you need to get the word out about your virtual store. You'll learn that a lot of traditional advertising strategies are being applied in new ways on-line, and you'll meet some of the advertising agencies that are moving into the virtual realm. You'll see that there are a variety of ways to promote your virtual store: Usenet groups, E-mail, on-line forums, Web banners, and print advertisements, to name a few. You'll learn the most successful ways to present yourself to potential customers in these milieux.

The Diversity of the On-line Market

Remember that the Internet is not a single, gigantic market, but a collection of markets. Some are large, some are tiny. In fact, many companies spend fortunes to pinpoint the kinds of niche markets you can find for free on-line. You can find radical, conservative, and middle-of-the road viewpoints. You can find investors and con artists. In fact, the only thing many Internet users have in common is their skill with a keyboard and a mouse.

The greatest strength of Internet advertising is that you can pick, from this great diversity, exactly the prospects you'd like your message to reach. In fact, if you offer a Web site, your prospects will *self-select;* that is, if you promote your site and if they like what you have to offer, they'll come to you.

It's also important to keep in mind that, on the Internet, borders don't matter. It's no more difficult to reach prospects in other countries than in your own, although at this point, most messages on the Internet (75 percent to 85 percent) are in English. However, in many other countries, people speak English in addition to the native language. For instance, the Japanese educational system provides six years of written English instruction, and the Japanese are highly likely to buy from other countries. So just because your virtual store is presented in English, do not think that your audience will consist of native English speakers only. When you think of advertising and promoting your virtual store, think of this as an *international* program.

Advertising on the Internet

In comparison to traditional advertising, Internet advertising can be very confusing. Old-school marketers may find not just the technology jargon overwhelming, but also the fact that ad campaigns can be developed overnight, customized information can be delivered inexpensively, and advertisements can be distributed in multiple ways, all on-line.

Another point of confusion around advertising on-line is that several of the well-established "facts of life" regarding advertising do not work on-line. In fact, as you will see in the sections that follow, on-line advertising is in direct contradiction to these facts. Both in print and radio/television advertising, the more often consumers see an ad, the higher their propensity to act on it. Most people get a sense of comfort and familiarity from seeing, for example, a car ad many times. If you are told that Volvos are safe by the same TV ad showing happy children in the back seat, you may finally choose to buy a Volvo.

With banner ads on the Internet, the propensity of consumers to act on a particular ad is highest the first few times they see the ad. If the ad is not acted on after the fifth or sixth time, chances that it will be are close to none. Furthermore, unlike TV ads, seeing the same banner ad over and over does *not* provide a sense of comfort and familiarity. It starts annoying the consumer. The virtual merchant who decides to use banner ads must keep this in mind and change the creative layout and location of banner ads often.

In radio/television and print ads, there is often a several-month time lag in the effectiveness of the ad, following its first appearance. There is also a several-month effectiveness period after the ad has stopped running. It takes several impressions, both in print and radio/TV, for the subconscious mind of a consumer to grasp the message that is being advertised and to take action on that message. Likewise, after the ad is off the air and out of print, the effect of the advertised message lingers in the subconscious minds of consumers and they may still act on the message. This is in direct contrast to Web banner advertising, on which consumers will take action immediately upon initiation of the campaign. The meaning of consumers "taking action" is also quite different in a Web context and will be discussed later in this chapter.

MYTH: *The Internet is the best new advertising medium to come along since television.*

There is a very big difference between traditional advertising and the Internet. Advertising is a passive activity in which you receive the message without actively searching for it.

The Internet is anything but passive. Nothing happens on the consumer's screen until a key is pressed or the mouse is clicked. Internet users value this greatly. They want to be in control of what happens on their screens, what messages they get. The last thing they want is advertisers creeping up on them when they are not ready to receive these messages.

The on-line world is an interactive medium and should not be thought of in terms of television advertising, which is a broadcast medium. The Internet is a narrowcast medium, similar to direct mail or specialty print magazines, with one major difference: Advertisers' messages can be communicated only if consumers choose to hear them.

Intrusive or traditional advertising, as we know it, has not been successful in the on-line world. Prodigy was the pioneer in this area in the early 1990s, when advertisers started using it as a venue to reach the more than one million users. Though advertisers were very willing to pay for this audience, Prodigy users were not willing to be at the receiving end. They found the ads intrusive, and Prodigy's user base showed its displeasure by switching to the competing on-line services, AOL and CompuServe.

Byron Abels-Smit, of Aspen Media, once observed, "The Internet is not just a new medium, but a new *kind* of medium. It's like when television was new, at first advertisers treated it like print. Early TV commercials were just type and a voiceover. That only changed as people learned how to effectively use television for marketing. Newspaper rules didn't apply for TV. In the same way, print media and TV rules don't apply to the Internet."[1]

What are the key features of advertising on the Internet?

- ◆ It's fast.
- ◆ It's inexpensive.
- ◆ It's multifaceted.

The following sections explain these ideas in more detail.

It's Fast

No other advertising medium can match the Internet's ability to deliver advertising messages quickly. The process of conceptualization and implementation of an ad and the resulting customer response can happen within a matter of hours—and speed is important on the Internet. Customers on-line are accustomed to fresh, accurate information and near-instant responses.

You'll definitely be judged by the quickness and accuracy of your responses to any customer feedback. For that reason, it's probably worthwhile to staff your virtual store with someone who can respond to customer E-mail and inquiries as rapidly as possible—much like staffing an 800 number.

It's Inexpensive

Compared to the cost of direct-mail advertising, which averages 50 to 75¢ per piece, you can create an impression for as little as 10¢ per unit in an E-mail advertisement. That figure approaches the average cost of specialty print advertising, at approximately 5¢ per impression.

More important, you can deliver long copy for the same price as short copy, and on the Internet, long copy sells! Information-hungry Internet users want all the information they can get about your products and services. More information is better. Also, the cost of updating your information is negligible, unlike, for example, the cost of printing thousands of brochures and flyers every time your prices change. All you pay for is the time spent updating your site on the Web.

It's Multifaceted

On the Internet, there are so many ways to get the word out about your virtual store, some of which might surprise you. All are new in concept, going where no ads have gone before. To be an effective Internet advertiser, you'll want to be comfortable with Gopher, ftp, news groups, E-mail lists, the Web, and the on-line services such as AOL and CompuServe, because all of these can serve as platforms for your message.

For instance, you can participate in *Usenet news groups* whose discussion topics are related to your line of business, politely answering any questions that may be posted. The point of this method is not to make your answer an advertisement for your store, but to provide free, professional information as a way of drumming up business. Unlike magazine readers, Internet users are highly sensitized to advertising and often do not welcome blatant ads, but they perceive the value of and respond with gratitude to relevant information presented in a helpful manner.

A number of "free E-mail" services exist on-line that accept advertising to be seen by their members. These E-mail services, such as Juno Online Services and FreeMark Communications, believe that users will supply demographic data and tolerate intrusive advertising for access to free E-mail. Subscription mailing lists (ListServs) may also allow E-mail advertising of your goods and services, as long as they are in keeping with the needs of the subscribers.

Other advertising ideas include screen savers that advertise your company and products or multiplayer game sites that incorporate your brand into the flow of the game. Sound far-fetched? Here's an example.

Last year, 223,599 users registered at the Riddler entertainment site (www.Riddler.com), which allows single players or multiple-player teams to compete for cash awards and prizes sponsored by advertisers. The Riddler site features riddles, crossword puzzles, and trivia contests, all sponsored by companies such as AT&T, NBC, Snapple, Random House, and Lycos.

At Riddler, the advertisers' messages are integrated into every game, and their brand identities are part of the prize tokens that players collect when they win. According to Interactive Imaginations (I I), the company that sponsors the Riddler site, an average player spends about an hour for each visit, thus generating dozens of ad impressions.

When users register at the Riddler site, they must provide demographic information that allows sponsors to customize and target messages to qualified consumers. Prizes also are customized to fit the lifestyles of specific players. For instance, prizes previously awarded have included Toyota RA V4 sport utility vehicles, music compact disks from Capitol and Atlantic Records, vacations, and cash.

Interactive Imaginations will develop exclusive customized games for advertisers, with packages beginning at $10,000 to design, manage, and maintain the game. Michael Paolucci, president of I I, characterizes the company as "an extension of Madison Avenue, not just a technology company."[2]

There's a burgeoning group of developers creating interactive screen savers that include advertising messages. One such company, Freeloader, downloads advertising and other content from Web sites onto a personal computer (PC). While a screen saver is running, five hot buttons at a time appear on the user's screen, running for about 15 seconds each. If a user clicks on any of the hot buttons, the software automatically takes the user to the stored advertising that has been downloaded previously onto his or her PC. A standard ad package that features a screen saver and welcome page promotion costs about $11,000. A premium ad sponsorship, which offers movie and sound clips, large color pictures, and screen saver promotions, starts at $21,000.[3]

The marketing community will be watching with great interest to see whether these new interactive advertising strategies are effective in creating brand recognition and increasing consumer purchases on-line. Since the first wave of Internet advertising based on traditional ads from print and TV fell flat, everyone is waiting to see whether these ideas will succeed.

Web Banners—Are They Worth It?

One of the most specific types of Web advertising is the Web banner, which amounts to buying space on someone else's Web site to advertise your product or service. Banner ads are usually small in size, so the message can be only about one sentence long, and more often three or

Internet Shopping Network Talks about On-line Advertising

A recent survey ranked ISN third among all Internet advertisers—after AT&T and Netscape. ISN advertises heavily on-line, and it was one of the first to do so. One of its earliest on-line ads appeared on HotWired (when HotWired used to accept advertisements). Interestingly enough, ISN formerly advertised off-line for its on-line site, but at present it's switched everything onto the Net. "It makes sense for us, since we're 100% an on-line business," says Bill Rollinson, cofounder of ISN.

ISN participates in setting up reciprocal hot links with other sites. Rollinson says, "I know it goes against conventional wisdom, giving away your customers, but I think you do customers a disservice if you don't link out. I'm a firm believer in links both ways."

Another way ISN generates interest in its on-line store is by judicious use of proactive E-mail, after asking the customer's permission. For instance, if a customer buys a printer, he or she might receive an e-mail about a special price on toner cartridges for that printer. E-mail also can be sent regarding weekly specials and holiday items.

Rollinson offers some insight from the lessons ISN has learned about on-line advertising. First, as in any advertising, the more targeted your ads, the better the likely result. "The Net really lets you target," he points out, citing news groups and other ways to reach customers with specific interests. Rollinson notes that "the customer is really in control in this medium, and careful targeting allows them to react." He adds that on-line advertising is exciting because the Internet provides for immediate feedback: "It's exciting to track how the ads are doing, and there's not the waste of paper costs or mailing costs."

four words. In addition to the message, banner ads provide a hot link to your virtual store, which is like having an elevator from the high-traffic store on Main Street directly to your store. Potential customers need to take action (click the button) to get to your store, but at least they have a way to get to you. You'll want to consider Web banners as an effective on-line advertising alternative.

TIP   *How do you set up a Web banner? First, go to a Web site that sells them, such as Yahoo or Netscape. Many of the virtual stores covered in sidebars have purchased Web banners on search sites such as Yahoo. As this book goes to print, a Web banner costs from $15,000 to $40,000 for three months.*

At some sites, you can buy a banner on a specific page, in a manner analogous to how a magazine sells an advertisement on a specific page in the back section. Also like magazine advertisements, Web banners have specific dimensions that sell for different prices.

Some Web banners can be as small as a button with a hot link, which says, for example, "Click here to go sailing," and links the customer to the SailAmerica Web site. (Examples of advertisements like this one may be found in the Knight-Ridder site's Travel section.)

Some sites, such as Yahoo (see Figure 5.1) and C-Net rotate the banner's Web spot. For instance, week by week it might appear on the first page of the site, then the second page, then the third page, then back to the first page. Site managers who use this technique feel that the banner and the site remain fresh for repeat traffic by rotating the advertisements in this way.

Overall, Web banners are a very attractive way to get part of the traffic of a popular site to see your advertisement and have the opportunity to

Figure 5.1   Web banner ad.

Virtual Vineyards: Built on Internet Advertising

Virtual Vineyards (Figure 5.2) is one of the all-time greatest success stories of Internet retailing. It's been in business strictly on the Internet since January 1995, selling fine wine and gourmet food items to customers worldwide.

Robert Olsen, president, estimates that Virtual Vineyards spends 10 to 20 percent of its revenues on advertising. The company has done a lot of advertising on-line, primarily in the form of Web banners purchased at sites such as Yahoo and InfoSeek, as well as some lesser lights. It also advertises on AOL and CompuServe. Other means of getting customers to its virtual store site include

Figure 5.2   Virtual Vineyards.

Continued

promotions through Internet Service Providers (ISPs) and joint marketing with other companies. It has hot links to two or three sites, including Wells Fargo Bank and CyberCash, for customer convenience. Because of its success, many sites have hot links to Virtual Vineyards, says Olsen, "From 30 or 40 to hundreds. They don't tell you anymore when they link to you."

Olsen feels that the company's on-line advertising efforts have been "modestly successful." Virtual Vineyards is in the process of increasing its off-line advertising, because the customer acquisition cost off the Web is about half of the cost on the Web.

Virtual Vineyards accepts payment "any way they want to make it—online, offline, whatever. We've never received cash, but we would take it," Olsen quips. Virtual Vineyards was one of the first merchants to adopt CyberCash as a payment method.

"We've found the Internet to be an opportunity for value-added selling, not just low cost," Olsen concludes. This company is definitely in the arena for the long term.

visit your virtual store. For instance, if a site gets one million hits per week, and you get 10 percent of that traffic to your store through a direct link, you have 100,000 potential customers visiting your site each week. And all of those customers have seen your brand name at least once, whether or not they decide to visit your site.

One thing about the Internet—it makes it easy to measure how many customers actually are visiting your store. You can use several methods to find out which customers are coming to your store site and where they are coming from, thus you can see very quickly which advertisements are working best for you. These measurement tools are discussed in Chapter 4 and in Appendix A.

Traditional Advertising for Web Goods

Traditional advertising and promotion also are important in setting up your virtual store. Advertising only on the Internet is like preaching to the choir. Also, the 1-inch by 5-inch space of a Web banner has not yet been proven as an effective way to make a genuine impression on the customer. In addition to Internet advertising, then, you'll want to place advertisements in the physical world.

Print advertisements for on-line goods and services have proven effective. For example, Netscape has taken out full-page advertisements in *The Wall Street Journal.* Netcom, an Internet Service Provider, has a consistent program of print ads. General business publications, such as *The Wall Street Journal,* recognize this and provide special advertising sections for Internet-oriented businesses.

In addition to daily journals, you'll want to place advertisements in Internet-related magazines, such as *Internet World.* These magazines reach a large audience of sophisticated consumers who are highly likely to shop on-line in the near future, if they aren't already doing so.

Finally, you need to advertise your business in the traditional venues specific to your business, even if you have only a virtual store. If you are in the exotic animal business and have no sales channel other than your virtual store, named exotics.com, take out a print ad or two publicizing your Internet address in the publications dedicated to exotic animals. You will be surprised how many yak and emu owners who read those magazines have Internet access. They will find out about you through the publication and visit your virtual store. With a name like exotics.com, if you rely only on Internet advertising, you may attract a very different crowd than you had in mind.

Advertising Agencies in the Interactive World

This section gives profiles of and advice from four top advertising agencies working in the on-line world. Although three of these agencies, CKS Interactive, Poppe Tyson, and Winston Advertising, have a lot of experience with technology, they are traditional agencies learning new ways to advertise in the on-line environment. One agency, NarrowLine, was founded solely to create placement for Internet advertising.

David Carlick at Poppe Tyson suggests that you ask yourself the following important questions when looking for an Internet advertising agency:

- Do they have enough expertise and commitment to the medium that I won't become their guinea pig?
- Is the chemistry good between us?
- Can they understand my business?
- Do I like their work?
- Does my budget match their requirements?

In general, Carlick advises you to avoid agencies that seem intimidating or act as if they know more than you do.[4]

CKS Interactive

CKS Interactive, of Cupertino, California, got into the business of on-line design in 1987, beginning with Hypercard training stacks for Apple Computer, which it saw as a tremendous opportunity to add value to Apple's product and create a branded experience that users would associate with support and friendliness, with no effort from Apple. CKS Interactive is a division of CKS Group, a company of about 250 employees worldwide, which provides more traditional integrated marketing communications. It's developed Internet sites for well-known clients such as Clinique cosmetics.

John Holland, on-line strategist at CKS Interactive, points out, "The Internet allows a lot of flexibility in the type of environment you create. It also allows for reciprocal link relationships. And you can author very quickly. In contrast, the online services such as AOL offer incredible reporting. And there's a lot of equity in the AOL brand right now. It's a great place for smaller businesses, because they can rely on the AOL brand to give them credibility while they're getting started."

CKS Interactive recommends that any virtual store should quickly communicate the possibilities that a customer will find there. "Consider the idea of walking into a cocktail party," Holland offers. "You see a table of food, there's a band playing, and there's a group of people having an intimate conversation. Usually the host or hostess greets you with some sort of a brand message—'Nice to see you, so glad you could make it.' Although the new guest can't see everything that's happening at the party in that first glance, he or she gets a pretty good feel for what kind of things to expect from the event." People at Web sites are actually having a branding experience.

A branding experience on the Web has some unique components. "We encourage our clients to consider what an incredibly powerful branding environment the interactive experience can create," says Holland. "First, the experience usually is initiated by the customer. Then, the click stream and navigation of the environment express the customer's level of interest and communicates to the company; to deliver a powerful experience, the company can anticipate and send back what the customer wants. When this kind of interaction is established, most unique of all is the back and forth 'pumping' action of the experience, like the systolic/diastolic action of the heart." As this back-and-forth flow occurs, customers feel as though they're having a very personal experience; there's a feeling of "agency" about the Web site—that the site is enabling this experience to occur. That's a powerful branding experience.

This approach is very different from the old model of branding, in which communication goes out from the company in magazines and TV ads and on packaging. The only response may be an eventual blip in consumer purchases or requests for information, maybe weeks or months later.

"If there's one thing we've learned about the current state of shopping on-line, it's that people don't shop on-line, they *buy* on-line," says Holland. "To change that, we need to learn to create an irresistible, faithful shopping experience on-line." For instance, how does a client such as The Sharper Image—that has built itself an image that relies on a really luxurious catalog—move that experience into cyberspace? The first thought might be to literally recreate that luxurious catalog experience on-line. But CKS Interactive recommends a *faithful* recreation, which is not necessarily a literal one: It captures the spirit of the store or the catalog, but it's not necessarily identical. In other words, the goal is to create a faithful new media representation of who and what you are.

To make a faithful recreation, we need to imagine ourselves *into* cyberspace. There's a sort of Disney imagineering thinking that will be required to form the seeds of the new shopping experience mandated by the new medium. Disney starts the imagineering process with money as no object; then, once a design is found, it is pulled it into line as something that's cost effective. That's a good way to approach creating an on-line site—except that, for shopping, imagineering, or "thinking outside the box," as it is sometimes called, will be about *creating utility.*

Following are some examples of on-line sites that CKS believes to be thinking outside the box:

- *The Girl Scouts.* A troop in Connecticut put up a Web site on Open Market and sold about $300,000 worth of cookies. It worked because people know what to expect from Girl Scout cookies. Ordering on-line became a no-brainer.

- *On Sale.* With the auction model, this company has perhaps come the closest to doing something really different on-line.

- *Firefly (www.ffly.com).* It's a music site, but it's not selling albums. The goal is to sell ad space, closely targeted to consumer preferences. It puts up a selection of ten albums, which you rate and submit. The second selection is likely to be much closer to your taste; the third set even more so. The site's goal is to build a profile of your tastes in music. But businesses such as Columbia House certainly could make use of that information.

The Firefly site has another interesting facet: It gives the consumer a *mirror,* a picture of himself or herself, a point which is in keeping with the widespread use of the Web for vanity sites. With sites like Firefly on the Web, not only can we tell the world about ourselves on-line, but the world can reflect us back to ourselves.

John Holland himself is the creator of Net Breakfast, a part of the CKS Interactive site that helps you keep up with things changing daily and weekly on the Web (see Figure 5.3). It's set up like a calendar, with links for each day of the week. If you follow the links "at breakfast every day," you'll have a good grasp of how certain key sites are evolving. Net Breakfast creates an intuitive system for organizing sites so we can keep up.

"Perhaps over time, the Internet will become a giant collection of affinity groups. As it grows bigger and bigger, it will feel less like a community. It's already lost some of that feeling for me since the old days," states Holland. "To me, the Net is measured anarchy."

As for the big picture, Holland says, "Our long-term strategy involves the gradual and careful acquisition and committed retention of our most

Figure 5.3   Holland's Corner on the CKS site.

qualified, most valuable customer relationships." What about the future of Internet commerce? Holland sees on-line transactions becoming "a series of constant, organic exchanges, more like an energy flow than a transaction. More like a wave than a particle," he adds, smiling.

Poppe Tyson

Poppe Tyson, of Mountain View, California (see Figure 5.4), has been in the advertising business for a long time, and it's been working on Internet advertising for about two years. The company specializes in advertising for the "considered purchase, things that someone tends to investigate before buying, such as automobiles, semiconductors, personal computers, barbeque grills, and maybe even a movie," says David Carlick, vice president. "What we're doing on the Internet is helping our clients fill the digital service gap for their customers. People now expect to see the latest product information, compare products and cost, find dealers, and order on-line. We can help with that.

Figure 5.4   Poppe Tyson.

The purpose of Web site building is to help the client manage their brand as a growing percentage of customers prefer to interact over the computer."

"The old view is that the Web is a medium, and Web sites deliver content. Our experience has shown that the Web is better viewed as an applications platform, in the way that a PC is a platform, and that Web sites are applications for marketing and sales. Some of those applications can imitate media, such as brochures, but the real value comes when the applications deliver services of value to the consumer."

Basically, Carlick divides the Web into two kinds of sites: service sites and affinity sites. At a service site, the customer can get real help or information about products and services. "It enhances the customer's knowledge and enjoyment of the product," says Carlick. "For example, the Weber Barbeque site we've done is a service site."

At an affinity site, the purpose is to create good feelings that are shared with the customer. For instance, the Poppe Tyson Valvoline site is an affinity site according to Carlick's definition. Motor oil isn't too glamorous in itself; therefore, the Valvoline site features games and auto racing pictures that help build affinity with the customer.

What about creating a site on the Internet versus using an on-line service? Carlick replies, "Our clients want to build sites that let them control the image of their brand—something they can't do as a subset of the AOL Web site. Ultimately, AOL is a great Web site, on-line connectivity, and Web access all in one—offering everything for one price—and their users can now access all Web sites that are built to the open Web site standard."

Another area in which Poppe Tyson seems to have a unique view is that it does not recommend the solicitous use of hot links, or, as Carlick says, "Welcome to my site, please leave." He recommends the use of hot links only if a complementary product or service is involved.

Carlick also had some interesting comments about the differences between advertising in print and advertising on-line: "In the media world we'd say 'What is the message we want to project?' but on-line we say 'What are the goals of the user? What will he or she want to see and investigate?'" Clearly, the on-line advertising is much more user-driven than previous media ads could ever be.

Winston Advertising

Winston Advertising, of Santa Clara, California, is an agency that specializes in promoting high-tech companies. Located in Silicon Valley, Winston has approximately 30 employees and its gross billings total as much as $25 million annually. Its clients include the likes of Hitachi Data Systems and Philips Electronics.

In the last year, Winston Advertising has moved into creating Web advertisements, such as banners, for its clients in addition to more traditional, off-line pieces. John Wickett, president of Winston Advertising, says, "Six months ago our revenues from Web advertising were zero. Now they're about $50K per month. I expect that 6 months from now they'll be $100K per month. That's not including revenues from creating Web sites." Winston Advertising also creates Web sites for clients who need them. The agency makes another $50,000 per month so far on creating and maintaining Web sites for its clients.

According to Wickett, "Our clients have moved from indifference to the Web into a view that a Web site is something without which they cannot do business. It's certainly going to change the way businesses interact." He points out that it's much easier and faster to get on-line and learn about a product or a client than to call someone up and ask for information or fill in one of those information cards in the back of a trade magazine, then wait until the material arrives in the mail a couple of weeks later. "By that time, you've almost forgotten about it," he concludes.

What Winston Advertising finds different about the Web is that customers can see results faster. "It's the most dramatic shift in this business in 25 years," Wickett says. "Typically, what ad agencies do doesn't impact this month's sales. It usually affects next quarter's revenues or next year's revenues, because it takes a while to create ads and get them into the media. For instance, a print ad usually take 4 to 6 weeks to create, then another 2 to 6 weeks are needed to get the ads into the publications. Web advertising enables us to have a short-term effect. For instance, one of our clients has a bundling deal this month with Netscape. We created a banner one night, it went up the next day, and they're already getting sales. A new client of ours, Gyration, has gone from 3,000 to 30,000 per month in sales this way."

Winston believes that the Web also has an effect on the way the advertising agency does business. "We get more time-to-market pressure. After all, for a banner that runs one month, if we can get it up 2 days earlier, that's 10% more selling time. We're beginning to work in new ways. Instead of the well-established steps we've used in the past to come up with creative concepts and narrow them down into successful print ads, we're starting to do more flexible things like sit down with the client, the project manager, and a graphic designer and come up with something for the Web, often in real time. Still, good thinking and strategy have an important role here. After all, it's easier to come up with an ad in real time if you've already settled on a clear concept to work with, such as 'safety and security.' "

Winston Advertising says that it will increase its revenues this way in the longer term, but its true goal is to increase its clients' bottom-line revenue. "If we make our client successful, we'll make more money. We believe in creating long-term relationships with our clients. We're willing to make an investment with smaller companies that will create growth opportunities for us, too," Wickett adds.

At this writing, Winston Advertising is working on developing its own Web site, primarily as a vehicle for better communication with its customers. "We want to create forums in which the customers can communicate with us and with each other."

NarrowLine

NarrowLine, of San Francisco, California, is an advertising placement company founded in 1996 to help agencies take advantage of the new possibilities available on-line. Tara Lemmey, president of NarrowLine, has a unique perspective on Internet advertising. She advises advertisers that the Internet does not behave like any other individual medium: It's not direct mail, it's not print ads, nor is it any other medium. What is it?

Lemmey's view is that Web advertising is most like shelf space in a store. Advertisers and distributors fight hard to obtain shelf space for their products. Why? Because shelf space provides brand awareness at the actual point of purchase. There's a good chance that a shopper will switch brands at that point if incentives—such as lower price, coupons, rebates, or other extras—are offered. Says Lemmey, "What people should worry about is building brand equity online, just getting your name up there, which is the equivalent of shelf space, not click through. The problem is about getting eyeballs onto your brand name, hoping that people who are shopping on-line will switch to your brand right then and there."

Why is brand equity on-line like shelf space in a store? Consider people who grocery shop on-line using the Peapod service. Usually, after the first few shopping sessions, they've made up personal lists of items they purchase regularly. Once those personal lists are set up, it's very hard to get people to change brands, because their shopping process has become *automated.*

As agent technology proliferates on the Internet, brand equity is likely to be more and more expensive to come by. Once personal lists in various areas of life are set up—magazine subscriptions on-line, games, news services—someone will have to do something very compelling to get shoppers to switch. *The shelf space has disappeared!*

Lemmey states that advertisers should not get hung up on click-through rates as the be-all and end-all of on-line advertising. She feels that brand awareness and positive predisposition toward a brand can be created on-line, "even though a person doesn't call an 800 number right then and there." So, although there is a direct component to Internet advertising, it's clearly not the same as direct mail or direct ads that encourage the customer to respond right away. *Moral:* Get your brand name up there on the shelf right away!

Hot Links—Back to Trading Baseball Cards

Hot links are a way to obtain inexpensive promotion and advertising on-line. We touched on this topic in the section on Web banners, but Web banners are paid advertisements. Hot links can be traded by developing relationships with other stores that have Web sites. The key element of using hot links successfully is creating an infrastructure with partner companies, so that a customer can traverse from site to site, finding goods and services that are desirable. A group of Web sites connected by hot links is a bit like a shopping mall without the physical boundaries. For example, a virtual store that sells wine might like to have a hot link to a store that sells gourmet chocolate or other fine food items.

TIP   *The idea of creating hot links is to link to other stores with whom you are not competitive, but whose goods and services might appeal to customers with the same demographics as yours. One store that sells wine on-line, Virtual Vineyards, has no hot links right now, although you might expect them to be linked with the equivalent of Brooks Brothers on-line. This is perhaps the greatest missed opportunity for on-line advertising right now. On-line merchants could be marketing themselves to their sister stores. Get together and package yourself as a hot-link location to your adjacent industries.*

Suppose I want to create a very upscale image on-line. I might market my virtual store to Tiffany's on-line site. If my site has a lot of traffic, both of us win: I get an upscale image, and Tiffany's gets more traffic to its Web site.

Early on, HotWired utilized hot links. It was one of the only sites to take advantage of this opportunity. Later, however, HotWired decided to charge for links, so became another Web banner site.

Promotions on the Internet

You'll want to consider offering promotions on the Internet, just as you would for any retail business. For instance, contests and sweepstakes can help generate customer interest in your site. You'll also want to plan various physical-world promotional activities, in which you give the customer something of value related to your virtual store. What will the customer consider something of value? Most companies have discovered that a T-shirt giveaway doesn't cut it, unless you're a cult phenomenon such as Interop was in the early days or Netscape.

So what can you give away? Something the customer already wants to buy. It is worth considering that information-based goods are very cheap to deliver. Your cost of goods delivered on-line is minimal, so why not give some away at a substantial discount for first-time buyers? For instance, you might offer a first-purchase coupon good for up to a 75 percent discount on your product or service.

Promoting the First On-line Purchase

Research has shown that after a customer buys once on-line, he or she is much more likely to do so again—but that first purchase is expensive in terms of advertising and promotional dollars. Instead of handing out tchotchkes, use some of your promotional budget to help customers finance their very first purchase.

Getting a customer to make that first on-line purchase is about as difficult as getting a customer to take that first cruise vacation in the real world. But people who take a first cruise are quite likely to take another, and another. . . . Likewise, it's relatively easy to get a customer to convert from America Online to Prodigy, compared to the difficulty of getting someone to sign on for that first time.

Similarly, in the mail-order business, once a customer has ordered from a catalog such as L.L. Bean or J. Crew, the propensity to order again goes up significantly. Thus, the catalog stores have a huge business in selling each other their mailing lists—lists of people who are proven catalog customers. Note that with all the public concern about privacy on-line, it might not make sense to offer your mailing list of proven on-line customers to other stores. Let customers control how their names are used.

Placing an on-line order requires some effort, so it makes sense to offer a bigger reward than you would in a physical store. For example, Virtual Vineyards might offer a particular wine at a huge discount to first-time customers—say $5 per bottle for a $20 bottle of wine. After that first bottle, it's easier to spend $20 for a second or third bottle.

Juno Online Services (www.juno.com), a free E-mail service, conducted a nine-month beta test of its advertising-based E-mail system with about 5,000 participants. All the users typically logged in once per day. Juno is set up as an off-line service; that is, users read their mail off-line, going on-line only to retrieve incoming mail or dispatch their own mail. While the user is downloading new mail or uploading outgoing messages, a special (premium-priced) advertisement appears on the screen for a few seconds. Messages from 15 initial advertisers, including Quaker Oats, Land's End, Snapple, Welch's Juices, *Wired* magazine, Swatch watches, Mirimax films, and Oki printers,[4] appeared on each E-mail page.

FreeMark, a competitor of Juno, also offers a free E-mail service sponsored by advertising. Like Juno, Freemark puts advertising on every E-mail screen by matching the customer's profile with the advertising message. Advertisers on FreeMark include Campbell's Soup, RJR Nabisco, the Verve jazz music label (part of Polygram), *Wired* magazine, and CMP Consumer magazines (computer-related publications). FreeMark's claim to fame is that it avoids privacy issues with its promise never to release the names of users to advertisers and never to sell lists of names. However, when a user responds to an advertiser's on-screen advertisement or requests more information, that user's name does become available.[5]

Couponing

Couponing in the physical world is a tried-and-true merchandising tool. Both in-store and out-of-store coupons are used by consumer products companies for promoting brand switching.

In the service world, the airline industry revolutionized couponing by using "value gifts" through airline miles. This is also a sort of couponing. But unlike the traditional coupons for hard goods that promote brand switching, these coupons promote brand loyalty, meaning that you get more of a service or product the more you use it.

Amazon Books

Amazon Books has been in business since July 1995, selling books on the Web. Although it hasn't yet posted a profit, the company is racking up $5 million in sales for 1996, a figure that surpasses most Barnes and Noble superstores.[6]

Amazon.com advertises both on-line and in other media. It doesn't reserve a specific percentage of revenues to spend on advertising, preferring to look for opportunities as they come up. Currently, it advertises on search engines and other areas that attract people who are likely to buy books. It has no hot links to other sites. Amazon has an Associates program for other sites to recommend books; links to Amazon earn a referral fee. "Right now, we're selling a lot just from word of mouth on the Web," says Leslie Koch, spokesperson for Amazon Books. The amazon.com site on the Web has become an underground sensation for book lovers all over the world (see Figure 5.5).

What Amazon.com offers that people really like are two customized services:

◆ An editorial service for people looking for books in a specific genre.

◆ A mailing list to notify customers when books become available in certain interest areas, such as stamp collecting or books by a certain author.

For authors, Amazon offers a questionnaire that works as an on-line interview. The author can annotate individual entries in the Amazon book catalog.

Amazon accepts VISA, MasterCard, and check, either on-line or by phone, for those who prefer not to enter their credit card information on-line. Most sales take place on-line, using the Netscape secure server.

Continued

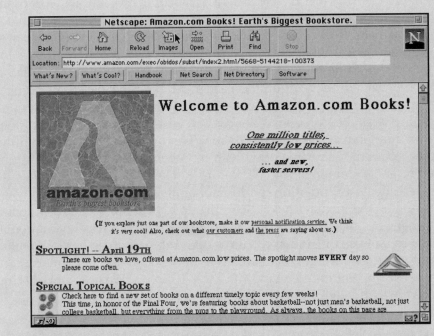

Figure 5.5 Amazon.com.

Amazon.com is definitely in the business for the long term. As the Internet grows, says Leslie Koch, "I see us growing with that. We offer a service that's different than you get going to a conventional bookstore. We're a Web-enabled business—we're thinking about how people are not served by the ways books are distributed and sold now. We expect business to grow as access grows and as we learn more about our customers' needs."

You can use coupons in the virtual world both to establish brand loyalty and to promote switching to your brand. There are no reasons why you cannot give "frequent-flyer miles" at your virtual store. This is especially easy if you collect revenues through the subscription method.

Electronic wallets, like those described in Chapter 3, eventually will be able to hold electronic coupons. If you are working with a payment service provider, such as CyberCash, First Virtual, or DigiCash, ask them if they can set up a couponing program for you.

CyberCash and Rocket Science Games are working on a consumer promotion program, called Rocket Fuel. Consumers will receive coupons for free interactive game play in Rocket Science's Virtual Rocket Arcade on the Internet each time they purchase a game in the physical stores. Rocket Science will also run its own "Rocket Flyer Miles" program. Consumers, who will pay as they play via CyberCoins, will accumulate Rocket Flyer Miles as they play at the Rocket Arcade. The Rocket Flyer Miles will be used for free game play, free download of new characters, game environments, or game elements. Jim Wickett of Rocket Science Games sees its virtual arcade as a promotion- and merchandising-driven site. "We want our customer, the Virtual Rocket Scientist, to look at our arcade as a social spot to hang out. We plan on creating loyalty and increasing the frequency of visits by the use of tried and true couponing that gives our customers more of what they want, great game play in a social setting. Arcades are fun because you get to interact with others like you. We are now offering that to kids in an environment their parents approve of, their homes."

MYTH: *The entities that will really be successful in the virtual world will be large corporations.*

There is no doubt that large corporations, especially those with successful brands, will have an edge on the Internet. But success is not limited only to large corporations, especially in the services area, where franchises use a corporate name but the actual service provider is unknown.

In the real world, franchises provide the element of trust for the service-based industries. No matter where you are in the world, you know what a McDonald's hamburger will taste like. Franchisees are willing to pay high fees for immediate name recognition. The typical Internet user, however, is a lot more willing to look behind the cover, past the franchise brand, to the actual service providers' credentials and quality.

Do not think that the name of a large company ensures instant success. Several small companies on the Internet have had successes above those enjoyed by large companies—for example, eTrade has been the stock brockerage of choice, not Charles Schwab.

Four Functions Your Virtual Store Must Perform

You don't need to be a large corporation to be successful in the virtual world. What you need is a complete, functioning virtual store that offers quality products and services. Following are four categories of things that a complete virtual store should be able to do. Every store must be able to do the first two of these—otherwise, it's not really a store. Depending on the kind of virtual store you are establishing, the last two may not apply to you.

1. *Show your products and services.*   Every virtual store must be designed to highlight the products and services available. Even a virtual store site such as FedEx highlights the delivery service because it shows all the packages en route.

2. *Process orders and inquiries.*   Since the Internet is such an information-oriented environment, it's imperative that your virtual store be equipped to answer inquiries and provide additional information to prospective customers.

3. *Process payment transactions.*   If you're not just answering inquiries, you'll want to accept some form of payment—credit cards, checks, cash, or electronic cash. The question is whether you'll accept payment directly on-line or use another medium, such as telephone or faxed credit card information. The biggest challenge in accepting on-line payment is security—both having it and letting your customers know that you have it. A possible solution is to secure Web browsers that can offer security in transferring credit card data and other sensitive information on-line.

   Also, accepting payment means you'll probably need an account with a merchant bank, or you'll need to work with a hosting service such as First Virtual that can handle those details on your behalf. (For more information about choosing the best payment options, refer to Chapter 6.)

4. *Deliver your products and services over the Net.*   For information-based goods, on-line delivery is usually the least expensive option. It makes sense to deliver bits over the net-

work, whether those bits are video clips or chapters of a book. For a virtual store that sells durable goods, of course, on-line delivery doesn't make sense. However, it might be a nice touch to send an order confirmation message by E-mail.

The biggest challenges you'll face in delivering goods on-line are:

♦ Secure delivery methods—You'll want to be sure that your product reaches your customer unaltered and that no one has made illegal copies along the way.

♦ Export restrictions—Depending on the nature of your product or service, you may face restrictions from the laws of your country or those of your customer's country. Just within the United States, for example, it's illegal to ship alcoholic beverages into several states.

♦ Copy protection—Copy protection prevents customers from reselling your products without your permission. Many publishers and large organizations are looking at this problem, and some technological copy protection solutions are likely to be available in the near future.

Tips on Effective Use of Internet Advertising

Following are some concrete steps you can take to ensure that your virtual store doesn't look like you just scanned in your catalog pages or existing brochures overnight.

♦ *Spend time on the Internet yourself.*   There's no substitute for "getting your hands dirty" to learn how to use the Internet, particularly the Web, as an effective marketing tool. Try out an on-line service; read and perhaps contribute to an on-line discussion group; buy something at someone else's virtual store (perhaps one of the ones mentioned in this book.)

♦ *Remember that Internet advertising is only a part of your overall marketing strategy.*   Keep your on-line advertising efforts as one color in your palette. Don't forgo traditional advertising and marketing channels—at least not until you've got proof that your Internet marketing can sustain your business on its own. Coordinate your on-line efforts as part of a campaign that helps you achieve your overall business goals. Keep your business objectives firmly in mind; don't be dazzled by technology. Do, however, be sure to promote your virtual store in your print advertising and through on-line publications. You can think of your Web address (URL) in the same way as your business's 800 number and publicize it accordingly.

♦ *Go for a clear, measurable response from customers to your on-line advertisements.*   As in print advertising, some ads are designed to create a positive predisposition toward your products and services, while other ads are designed to promote a quick and direct response. Make sure your on-line ads are well designed and have specific goals in mind.

No matter whether you advertise in print or on-line, you'll need some persuasive writing to get your message across. If you're just starting out and haven't had much experience with writing about your products or services, that can be a tall order. The following section offers some pointers that can set you on the right track in the on-line arena.

Getting Your Message across Clearly on the Internet

Your goal in creating a *home page,* which is the first page a customer sees at your virtual store, is to draw the visitor into your site. You can think of the home page as a directory, telling people what they'll find at your store, what's new, and how to get to each part of the store. Contact information also should appear on the home page, including a phone number, fax number, postal address, and E-mail address. You want to provide as many ways as possible for the customer to get in touch with you.

After the home page, you can come to the point of your company's message. In fact, you should do so as powerfully as possible. How do you make your message powerful?

♦ Know your company's competitive advantage. Be prepared to state specifically, in one short sentence, what distinguishes your store from those of your competitors.

- ◆ Understand the key benefits of your products and services. Be prepared to state them in a way that (1) conveys your competitive advantage most clearly, and (2) prioritizes them so that they have the most impact on Internet customers.

- ◆ Decide which information best supports the customer's buy decision, based on your company's competitive advantage and the key benefits of your products and services. For instance, if service is a hallmark of your company, you'll want to include customer testimonials. Provide product data sheets, technical support phone numbers, lists of authorized dealers and distributors for your product, contact information for sales representatives, and so forth. By doing so, you'll also appeal to as many types of shoppers as possible. (See Chapter 3 for a discussion about the different types of shoppers.)

- ◆ Tactically deliver your information, the message, and supporting information you so carefully crafted in the first three steps: Design a virtual store that creates the most convenient and pleasant shopping experience possible for your customers. Create shopping scenarios that give the customer a sense of control and interaction, because it's been proven that people who feel in control learn more and retain more of what they read. One way to do that is to provide as many opportunities as possible for feedback, such as an E-mail address link at the bottom of every page. Combine this pleasant shopping experience with your powerful message, to be found in some form on each and every page, and your virtual store is well on its way to success.

- ◆ Based on your earlier decisions about competitive advantage and key benefits, along with your design for a pleasant shopping experience that appeals to a variety of customer types, specifically create the Web pages, the customer mailing lists, the databases, and so forth, that support your model of who your company is and who your customer is. It's powerful to imagine real people out there who want what you've got. Put the pages on the Web, start your ad campaign, and you're ready to go.

On-line Dating Service Makes Excellent Use of Success Stories

Here are some examples of how success stories can add a personal touch and lend credibility to your virtual store. Like any personal ad, an on-line dating service must overcome a certain amount of resistance, so it makes terrific success stories a part of the store. For example:

Just thought you might like to know that myself and another member have "connected" using [your service]. When one thinks of the odds of the two of us actually meeting WITHOUT [the service], it is slightly overwhelming. She was born in Austria, I in Italy. I came to Canada, She stayed in Austria and eventually moved to the States (Florida and Washington). We have been exchanging email daily (indeed sometimes 3 or 4 times daily) and have met on a couple of occasions. Whether or not this will blossom into a long term relationship I don't know. But for those of us who are interested in meeting people from a broad spectrum of backgrounds, [your service] provides a safe and alternative venue. Carry on Mcduff!!

Or this one, a heartwarmer:

On January 22, 1996, I responded to a profile of a man from Sweden (I live in Calgary, Alberta—Canada), and surprisingly enough our personalities really clicked. We moved from e-mail correspondence into telephone calls on February 3, 1996. Every day we seemed to become closer to the other, and on the 15th of February, I decided that I really wanted to meet this man.

On March 29th I boarded Canadian Airlines CP099 and flew to Stockholm via London. This was my first trip via air and I was a bit nervous about the flight. The flight was a breeze compared to my first visit in Heathrow Airport! What a nightmare! I have

Continued

never been so confused in all my life about where I was to go to board the Scandinavian Airlines. Well I finally maneuvered my way to the right terminal and boarded SAS for the final leg of my journey to meet Sture.

My flight arrived in Stockholm at 5:45 P.M. and being really tired and anxious to walk, I zoomed out of the plane and ran right past Sture—who ended up having to chase me through the airport! When he finally caught my attention—I threw my arms around him and kissed him! He was very nervous, and I was very tired—great combination!

We spent a week in Stockholm and then headed up north to the Arctic Circle to visit his mother and we hit it off really well. I love his family.

On April 9th, Sture asked me to marry him and I accepted. He put a ring on my finger on the 14th of April and on April 15th, I sadly boarded my flight to return to Calgary—many tears were flowing. We didn't anticipate seeing each other again until July.

Upon arriving back in Calgary, I made an appointment with the Swedish Consulate and started the paper trail for emigrating to Sweden. And Sture is doing the same with Canada. It will be nice to be able to choose which country we want to remain in.

The fickle finger of fate intercepted for us and on April 18th the company Sture worked for shut down the office in Sweden and left Sture available to look for other opportunities. The position he had in Sweden was extremely stressful and what was initially a bad experience turned out to be a blessing. With free time available, he boarded a plane and came to me in Calgary on the 26th of April. It was a very emotional day for both of us, as so much had happened in our lives in 2 very short weeks.

My family adores Sture and so things are moving rapidly towards the day that we will be together permanently.

As you can see, part of the appeal is that the stories are written in the customer's own words, without editing or interruption.

The basis of all this advice is to help you increase your customers' sense of *involvement* with your virtual store and your products. If you think of your store as a conversation (perhaps a persuasive one) with your clients, rather than a presentation, you're on the right track. When you've succeeded in getting your customers involved with your site, remember that they'll take your messages much more personally than they tend to do in print media. Expect some strong responses, perhaps even some angry ones if they don't like what you're doing. Welcome all kinds of feedback and incorporate it into improving your store.

TIP *Be sure that any support personnel who handle customer feedback are well versed in Netiquette. As Howard Rheingold, author of* The Virtual Community, *states, "Netiquette is not just about the niceties of behavior or avoiding behavior. Netiquette is like the double line in the middle of a highway." Virginia Shea's book,* Netiquette, *is well worth reading. Chapter 7 in this book contains further discussion about Netiquette.*

Closing Thoughts

Internet marketing is a new beast. The on-line world resembles direct marketing, telemarketing, and shelf space, all rolled into one. No one quite knows how to make Internet advertising work, and lots of new, interactive ads are being tried out.

In general, Internet advertising gives a much quicker response than traditional advertising, because the customer can send feedback. It's easy to see whether a particular advertisement is working or not, in just a matter of days, not months.

Internet advertising also generally is less expensive than traditional advertising, such as direct mail, because printing and mailing costs are nonexistent. And you can reach across international boundaries effortlessly, as long as you're careful to keep informed of local laws and customs.

It's important to get your name "up in lights" on-line to build each prospective customer's recognition and help establish trust in your vir-

Another idea for reaching your customers is to send them greeting cards for birthdays or other special days. A company called Greet Street lets you choose a greeting card on-line and inscribe your message. The card is sent out automatically at the right time, and cards can be scheduled up to a year in advance. At this writing, Greet Street is about to launch a service to deliver digital greeting cards anywhere on the globe, by E-mail. A typical digital card from Greet Street includes animation, images, and music, along with a personalized message. Card prices start at $1.95. Currently, Greet Street does 80 percent of its business on AOL, but the Web business is growing, and it should really take off with these new digital greeting cards.

Doctors, dentists, and other professionals who like to remind clients about regular visits or those who just want to send a nice greeting for any occasion now have a way to do that in the physical world with help from Greet Street's automatic reminders or on-line by E-mail for about the same price. In other words, you could utilize a service like Greet Street quite effectively to help you with Internet marketing for your virtual store.[7]

tual store. If nothing else, seeing your name there day after day builds a reassuring sense of stability. You can use many avenues to get your message across, from news groups to digital greeting cards. As long as you've crafted a message and a shopping experience that conveys the unique benefits of your product or service and have not just slapped a bunch of existing brochures up onto the Internet, you're likely to create a successful image that leads you toward profitability.

CHAPTER SIX

ACCEPTING VIRTUAL PAYMENTS: SELECTING METHODS THAT ARE RIGHT FOR YOU

Topics presented in this chapter:

- ◆ Accepting On-line Payments
- ◆ Working with Your Merchant Bank
- ◆ Payment Service Providers Today
- ◆ Certificate Authorities
- ◆ Digital Signatures
- ◆ Small Businesses: How to Become a First Virtual Merchant

When setting up your virtual store, you're starting a business like any other. You'll want to accept payment in as many forms as your customers can offer it. What payment options are available on-line? Basically, the same ones that are available off-line: credit cards, checks, and cash.

This chapter covers existing on-line payment options and helps you select the best ones for your virtual store. It discusses on-line credit card payments and the emerging standard from MasterCard and VISA. It also includes some discussion of various forms of digital money and some providers that offer financial transaction services for electronic cash: CyberCash, DigiCash, and First Virtual.

After reading this chapter, you'll understand what your options are for accepting payments in your virtual store: 800 numbers, digital cash, credit cards submitted on-line or off-line, and so forth. You'll learn the basics about encryption and why it's important for on-line transactions. This chapter also gives you practical advice about the SET standard and how to become a merchant accepting digital cash, as well as step-by-step information on how to set up an account at a merchant bank.

This chapter discusses mainly on-line payment options, but don't forget that you can still offer your customers the more familiar means of payment: calling an 800 number, mailing in a check, or, for nearby customers, cash-and-carry. Also, you'll read in this chapter some interesting variations on how payments are accepted on-line, ranging from unencrypted transmission of credit card information (probably not the safest alternative) to using E-mail to confirm purchase requests before an order is filled. You may want to follow the example of Alamo Rent-A-Car, profiled later in his chapter, and set up your virtual store without accepting on-line payments, then add that capability later if it seems appropriate.

Accepting On-line Payments

In the physical world, consumers and merchants have a variety of payments to choose from when it comes time to make a payment. Even though the United States uses credit cards more than any country, as you can see from Figure 6.1, other payment methods are very significant and have larger market shares. In the virtual world, the same types of options need to become available for both virtual store owners and their consumers for electronic commerce to take off.

The most common form of on-line payment today is the credit card. However, as reported in Chapter 1, research shows that many customers have doubts about the security of using credit cards on-line. A number of efforts are underway to make on-line transmission of credit cards more secure. Perhaps two of the most notable are the Netscape secure Web browser software from Netscape Communications and the Secure Electronic Transfer, or SET, standard created by MasterCard and VISA.

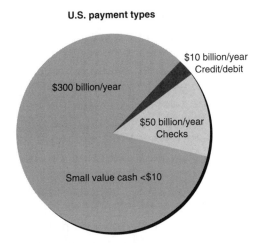

U.S. payment types

$10 billion/year
Credit/debit

$300 billion/year

$50 billion/year
Checks

Small value cash <$10

Figure 6.1   U.S. payment types.

Electronic Credit Card Transactions

The risks associated with an electronic credit card transaction on-line are similar to the credit card risks in the physical world. Essentially, any time someone has access to your credit card number, you run the risk of that person committing a fraudulent purchase in your name. Luckily, most people are honest. However, you should be aware that, of the fraud that does occur, over 60 percent is perpetrated by merchants illegitimately using their customers' credit card numbers.

On-line, it's possible that hackers could obtain access to your credit card number as it is transmitted to an on-line store. That's why stores that accept credit cards on-line usually offer some form of encryption protection. It's a bad idea to transmit credit card information in the clear over the Internet—or to ask your customers to do so.

On-line use of credit cards has been discussed quite extensively in the media, because some people feel that no encryption system is safe enough to prevent fraudulent use of credit card information. However, the technology does exist to virtually guarantee the security of credit card use. Several efforts have been made in the last few years to create on-line security standards for credit card processing. For example, MasterCard and VISA are working together on the SET specification, which offers excellent protection.

The Secure Electronic Transaction (SET) Standard

Financial institutions have a strong interest in accelerating the growth of electronic commerce. Although electronic shopping and ordering does not require electronic payment, a much higher percentage of these transactions are carried out using credit cards instead of cash or checks (see Chapter 1 for supporting data). This situation holds true in the consumer marketplace as well as the commercial marketplace.

Two major financial institutions, VISA and MasterCard, have jointly developed the Secure Electronic Transaction protocol as a method to secure credit card transactions over open networks. SET is being published as open specifications for the industry. These specifications are available for application to any credit card payment service, and they may be used by software vendors to develop applications.

In general, payment systems and their member financial institutions will play a significant role in building on-line commerce as they establish open specifications for credit card payments that:

+ Provide for confidential transmission
+ Authenticate the parties involved
+ Ensure the integrity of payment instructions for goods and services order data and authenticate the identity of the cardholder and the merchant to each other

The SET protocol meets these criteria, using cryptography (described later in this chapter) to:

+ Provide confidentiality of information
+ Ensure payment integrity
+ Authenticate both merchants and cardholders

SET changes the way that participants in the payment system interact. In a face-to-face retail transaction or a mail-order transaction, the electronic processing of the transaction begins with the merchant or the acquiring bank. However, in an SET transaction, the electronic processing of the transaction begins with the cardholder. That is, the transaction is initiated from the customer's computer, whenever he or she desires to make a purchase on-line.

Seven major requirements for on-line commerce are addressed by SET, as follows:

1. Provide confidentiality of payment information and enable confidentiality of order information that is transmitted along with the payment information.
2. Ensure integrity for all transmitted data.
3. Provide authentication that a cardholder is a legitimate user of a branded credit card account.
4. Provide authentication that a merchant can accept branded credit card payments through its relationship with an acquiring financial institution.
5. Ensure the use of the best security practices and system design techniques to protect all legitimate parties of an electronic commerce transaction.
6. Ensure the creation of a protocol that is neither dependent on transport security mechanisms nor prevents their use.
7. Facilitate and encourage interoperability across software and network providers.

Anyone interested in the processing of credit card transactions on electronic networks (including vendors developing software to interoperate with implementations of SET from other vendors) may obtain a copy of the SET specification from the VISA or MasterCard Web site (www.visa.com or www.mastercard.com). Besides VISA and MasterCard, advice and assistance in the development of the specification was provided by GTE, IBM, Microsoft, Netscape, SAIC, Terisa, and VeriSign.

The SET specification enables greater credit card acceptance on-line, with a new, higher level of security that encourages consumers and business to make use of credit cards in this emerging market. If you are considering accepting credit card payments on-line at your virtual store, the following section offers guidelines as to what any on-line credit card payment system must offer to provide sufficient security for you, the merchant, and for your customers. Each feature is described, then the SET implementation of the feature is given as an example.

Basic Requirements for On-line Credit Card Transaction Security

These basic requirements must be fulfilled by any system such as SET that offers credit card transaction services over an open network such as the Internet:

♦ *Confidentiality of information.* To facilitate and encourage electronic commerce using credit cards, it is necessary to assure cardholders that their payment information is safe and accessible only by the intended recipient. Therefore, card-holder account and payment information must be secured as it travels across the network, preventing interception of account numbers and expiration dates by unauthorized individuals.

On-line shopping: In today's on-line shopping environment, credit card payment instructions are often transmitted from cardholders to merchants over open networks with few or no security precautions. However, this account information pro-vides the key elements needed to create counterfeit cards or fraudulent transactions.

Fraud: While it is possible to obtain account information in other environments, there is a heightened concern about the ease of doing so with public network transactions. This con-cern reflects the potential for high-volume fraud, automated fraud (such as using filters on all messages passing over a net-work to extract all credit card account numbers out of a data stream), and the potential for mischievous fraud that appears to be characteristic of some hackers. The transmission of account information in a relatively unsecured manner has trig-gered a great deal of negative press to date.

With SET: Confidentiality is ensured by the use of message encryp-tion.

♦ *Integrity of data.* The transaction system must guarantee that message content is not altered during the transmission between originator and recipient. Payment information sent from card-holders to merchants includes order information, personal data, and payment instructions. If any component is altered in transit, the transaction will not be processed accurately. To eliminate this potential source of fraud and error, the system must ensure that the contents of all order and payment messages received match the contents of messages sent.

> *With SET: Payment information integrity is ensured by the use of digital signatures.*

♦ *Cardholder account authentication.* Merchants need a way to verify that a cardholder is a legitimate user of a valid branded credit card. A mechanism that uses technology to link a cardholder to a specific credit card account number will reduce the incidence of fraud and therefore the overall cost of payment processing. The transaction system should define a mechanism to verify that a cardholder is a legitimate user of a valid credit card account number.

> *With SET: Cardholder account authentication is ensured by the use of digital signatures and cardholder certificates. Note that SET does not define the process whereby a financial institution determines if an individual is a legitimate user of an account.*

♦ *Merchant authentication.* The transaction system must provide a way for cardholders to confirm that a merchant has a relationship with a financial institution that allows that merchant to accept payments. Cardholders also need to be able to identify merchants with whom they can securely conduct electronic commerce.

> *With SET: Merchant authentication is ensured by the use of digital signatures and merchant certificates.*

◆ *Interoperability.* The transaction system must operate on a variety of hardware and software platforms and must include no preference for one over another. Any cardholder with compliant software must be able to communicate with any merchant software that also meets the defined standard.

> *With SET: Interoperability is ensured by the use of specific protocols and message formats.*

In any such transaction system for on-line processing of customer-generated orders, these elements do not function independently; all of these security functions must be implemented.

SET Addresses Use of BankCards Only

The SET specifications address a specific portion of the message protocols that are necessary for electronic commerce: those parts that use or impact the use of credit cards on-line. To provide maximum convenience for your customers, you'll also wish to look into electronic cash and checks as alternatives to credit card payment. The following sections briefly describe those alternatives.

For the first time, with the MasterCard/VISA SET standard, the credit card companies are bearing a portion of the risk associated with on-line transactions, because they are dealing with customer-initiated transactions. As we move forward with alternative payment methods, such as electronic checks and coin, it becomes less clear who bears the risk. Luckily, electronic cash and checks are inherently low-risk payment methods where the merchant is concerned.

Several vendors are beginning to offer on-line checks, cash, and coin payment services. Among them are CyberCash and DigiCash, each profiled later in this chapter. Like the credit card companies, these electronic cash and coin payment service providers are taking on some of the risk inherent in any on-line sales transaction.

A Typical Credit Card Transaction Flow On-line

Figure 6.2 shows a typical credit card transaction flow for an on-line merchant who is using the credit card service from CyberCash. The con-

Merchant's-Eye View of the Electronic Shopping Experience

From the standpoint of payment processing, the electronic shopping experience can be divided into several distinct steps.

Step	Description
1	The customer browses for items. This step may be accomplished in a variety of ways, such as: ◆ using a browser to view an on-line catalog on the merchant's World Wide Web page, ◆ viewing a catalog supplied by the merchant on a CD-ROM, or ◆ looking at a paper catalog.
2	The customer selects items to be purchased.
3	The customer is presented with an order form containing the list of items, their prices, and a total price including shipping, handling, and taxes. This order form may be delivered electronically from the merchant's server or created on the customer's computer by electronic shopping software. Some on-line merchants may also support the ability for a customer to negotiate for the price of items (such as by presenting frequent shopper identification or information about a competitor's pricing).
4	The customer selects the means of payment.
5	The customer sends the merchant a completed order along with a means of payment.
6	The merchant requests payment authorization from the customer's financial institution.
7	The merchant sends confirmation of the order.
8	The merchant ships the goods or performs the requested services from the order.
9	The merchant requests payment from the customer's financial institution.

Even though these steps have been described as occurring in a specific order, variations are possible. The SET specification focuses on steps 5, 6, 7, and 9, when the cardholder chooses to use a credit card as the means of payment. Other payment services would take care of electronic check or coin payments tendered by the customer.

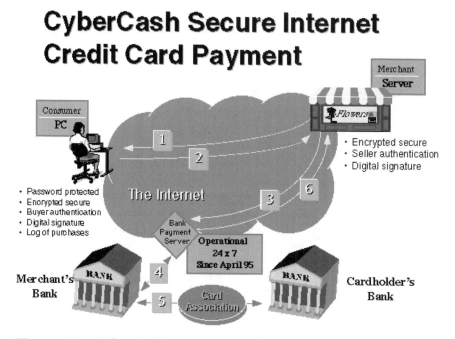

Figure 6.2   CyberCash's transaction flow.

sumer has been shopping at the merchant's virtual store. She chooses the items she wants to purchase.

Step 1:   The merchant sends over an electronic invoice for those items, totaling the prices and adding shipping and tax to it.

Step 2:   The consumer chooses to pay with her electronic wallet. The wallet on her desktop is activated. Her credit card information and her accepted amount of payment is sent to the merchant in encrypted form, without her having to type it in again.

Step 3:   The merchant receives this encrypted package, attaches her merchant information and the amount of the transaction to it, and sends it, all encrypted, to his merchant bank's Internet Payment Server.

Step 4:   At the merchant bank's Internet Payment Server, the messages are taken off the Internet and decrypted, and an authorization request is sent to the bank that issued the consumer her credit card for the amount of the transaction.

Step 5:   The issuing bank of the credit card sends an authorization code for the value of the transaction to the merchant's bank, verifying that the consumer has enough credit on her account to complete this transaction.

Step 6:   The merchant's bank sends this authorization code back to the merchant, over the Internet.

All this happens in less than ten seconds while the consumer and merchant are on-line. In case the credit card is not good for that value of transaction, the merchant has the ability to ask for another card number, just as at physical stores or restaurants, without losing the sale.

Electronic Cash and Checks

On-line checks are in several ways superior to their off-line counterparts. For one thing, they are drawn on funds that have already been collected and are held in escrow accounts. From another, there is nearly no float with an on-line check, since electronic settlement can be virtually instantaneous.

Electronic check transactions carry somewhat less risk than check transactions in the physical world, because an electronic check is drawn on cleared funds held in an escrow account at a participating bank. Furthermore, the opportunity for immediate settlement reduces the elements of risk even further for on-line merchants, provided that the merchant bank operates with an immediate, or at least daily, settlement model.

On-line cash is an interesting topic. It provides the same anonymity as physical tender, but the parties to a transaction need not meet face-to-face at all. Some governments and other official agencies fear that it might contribute to the growth of illicit activities on-line. Some suggest that a more sensible view is to limit very large cash transactions on-line but allow smaller transactions freely, since they are so convenient.

Electronic Coin

The demand for instantaneous delivery of electronic goods for small denominations of money is satisfied with on-line transactions, which can be referred to as electronic coin transactions or minipayments. These transactions, of less than $10 and possibly less than a penny, open up new opportunities for buyers and sellers.

A broad range of electronic goods and services can be offered, such as software, information, graphics, games, published articles and pictures, music and videos, Web access, and consulting and professional services. With electronic coin, merchants have a way to offer electronic goods and services for small amounts of money. This is an alternative to subscription models and is more cost effective than taking credit card payment for small denominations. In addition, the payment is assured and instantaneous. An electronic coin transaction involves little risk, since the amount of money exchanged is small, and the payment process allows for immediate settlement.

In CyberCash's implementation of electronic coin, called CyberCoin, these transactions are facilitated by the fact that the merchant and consumer do not have to have a prior relationship. Consumers hold coins in their electronic wallets, which can be used at any merchant accepting such payment. This is the virtual analogue to the chewing gum purchase at the checkout stand, where the decision is often impulsive and not based on any preexisting relationship with the merchant, and returns are not a consideration.

Working with Your Merchant Bank

It's important to realize that there is some delay between deciding to set up a virtual store and accepting your first credit card payment on-line. After submitting a merchant application, the approval process can take up to two months.

Example: Becoming a Merchant with Wells Fargo Bank

Although these steps were written with a Wells Fargo merchant bank in mind, setup procedures for other banks are likely to be similar.

1. The first step in becoming a merchant at Wells Fargo is to visit the bank, taking with you a copy of your corporation's articles of incorporation and your federal tax identification number

provided by the Internal Revenue Service. If you're a sole proprietor, you'll need a copy of your business license.

2. You can complete all the paperwork at the bank, with the help of a new accounts representative.

3. At Wells Fargo, it takes about one week to get your business set up for processing credit card payments (such as VISA, MasterCard, and AMEX). That basic credit card service will cost you about $25 per month, plus a transaction fee of 10¢ per item.

4. If you need other services, such as payroll deposit, the setup process takes an additional week. That service costs about $95 per month plus the 10¢-per-item transaction fee, on top of your other $25 per month for processing credit card transactions. This service also requires a $125 setup fee.

5. For some services, such as having your company's payable checks clear through an East Coast affiliate to take advantage of float time, setup time for your account can take up to a month.

These times and cost estimates were obtained from a specific bank just to give you an example. Other banks may require different fees and may take more or less time to set up your account. Regardless of how your business is set up, on-line or in the physical world, the banking on the back end is pretty much the same.

As you can see in step 5, many banking issues center around when *settlement* is done. Settlement is the actual exchange of money between accounts—the money moves from the customer's bank into the merchant's account. Settlement can be done in a batch system or at the end of each day. In virtual payment systems, settlement theoretically can occur instantaneously. However, there are advantages to waiting, especially when you're on the paying end. On the receiving side, clearly, end-of-day settlement is preferable for merchants, since they often can get their money faster.

Most merchant banks currently do batch settlement. As on-line settlement becomes more common, more banks will be moving to end-of-day settlement. The banks incur no additional cost for doing end-of-day settlement. They need not add new technology or resources, since the technology provider (for example, CyberCash) actually carries out the settlement transactions.

Another issue is authorization. For instance, the risk associated with any payment returns changes at the point of authorization from the merchant to the bank.

Today's Electronic Check and Cash Payment Service Providers

Several business are developing in the area of on-line payment services. Some of these businesses focus on payment services for consumers and some for merchants; some focus on providing payment services to banks and other financial institutions. Some focus primarily on one form of payment, such as electronic cash or credit transactions, while others provide a broader array of services and facilities.

This section presents profiles of some of the major providers of on-line payment services today. It compares and contrasts their strengths. You can find detailed information about how to set up merchant accounts with these providers in Appendixes B–D of this book.

CyberCash

CyberCash (Figure 6.3) was founded in 1994 by William Melton, founder of Verifone, and Daniel Lynch, founder of Interop, along with Steve Crocker, and the author. It has become one of the leading developers of software and services for secure Internet payment. CyberCash provides software for consumers, merchants, and banks, utilizing some of the most secure technology available in the world.

CyberCash provides cost-effective, convenient, and rapid solutions for processing financial transactions on the Internet. Its innovative solutions are designed to integrate fully with existing transaction processing systems used by banks and other financial institutions.

In early 1995, CyberCash released its first electronic wallet, which provides consumers with secure credit card transmission over the Internet. CyberCash creates Internet counterparts for all familiar payment methods: credit cards, checks, and coins. The CyberCash payment solutions enable monetary exchanges not only among businesses and financial institutions, but also among individuals, by means of:

- ◆ *Credit cards.* CyberCash's Credit Card Service provides secure transport of credit card information over the Internet

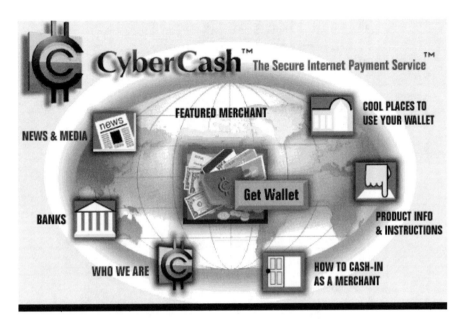

Figure 6.3   CyberCash.

directly into the majority of existing credit card processing networks and protocols. It also provides capabilities for merchant and consumer authentication. CyberCash supports the SET standard for credit card payments.

◆ *Electronic checks.*   The CyberCash Electronic Check Service allows instantaneous transfer of funds between individuals, between businesses, and between individuals and businesses without the risk of bouncing or forgery.

◆ *Small payments.*   CyberCash's CyberCoin service allows for low-denomination payments to be made rapidly and efficiently over the Internet. Amounts less than $10 can be transferred securely and conveniently. Payments as small as 25¢ are cost effective.

DigiCash

DigiCash (Figure 6.4), a corporation from The Netherlands, was founded in 1990 by David Chaum, who now serves as its managing director. Dr. Chaum created a patented extension of digital signature technology,

Figure 6.4   DigiCash.

called the *blind digital signature,* which allows a digital signature to be verified without revealing the identity of the sender. The primary benefit of the DigiCash payment system is the ability to make electronic payments anonymously.

Since its founding, DigiCash has been among the pioneers in development of electronic payment mechanisms that provide security and privacy for open, closed, and networked systems such as the Internet. DigiCash's first product was a road toll system developed for the Dutch government. It is now being tested in Japan and marketed in other countries.

DigiCash has developed a number of other technologies by working with leading organizations. For example, MasterCard has licensed Digi-Cash technology for a demonstration system implementing the first smart-card chip mask technology meeting the latest EMV (Europay, MasterCard, VISA) standard. These advances provide dynamic public-key authentication using the least expensive smart-card chip available.

DigiCash designed cards that included prepaid cash replacement functions and loyalty schemes, access control, and other applications for MasterCard's credit/debit systems. DigiCash's advances in security and reliability are integrated into the design. DigiCash developed a complete system, including terminals, PIN pads, host computer, and all related software. Cooperation is ongoing.

Switzerland-based Crypto AG, the leading international manufacturer and distributor of cryptographic devices, nonexclusively licenses DigiCash encryption technology. For ultrafast processing of transactions, DigiCash developed a modular family of high-speed encryption boards, which is manufactured and marketed by this licensee.

European Commission Project CAFE, founded and chaired by Dr. Chaum, is based on DigiCash technology implemented as a cross-border electronic wallet. This technology works with smart cards and infrared point-of-pay electronic wallets. The project consists of a consortium of firms including Gemplus, France Telecom, and PTT Netherlands. Project CAFE was selected by the European Commission to install a trial card and electronic wallet system in its headquarter buildings in Brussels, which began in the third quarter of 1995.

The DigiCash E-cash system is being implemented in the United States by Mark Twain Bank. DigiCash technology is especially appealing for use in smart cards—credit card–sized storage devices that carry monetary value and can be inserted into a specialized computer slot for loading or unloading digital money—which are finding increasing acceptance within the United States.

First Virtual

First Virtual Holdings (Figure 6.5) was formed in early 1994 by Lee Stein and Einar Stefferud and several other Internet veterans. Its payment and security technology has been architected and developed by Nathaniel Borenstein and others. The first product offering from First Virtual was an Internet payment system, which was developed quietly and publicly announced as a fully operational open Internet service on October 15, 1994.

First Virtual's system differs in many ways from all other proposed approaches to Internet commerce—most notably in the fact that it does not rely on encryption or any other form of cryptography to ensure the

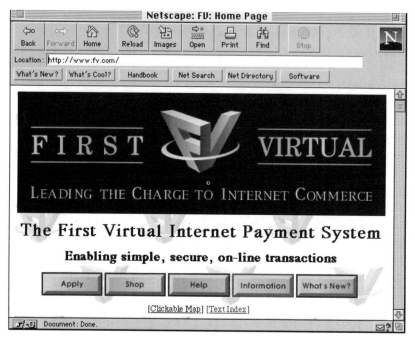

Figure 6.5   First Virtual.

safety of its commercial transactions. Instead, safety is ensured by enforcing a dichotomy between nonsensitive information (which may travel over the Internet) and sensitive information (which never does) and by a buyer feedback mechanism built atop existing protocols.

In a nutshell, First Virtual relies on E-mail for placement and verification of on-line orders and utilizes credit card transactions primarily. Its payment system is built on top of preexisting Internet protocols, notably the SMTP/RFC822/MIME (E-mail), telnet, finger, ftp (file transfer), and HTTP (Web) protocols. Because those protocols are not secure in the sense that they carry no strong proofs of identity, it is necessary to design a payment system in such a way as to provide much stronger guarantees. While others have focused on achieving this goal using cryptography, First Virtual designed a higher-level protocol based on E-mail callbacks.

In the First Virtual system, a buyer and seller may meet and decide to transact business in any manner they desire. While this often occurs when a buyer browses a seller's Web page, it also frequently happens by

E-mail, ftp, Internet Relay Chat, or even off-Net entirely, and it could easily happen in the future via protocols that do not exist today. Once the buyer and the seller have an intent to do business, they submit a transaction to First Virtual. That transaction can be submitted via standard E-mail or via a new protocol, SMXP, designed by First Virtual for real-time exchange of MIME (E-mail) objects.

When First Virtual is asked to process a financial transaction, it looks up the buyer's Virtual PIN™ (account identifier) in its database, and finds the buyer's electronic mail address of record. An E-mail message is dispatched to the buyer, asking the buyer to confirm the validity of the transaction and his or her commitment to pay, which the buyer can respond to with a simple answer of "yes," "no," or "fraud." Only when the buyer says "yes" is a real-world financial transaction actually initiated. Simple attacks based on Internet "sniffing" are rendered unappealing because their value is sharply limited by the fact that a Virtual PIN or First Virtual ID is not useful off the Net and requires E-mail confirmation for use on the Net. More sophisticated attacks require criminals to break into the victim's computer account and monitor the victim's incoming mail, a crime that is much more easily traced. It is also worth noting that such a break-in would also probably yield access to the victim's encryption keys in any commerce schemes that make use of public key cryptography for encryption.

In First Virtual's system, the valuable financial tokens that underlie commerce—notably credit card numbers and bank account information—never appear on the Internet at all. Instead, they are linked to the buyer's Virtual PIN by First Virtual when the customer applies for a First Virtual account, a procedure that involves an off-Internet step for the most sensitive information. Currently, the sensitive information is provided by either an automated telephone call (for buyers to provide their credit card numbers) or by postal mail (for sellers to provide their bank account information). However, it would also be possible to provide the Virtual PINs automatically en masse to buyers—for example, by direct mailing from the credit card issuers, as is done with traditional ATM PINs.

The exclusion of the most valuable (to criminals) information from the Internet data stream eliminates any need for encryption, which in turn eliminates the need for any nonstandard software on the buyer's end. Ordinary E-mail—the lowest common denominator of Internet connectivity—is all that anyone needs in order to participate. The simplicity of this approach gained First Virtual more than a year's head start in the marketplace on the encryption-based approaches and greatly lowered the entry barrier to anyone wishing to become a First Virtual user.

Another unusual feature of the First Virtual system is that it is explicitly designed for entrepreneurs. There is no screening process for sellers, allowing anyone on the Internet to open a new business. The system even includes an automated information server, the InfoHaus, that will (for an additional fee) make information continuously available for sale by Web, ftp, and E-mail, even for sellers who do not have their own Internet servers. First Virtual's InfoHaus is a leading example of a hosted on-line service for merchants. It is especially designed for merchants who sell information-based goods, and it can accommodate small payments, on the order of $1 per page, effectively.

Later in this chapter, you can read a summary of how to become a First Virtual merchant. Further details, including terms and conditions are provided in Appendix C.

Digital Signatures

The basis for secure, encrypted financial transactions on-line is the *digital signature.* Digital signatures, which are based on encryption technology, were developed at Stanford University in 1976 by Whitfield Diffie, a mathematician. (For an in-depth discussion on companies offering digital IDs and signatures and their legal implications, see Chapter 7.) Using digital signatures, the recipient of an encrypted message can positively identify the sender, because a message encrypted with a certain key can be decrypted only by a corresponding (but different) key. Digital signatures form the basis for public-key cryptography.

When a message can be encrypted with two keys—a public key and a private key—instead of just one key, the risks associated with transmitting a secret key to everyone who needs to know it are eliminated (see Figure 6.6). Furthermore, since a message encrypted with a public key can be decrypted only by the associated private key, and vice versa, two-key cryptography virtually guarantees the identities of the sender and receiver. Digital signatures are now being supported in some court cases.

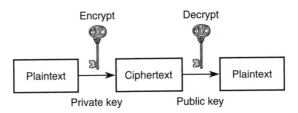

Figure 6.6   Two-key encryption.

CyberCash licenses its public-key cryptography technology from RSA Data Security. The initials RSA stand for Drs. Rivest, Shamir, and Adelman, who developed a commercially viable implementation of public-key cryptography.

SET and Digital Signatures

SET uses a distinct public/private key pair to create the digital signature. Thus, each SET participant possesses two asymmetric key pairs: a *key exchange* pair, which is used in the process of encryption and decryption, and a *signature* pair for the creation and verification of digital signatures. Note that the roles of the public and private keys are reversed in the digital signature process, where the private key is used to encrypt (sign) and the public key is used to decrypt (verify the signature).

Encryption

Generally speaking, the encryption process for Alice to send a message to Bob consists of the following five steps:

1. Alice runs the property description through a one-way algorithm to produce a unique value known as the *message digest.* This is a kind of digital fingerprint of the property description and will be used later to test the integrity of the message.

2. She then encrypts the message digest with her private signature key to produce the digital signature.

3. Next, she generates a random symmetric key and uses it to encrypt the property description, her signature, and a copy of her certificate, which contains her public signature key. In

Technology Note: Public-Key Cryptography

Public-key cryptography is based on the idea that it is very difficult to find the factors of a large prime number. A grossly simplified example[1] may serve to illustrate the basic concepts clearly. To begin, select two (usually very large) prime numbers, p and q. For the sake of this example, let $p = 7$ and $q = 13$. Thus, $p \times q = 91 = n$.

The encryption key, e, must have no factors in common with $(p - 1)(q - 1)$:

$$(p - 1) \times (q - 1) = 6 \times 12 = 72$$

Select e at random to be 43. Choose d such that:

$$ed = 1 \bmod 72$$

Using Euclid's algorithm, a standard mathematical formula, d is calculated to be 67.

The public key is the pair (n,e), in this case (91, 43); the private key is d, in this case 67. The factors p and q must be kept secret or destroyed, since if anyone could factor n into p and q, the private key, d, could be obtained.

How would I encrypt a message using my new key? Suppose Bob wants to send me a message—call it m. Bob would use my public key (91, 43) in this way:

Bob creates the ciphertext c by exponentiating: c = m43 mod 91. To decrypt the message, I also exponentiate, using my private key: m = c67 mod 91. Since I am the only one who knows d, my private key (in this case 67), I am the only one who can decrypt Bob's message.

order to decrypt the property description, Bob will require a secure copy of this random symmetric key.

4. Bob's certificate, which Alice must have obtained prior to initiating secure communication with him, contains a copy of his public key-exchange key. To ensure secure transmission of the symmetric key, Alice encrypts it using Bob's public key-exchange key. The encrypted key, referred to as the *digital envelope,* is sent to Bob along with the encrypted message itself.

5. Finally, she sends a message to Bob consisting of the following: the symmetrically encrypted property description, signature, and certificate, as well as the asymmetrically encrypted symmetric key (the digital envelope).

Decryption

Likewise, the decryption process for Bob, when he receives Alice's message, consists of the following five steps:

1. Bob receives the message from Alice and decrypts the digital envelope with his private key-exchange key to retrieve the symmetric key.

2. He uses the symmetric key to decrypt the property description, Alice's signature, and her certificate.

3. He decrypts Alice's digital signature with her public signature key, which he acquires from her certificate. This recovers the original message digest of the property description.

4. He runs the property description through the same one-way algorithm used by Alice and produces a new message digest of the decrypted property description.

5. Finally, he compares his message digest to the one obtained from Alice's digital signature. If they are exactly the same, he confirms that the message content has not been altered during transmission and that it was signed using Alice's private signature key. If they are not the same, then the message either originated somewhere else or was altered after it was signed. In that case, Bob takes some appropriate action such as notifying Alice or discarding the message.

Dual Signatures

Just as DigiCash introduced an extension of digital signatures, called blind digital signatures, that enabled its electronic cash technology, SET has introduced a new application of digital signatures—namely, the concept of dual signatures. To understand the need for this new concept, consider the following scenario: Bob wants to send Alice an offer to purchase a piece of property and an authorization to his bank to transfer the money if Alice accepts the offer, but Bob doesn't want the bank to see the terms of the offer nor does he want Alice to see his account information. Further, Bob wants to link the offer to the transfer so that the money is transferred only if Alice accepts his offer. He accomplishes all of this by digitally signing both messages with a single signature operation that creates a dual signature (see Figure 6.7).

If Alice accepts Bob's offer, she can send a message to the bank indicating her acceptance and including the message digest of the offer. The bank can verify the authenticity of Bob's transfer authorization and ensure that the acceptance is for the same offer by using its digest of the authorization and the message digest presented by Alice of the offer to validate the dual signature. Thus the bank can check the authenticity of the offer against the dual signature, but the bank cannot see the terms of the offer.

Figure 6.7   Dual signature.

How SET Uses Dual Signatures

Within SET, dual signatures are used to link an order message sent to the merchant with the payment instructions containing account information sent to the acquiring bank. When the merchant sends an authorization request to the acquiring bank, it includes the payment instructions sent by the cardholder and the message digest of the order information. The acquiring bank uses the message digest received from the merchant and computes the message digest of the payment instructions to check the dual signature.

Certificate Authorities

This section describes the technology and mechanics surrounding a certificate authority. (For a more in-depth discussion on the legal issues surrounding certificate authorities, see Chapter 7.)

Before Bob accepts a message with Alice's digital signature, he wants to be sure that the public key belongs to Alice and not to someone masquerading as Alice on an open network such as the Internet. One way to be sure that the public key belongs to Alice is to receive it over a secure channel directly from Alice. However, in most circumstances this solution is not practical.

Technology Note: Generation of a Dual Signature

A dual signature is generated by creating the message digest of both messages, concatenating the two digests, computing the message digest of the result, and encrypting this digest with the signer's private signature key. The signer must include the message digest of the other message in order for the recipient to verify the dual signature. A recipient of either message can check its authenticity by generating the message digest on its copy of the message, concatenating it with the message digest of the other message (as provided by the sender), and computing the message digest of the result. If the newly generated digest matches the decrypted dual signature, the recipient can trust the authenticity of the message.

An alternative to secure transmission of the key is to use a trusted third party to authenticate that the public key belongs to Alice. Such a party is known as a *certificate authority* (CA). The CA authenticates Alice's claims according to its published policies. For example, a CA could supply certificates that offer a high assurance of personal identity, which may be required for conducting business transactions; this CA may require Alice to present a driver's license or passport to a notary public before it will issue a certificate. Once Alice has provided proof of her identity, the CA creates a message containing Alice's name and her public key. This message, known as a *certificate,* is digitally signed by the CA. It contains owner identification information, as well as a copy of one of the owner's public keys (key exchange or signature). To get the most benefit, the public key of the CA should be known to as many people as possible. Thus, by trusting a single key, an entire hierarchy can be established, in which one can have a high degree of trust (see Figure 6.8).

Certificate authorities will be a necessity in the era of the virtual store. Just because I say I am Jane Doe and produce her private key, who's to say I didn't steal it from Jane or pay her a large sum of money to rent her key? If no one knows what Jane Doe looks like, I could commit any sort of crime in her name or withdraw all the money from her bank account. CAs must exist to help establish and maintain the link between on-line identity and physical identity, for the purposes of doing business and enforcing the law.

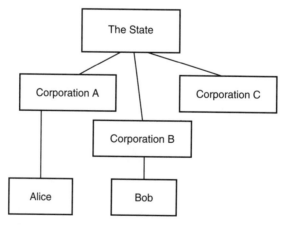

Figure 6.8   Certificate hierarchy.

In some cases, a local government will act as a certifying authority, much in the way a government grants passports nowadays. In other cases, trusted independent entities will be established to certify that the holders of certain public keys are indeed who they claim to be. Each certificate authority has a key with which it encrypts all certifications.

One of the most important aspects of becoming a certificate authority is to make sure that your key is never compromised. If such a thing were to occur, criminals could gain the ability to make any sort of document look official or masquerade as someone else. Whenever a key is compromised, it is placed on a list of revoked keys until it expires. All encryption keys expire, much like credit cards, and for much the same reasons. Eventually, any encryption key can be broken, so for security reasons everyone gets a new key approximately every two years.

Import/Export Issues for SET

A number of governments have regulations regarding the import or export of cryptography. As a general rule, these governments allow cryptography to be used when:

- the data being encrypted is of a financial nature;
- the content of the data is well defined;
- the length of the data is limited; and
- the cryptography cannot easily be used for other purposes.

The SET protocol is limited to the financial portion of shopping and the content of the SET messages has been carefully reviewed to satisfy the concerns of governments. As long as software vendors can demonstrate that the cryptography used for SET cannot easily be put to other purposes, import and export licenses should be obtainable.

For more discussion about jurisdiction and other regulations, please refer to Chapter 7.

Returns

Returns are a very important issue for both customers and merchants of the virtual world. In these early stages, for trust to develop and for commerce to take off in the virtual world, consumers need the clear assurance that they can return the merchandise they buy on-line if it does not meet their expectations. Payment protocols such as SET will eventually give merchants the procedures to process returns, as they do in the physical world.

Returns are relatively simple to understand for hard goods. They become more complicated when the items sold are soft goods, such as software, that have been delivered over the Internet. They become nearly impossible when the items are information, such as answers to legal consultations, where the value has already been transferred. As Albert Einstein once said, "A mind once stretched can never return to its former dimensions." Returns are an interesting aspect of managing the virtual store.

With Web-delivered goods there is the possibility of unethical conduct if customers return information-based goods after reading them, thereby avoiding payment. Should I even have the right to return information-based goods? Are newspapers returnable, for example?

What happens if a customer claims that goods were not delivered? This situation has cropped up because of some bugs in certain delivery systems. In early 1995, some customers claimed they never received certain goods and asked for their money back. The merchants had sent the merchandise in good faith; however, the delivery system had a bug that prevented it from delivering files larger than a certain size. Eventually everything got straightened out, but in the meantime there were some unpleasant discrepancies.

The Netbill solution has a good answer to the return problem: It uses a return receipt system that guarantees exactly what was delivered and when. This solution is more expensive, however, because it requires a return channel. Depending on what you're delivering and to whom, as well as what kind of service reputation you'd like to create, you might want to consider a return receipt system for your virtual store, using either physical or on-line receipts.

Virtual merchants must be willing to stand behind their goods and services for reasonable returns. This attitude will build trust and make the merchants reputable in the virtual arena. However, merchants should not be expected to process returns when payments are made using electronic coins. Coin and low-value cash transactions should be treated as final sales when they occur. A teenager who spends 50¢ for 15 minutes of computer game play should not expect to get money back 5 minutes into the game because he or she doesn't like it. The virtual world collectively needs to learn that there is a test of reasonableness that applies to returns.

Small Businesses: How to Become a First Virtual Merchant

For virtual stores too small to be accepted by a merchant bank, one of the best alternatives is to sign up as a merchant with First Virtual, which handles all the payment processing on your behalf. To become a First Virtual merchant, you need:

- ◆ A private E-mail account
- ◆ A bank account that accepts direct deposit via the U.S. Automated Clearinghouse (ACH) system.

Getting Your VirtualPIN

In order to sell with First Virtual, you need a seller's account ID, called a VirtualPIN, which will identify you within all FV transactions. The process of getting an account ID is simple and straightforward:

1. Complete an application on the First Virtual Web site.
2. Send a check for $10 to First Virtual. The address is included in the E-mail confirmation message sent to you after you complete your application.

   Important: Your check must be drawn on the account into which you want your proceeds deposited. The routing/transit numbers and account information on this check should tell First Virtual where to deposit your funds. (Please verify this with your bank. If necessary, attach a note with your check giving the correct numbers.)

3. First Virtual will send you an E-mail message when your seller's account has been activated, which generally requires about ten business days. This message will contain your seller's VirtualPIN (account ID), which you will need to build a storefront on the InfoHaus or to submit transactions to FV for settlement if you make sales on your own server.

Please note that:

◆ You may have as many VirtualPINs (separate seller's accounts) as you wish.

◆ Any VirtualPIN may be activated for selling, buying, or both.

◆ If you plan to open a storefront on the First Virtual InfoHaus, you must have a seller's VirtualPIN and a buyer's VirtualPIN.

TIP   *If you choose, you can use just one VirtualPIN, activated for both buying and selling. First Virtual recommends, however, that you keep your buying and selling VirtualPINs separate.*

◆ If you want to start selling quickly or open a store on the InfoHaus right away (without having to wait for your check to be received and processed), apply for a VirtualPIN and activate it for buying (which generally takes less than two hours). You may then use your buyer's VirtualPIN when selling, but you must activate this same VirtualPIN for selling, too. Any money owed from your sales will be held by First Virtual until this has been done.

◆ When you apply for your VirtualPIN, you must specify a *full name,* which will be seen by buyers with whom you do business. You are not required to use your actual name; you may use a pseudonym, nickname, or business name. If you will be setting up an InfoHaus storefront, First Virtual recommends that you use the name by which your storefront will be known.

Setting up a Storefront on Your Own Server

To set up a storefront on your own server you must first set up your World Wide Web or ftp server and stock it with your products, their descriptions, and clearly stated prices. You may submit a transaction manually to First Virtual, using E-mail or telnet. You will need to provide the following information about each sale:

◆ Buyer's VirtualPIN
◆ Seller's VirtualPIN
◆ Amount of the sale
◆ Currency (for example, U.S. dollars)
◆ Description of the transaction (such as the name of the item purchased)

First Virtual can also provide you with software you can install at your own site, which modifies your existing WWW or ftp server to automate the sale of information products and the submission of transactions.

Finally, sales using First Virtual can be automated using scripts you write yourself. For example, if you already operate a mail archive server that sends out files in response to messages, you can modify it easily to charge for files, by requiring that a request for a file include a buyer's VirtualPIN identifier to be charged.

Setting up a Storefront on the First Virtual InfoHaus

The InfoHaus is First Virtual's on-line mall for information products. On the InfoHaus, anyone can open an on-line store using common tools like E-mail and telnet. If you sell information products on the InfoHaus, all of the billing and collections are done for you automatically.

The *InfoHaus Seller's Guide* is a complete step-by-step guide to setting up your InfoHaus storefront. You can request the Guide by E-mail to: *infohaus-guide@fv.com,* or you can read the *InfoHaus Seller's Guide* on-line.

Alamo Rent-A-Car: A Cautious Approach

Alamo Rent-A-Car (Figure 6.9) has been operating its Web site since March 1995. In June of that same year, it began taking real-time reservations at the site. There's also an Alamo site on CompuServe, but at this writing it doesn't accept reservations.

Kellie Smythe, director of Electronic Distribution at Alamo, says, "It's not a major revenue impact for us yet, but it's a great opportunity in brand marketing. We can let the industry know we're on the cutting edge. And there's been so much free press in being one of the first travel sites online."

Interestingly enough, the Alamo site isn't accepting any money yet. It's even waived the credit card deposit normally required to make reservations on vans. It opted to focus on quick, efficient service. Within 7 to 10 seconds, a customer can obtain a rate and availability quote in the city of choice. When the customer clicks to confirm a reservation, he or she receives a confirmation number to be given when the car is picked up.

A customer also can enter a travel agent's number so that the travel agent gets credit for the rental. In fact, one of Alamo's main goals with the site is to create a better partnership with travel agencies by offering another alternative to the Global Distribution Systems commonly used by travel agencies, such as SABRE and Galileo. As Smythe puts it, "I don't see GDS going away, but the Internet offers an alternative." On Alamo's site, there's an area for consumers and a password-protected area for travel agents only.

At Alamo, there's still quite a sense of testing things out to see what works. Smythe states, "We're trying to determine what mix of business is best to bring up on the Internet. Who should we move over to this channel, or should we let people migrate on their own and determine the mix for us? You want to move customers to your most inexpensive distribution channel, whatever it may be."

Alamo is also testing out on-line advertising, but to date has relied mostly on traditional ads. The company has only a few hot links—so far only to its airline and hotel partnerships. Basically,

Continued

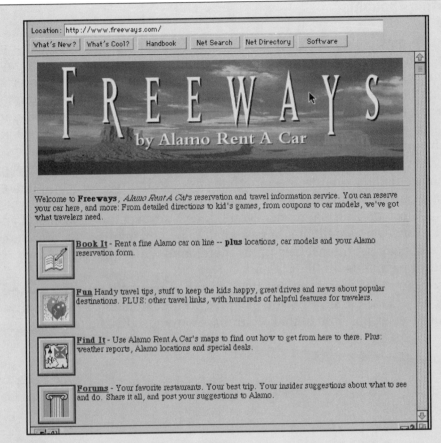

Figure 6.9   Alamo Rent-A-Car.

it's evaluating one step at a time, looking and testing as it goes. It's also weighing the potential benefits of creating a presence in other locations on the Net, such as AOL. Soon it'll be testing out credit card payments as well.

The Alamo site was built and is maintained externally, by a Web service provider. Outsourcing was a decision based on time, cost, and resources. Smythe concludes, "We had money and the resources, but not enough to get it done in the time frame we wanted."

Closing Thoughts

On-line payments require confidentiality, data integrity, customer and merchant authentication, and interoperability. For credit card payments, these characteristics are being fulfilled by the SET standard, which has been proposed by MasterCard and VISA but can be implemented by any financial institution. For electronic checks, cash, and coin payments, transaction service providers such as CyberCash, Digi-Cash, and First Virtual offer attractive opportunities. All of these service providers rely on the same underlying technology—public-key encryption and digital signatures—sometimes used in innovative ways, to create a secure environment for on-line commerce.

For most on-line payments, you'll need an account at a merchant bank; however, small businesses that may not qualify for merchant accounts can set themselves up as merchants with First Virtual, which handles payments on their behalf.

It's a good idea to accept as many forms of payment, on-line and off-line, as you can. That way, you can give your customers as many convenient ways as possible to make purchases at your virtual store.

CHAPTER SEVEN

UNDERSTANDING VIRTUAL LEGALITY

Topics presented in this chapter:

- ◆ Who Controls the Internet?
- ◆ Jurisdiction: National and International Laws
- ◆ Netiquette
- ◆ Digital IDs and Signatures
- ◆ Certificate Authorities and Key Escrows
- ◆ Copyright Protection
- ◆ Import/Export Laws
- ◆ International Money Movement and Currency Conversion
- ◆ Taxation

This chapter discusses legal issues that every virtual store owner needs to be aware of to operate a store successfully. The Internet store is different from a physical store by virtue of the fact that it is in an international environment the day it opens its doors. Because of this, there is a lot of confusion regarding laws and jurisdictions that bind it. Some assume that because the virtual store is in cyberspace, no laws of the physical world apply to it. This is further exaggerated by the fact that there is no single owner of the Internet. This purpose of this chapter is to dispel some of these assumptions and provide the store owner with a thorough understanding of the legal structure.

In addition to the legal issues, this chapter discusses the social structure of the Internet, which is in great part how the Net governs itself. The chapter also discusses several key topics that will be affecting the virtual store owner in the near future, though they may not be in full implementation today. Digital signatures, digital IDs, certificate authorities, and international currency conversation all fall under important developments that soon will be part of the virtual store owner's life.

After reading this chapter, you'll have a good understanding about who controls the Internet, the importance of your contract with your Internet access provider, and some of the Net's societies. You'll also get a sense for who has jurisdiction over your virtual store, though we expect this topic to evolve as more court cases are presented and tried. You will also have a good understanding of Netiquette and the dos and don'ts of social behavior on the Net.

You will have a basic understanding of binding electronic entities and be prepared to meet the legal issues that are evolving regarding digital IDs, certificates, and signatures. You will also have a realistic view of what laws hold true in the virtual world in the areas of copyright protection, import and export restrictions, and taxation. Finally, you will have a sense of what the future will bring to your Internet business in the area of international currency conversion and how you should prepare for it.

Who Controls the Internet?

The first problem with that question is that there is no one Internet. The Internet is a collection of interlinked networks that all speak the same technical protocols, called TCP/IP. Some networks in the United States are owned and operated by publicly traded companies, such as Uunet, MCI, PSInet, AT&T, and Netcom, and some are owned by universities and research organizations, such as NSFnet. Internationally, most are owned and operated by governments and their research and education dollars. Each time a new node is added to one of these networks, it is by definition added to the Internet.

Until recently the major backbone in the United States was owned and operated by the National Science Foundation, a U.S. government agency. In this precommercial era, the NSF dictated the rules and regulations regarding the activities permissible on the Internet. It was during this era that the Appropriate Use Policy (AUP) was in effect, restricting the kinds of traffic on the NSF backbone—thus on most of the Internet—to not-for-profit activities. During this era, private companies in the United States received their Internet access through nonprofit entities such as BARRnet at Stanford University. These companies, who were tied to the Internet through the universities, were encouraged to use the Net but limit their activities to research and development. As corporations saw the Internet as a commercial communications and commerce tool, a new group of companies emerged to fill the need for Internet-like services devoted to commercial activities. These companies, such as Netcom, Uunet, and PSI, who wanted to provide commercial Internet services, started building their own backbones to go around the NSFnet. They formed the CIX (Commercial Internet Exchange) and started routing traffic through each other's networks. In May 1995, the NSFnet ceased being the major backbone carrier. This resulted in a true network of networks, with no single entity ruling the Internet.

Today, an Internet packet may travel over networks owned and operated by five or six different entities on its way to its final destination. The Internet access providers do have their own policies that they explain to their customers prior to signing them up and write into contracts that get executed. These contracts form the first level of governing for the Internet. There are significant differences between these contracts, especially between the on-line service providers such as CompuServe and America Online, who have their proprietary networks in addition to providing access to the Internet, and the more commercially oriented Internet service providers such as Uunet and PSInet.

Your access to the Internet can be terminated immediately by the access provider if you violate the terms in these contracts. In addition to these contractual rules, there are the "understood" rules of Netiquette, the Internet's code of conduct, which we will discuss later in this chapter. Your Internet access provider may also choose to terminate your access to the Net if you violate this underlying code of conduct, such as by indulging in mass junk E-mail mailings. It is quite common for others on the Internet to go directly to your access provider and ask it to terminate your relationship when such abuse of the Internet takes place.

> **T**IP   *As of this writing, no commission or organization exists to regulate Internet access providers, so you may find a wide array of choices among the contracts that access providers may ask you to sign. As part of your shopping-around process for an access provider, look into the contracts and procedures in addition to the pricing structures.*

The Internet Society

The preceding discussion pointed out that each network on the Internet is owned and run by a different entity, which makes up its own contractual rules regarding its relationship with its customers. The Internet Society is the highly respected nonprofit organization that focuses on keeping the Internet interoperable. The Internet Society does not operate any of these networks, but it helps Internet access providers by providing technical guidance for interoperability and standard-setting capabilities. The Internet Society also works to educate the population at large about the Internet and provides help to developing nations as they try to gain access to the Internet.

There are several task forces and subcommittees that focus on specific tasks. The Internet Engineering Task Force (IETF) focuses on interoperability and technical issues as well as promoting standards. The Internet Architecture Board focuses on design and protocol issues.

If you plan on doing business on the Internet, it is wise to become a member of the Internet Society, for which membership costs are nominal.

The InterNIC

One of the main issues facing the virtual store owner is the store address, or the *domain name.* The closer your domain name is to your corporate or branded product name, the easier it will be for your customers to find you. An example would be keds.com versus striderite.com, since most consumers know Keds as a brand name. It costs very little to register your domain name, assuming that it is available to you.

You can check out your name of choice by contacting InterNIC, the organization that registers domain names and keeps track of them via a database searcher called Whois. If the name you want to use is already registered, you may be able to contact the party that registered it and see if you can buy the right to use it or take legal action against them. McDonald's Corporation was awarded the domain name "McDonald's" after attempting to buy it from the individual who had registered it previously with hopes of making a lot money from selling it to McDonald's. There is legislation in the works that will extend trademark treatment to domain names and disallow individuals from registering names that do not "belong" to them. InterNIC now requests that you give a reason why you want to register a certain name and disallows multiple registrations by the same entity for similar names.

Generally, your access provider will register your domain name with InterNIC for a nominal fee, usually under a few hundred dollars. If your access provider is not able to do this, contact InterNIC directly at admin@internic.net.

MYTH: *Laws that govern the real world do not apply to the virtual world.*

Virtual or not, laws apply. It is not true that no one rules the Internet. The governing bodies that govern your real-world operations will govern your virtual store. Do not look at your virtual store as an escape from legality and jurisdictions. Instead, be ready to deal with multiple jurisdictions, since the Internet, by definition, is an international environment.

Jurisdiction: National and International Laws

There has been a significant amount of confusion about whether existing civil and criminal laws apply to the Internet. Many Internet users share libertarian views and prefer that the government stay out of the Internet. The fact remains, however, that the laws that apply to your business in the physical world also apply to your business in the virtual world. Those businesses that have believed the opposite to be true have violated laws and been found guilty of fraud, negligence, false advertising, libel, and so forth.

The following pages address specific topics such as taxation, copyright protection, and contract obligations. The underlying message through all these discussions is that, as the virtual store owner, you must abide by the same laws at your virtual store that affect your business in the physical world. In addition, you need to be aware of other jurisdictions that may apply when you operate across state and national lines.

The Internet uses telecommunication lines to send E-mail messages and download Web site pages. When your customers come to your virtual store, they are using the telecommunication lines to receive your storefront information. You should therefore treat your virtual store as you would any communication you send out over your telephone lines.

To date, the U.S. government has not actively created many laws specific to the Internet. It is conceivable that Congress is waiting for substantial growth in usership as well as to let issues arise and policies shake themselves out. Another reason the government has taken more of a laissez-faire approach to the Internet and electronic commerce is that larger issues loom, such as money laundering and tax evasion.

We expect more and more specific government regulation in the next few years as legislators try to figure out how to legislate the virtual world. The law passed in the state of Georgia in May 1996 is a good example. The law is written to specifically prevent individuals from fraudulently representing themselves as someone else and makes this a clearly punishable offense. In addition, for the first time in the United States, this state law requires that Web site owners get permission from another site before they can link to it.

Furthermore, most technologists feel that the government just doesn't understand the Internet or what to do with it. This is about to change. There are several new laws and proposals before Congress to regulate the content available on the Internet. One example of this is the Communications Decency Act, which limits the content on the Internet to that deemed decent by Congress. Another is the Computer Fraud and Abuse Act, which, through its 1994 amendment, covers access without authorization to any Internet computer and makes this a felony.

As the virtual store owner, it is your responsibility to keep up with new legislation and to be an active voice by communicating your views to your representatives in Washington. The day your virtual store opens, it probably will be operating in a multistate and international environment. The laws that govern commerce in different states and countries vary greatly. It is your responsibility, as the virtual store owner, to be aware of restrictions.

> **T**IP   *Virtual Vineyards, which sells a collection of California wines from boutique wineries, realized that several counties in Texas as well as the whole state of Florida made the importation of alcoholic beverages illegal. Virtual Vineyards rightly accepted the responsibility of checking zip codes in shipping addresses to determine whether wine could be shipped into that address legally.*

There are also several "social" laws that vary greatly based on cultural differences. Recently, the Communications Decency Act has made it illegal to use so-called indecent language on-line in the United States. Although there is room for interpretation about the meaning of "indecent" in this case, some language is clearly indecent and should be avoided.

In Singapore and Japan, *Playboy* magazine is illegal. What is *Playboy*'s liability if a user obtains *Playboy* photographs on-line? In other words, in the new era of on-line commerce, if I can get to the store, who polices what I walk out with?

Some countries are attempting to control their citizens' access on-line. Germany restricted access to the Usenet news in November 1995, but reopened it in early 1996. Meanwhile, Singapore closed access to Usenet in early 1996.

The international nature of the Internet adds complexity to trademark infringements. It is hard to pinpoint exactly which jurisdiction should oversee a particular infringement.

Shopping around for Favorable Laws (Jurisdiction as a Commodity)

As commerce becomes international, it will become possible to shop around for laws favorable to a certain line of business or a profession. Just as it is popular in the United States to incorporate in the state of Delaware because its laws are favorable for corporations, it will one day be popular to incorporate or to operate under the jurisdiction most favorable to merchants in cyberspace. We are already witnessing this as virtual casinos open their doors to the world from their Internet servers placed in the Bahamas.

Encryption and Its Importance for Internet Commerce

Encryption, which ensures security on the Internet and therefore fosters commerce, is a highly debated topic in Congress when it comes to exportation. Currently, encryption technology is considered in the category of "military arms and weapons" and is restricted from export. This is a big hindrance to international commerce, because the availability of encryption would enable entities that do not know each other to conduct business and transact securely. There are competing viewpoints in Congress, but the one presented here (see sidebar) represents the thinking most liked by Internet insiders.

Netiquette

Netiquette is the etiquette or code of conduct that has been established for on-line conduct over the last 20 years. Internet communications are often text based and asynchronous (unlike a telephone communication, the two entities communicating via the Internet are not on-line at the same time), which therefore makes it hard to communicate emotions and social norms. Netiquette has evolved over time to add the human and social touch to on-line communications.

As a virtual store owner, you need to always respect and follow Netiquette. Internet users are quite vocal when they are dissatisfied or wronged and will let the world know of your wrongdoing. Just imagine having thousands of picketers in front of your physical store within a matter of hours. That can happen on the Internet if you violate the Netiquette rules. The Internet community governs itself through Netiquette. Though Internet users do not send you to jail, they can shut down your virtual store for a long time.

Following is a list of Netiquette rules, but the best thing to do is to use common sense. Never do anything on the Internet that you would not do at your physical store at a high-visibility site such as Madison Avenue in New York or the Champs Élysée in Paris. Just because no one is staring you in the eyes does not mean that they cannot see you. This Netiquette list focuses on what *not* to do. (See Chapter 5 for a detailed discussion of what is acceptable to do in marketing and advertising your virtual store.)

Available from http://www.senate.gov/member/vt/leahy/general/

LETTER FROM SENATOR PATRICK LEAHY (D-VT)
ON ENCRYPTION

May 2, 1996

Dear Friends:

Today, a bipartisan group of Senators has joined me in supporting legislation to encourage the development and use of strong,
privacy-enhancing technologies for the Internet by rolling back the
out-dated restrictions on the export of strong cryptography. In an
effort to demonstrate one of the more practical uses of encryption
technology (and so that you all know this message actually came
from me), I have signed this message using a digital signature generated by the popular encryption program PGP. I am proud to be
the first member of Congress to utilize encryption and digital signatures to post a message to the Internet.

As a fellow Internet user, I care deeply about protecting individual privacy and encouraging the development of the Net as a secure
and trusted communications medium. I do not need to tell you that
current export restrictions only allow American companies to
export primarily weak encryption technology. The current strength
of encryption the U.S. government will allow out of the country is
so weak that, according to a January 1996 study conducted by
world-renowned cryptographers, a pedestrian hacker can crack the
codes in a matter of hours! A foreign intelligence agency can crack
the current 40-bit codes in seconds.

Perhaps more importantly, the increasing use of the Internet and
similar interactive communications technologies by Americans to
obtain critical medical services, to conduct business, to be enter-

Continued

tained and communicate with their friends, raises special concerns about the privacy and confidentiality of those communications. I have long been concerned about these issues, and have worked over the past decade to protect privacy and security for our wire and electronic communications. Encryption technology provides an effective way to ensure that only the people we choose can read our communications.

I have read horror stories sent to me over the Internet about how human rights groups in the Balkans have had their computers confiscated during raids by security police seeking to find out the identities of people who have complained about abuses. Thanks to PGP, the encrypted files were indecipherable by the police and the names of the people who entrusted their lives to the human rights groups were safe.

The new bill, called the "Promotion of Commerce On-Line in the Digital Era (PRO-CODE) Act of 1996," would:

♦ bar any government-mandated use of any particular encryption system, including key escrow systems, and affirm the right of American citizens to use whatever form of encryption they choose domestically;

♦ loosen export restrictions on encryption products so that American companies are able to export any generally available or mass market encryption products without obtaining government approval; and

♦ limit the authority of the federal government to set standards for encryption products used by businesses and individuals, particularly standards which result in products with limited key lengths and key escrow.

Continued

This is the second encryption bill I have introduced with Senator Burns and other congressional colleagues this year. Both bills call for an overhaul of this country's export restrictions on encryption, and, if enacted, would quickly result in the widespread availability of strong, privacy protecting technologies. Both bills also prohibit a government-mandated key escrow encryption system. While PRO-CODE would limit the authority of the Commerce Department to set encryption standards for use by private individuals and businesses, the first bill we introduced, called the "Encrypted Communications Privacy Act", S.1587, would set up stringent procedures for law enforcement to follow to obtain decoding keys or decryption assistance to read the plaintext of encrypted communications obtained under court order or other lawful process.

It is clear that the current policy towards encryption exports is hopelessly outdated, and fails to account for the real needs of individuals and businesses in the global marketplace. Encryption expert Matt Blaze, in a recent letter to me, noted that current U.S. regulations governing the use and export of encryption are having a "deleterious effect . . . on our country's ability to develop a reliable and trustworthy information infrastructure." The time is right for Congress to take steps to put our national encryption policy on the right course.

I am looking forward to hearing from you on this important issue. Throughout the course of the recent debate on the Communications Decency Act, the input from Internet users was very valuable to me and some of my Senate colleagues.

You can find out more about the issue at my World Wide Web home page (http://www.leahy.senate.gov/) and at the Encryption Policy Resource Page (http://www.crypto.com/). Over the coming

Continued

months, I look forward to the help of the Net community in convincing other Members of Congress and the Administration of the need to reform our nation's cryptography policy.

Sincerely,

Patrick Leahy

United States Senator

1. *Never E-mail advertisements or sales literature to people unless they actively ask for it or give you permission to do so.* The biggest nightmare of the Internet community is that E-mailboxes will be filled with junk mail. In the physical world, junk mail has its printing and mailing costs. On the Internet, these are eliminated, which makes users even more worried about junk mail proliferation.

2. *Never post advertisements and solicitations to Usenet news groups, chat groups, and forums.* Certain Usenet news groups and forums may be perfect target groups for your marketing message. They provide narrowcasting capability for you as a store owner. But do not be tempted to take advantage of these groups by posting solicitations or advertisements. You will alienate yourself from these groups immediately. Instead, genuinely participate in these groups and offer information in a constructive way.

3. *Never make false representations of your products or services.* The Internet community prides itself on its intelligence and ability to see through things. More than 70 percent of Internet users have college degrees. They will catch your false representations and publicize them to the world.

4. *Stay away from imposture of any kind.* It is tempting to think that in the virtual world you can be anybody. In the early days, Cisco Systems (the company that sells most of the Inter-

net routers) had T-shirts showing a dog sitting at a computer and the caption read "On the Internet you can be a dog and no one will know it." This is a refreshing thought, but it does not work when it comes to commerce. Though many people on the Internet have multiple personas of both sexes, they expect the businesses they are dealing with to represent who they are honestly.

5. *Do not violate intellectual property laws.* We have allocated a section to this topic elsewhere. In short, treat intellectual property as you would in the physical world.

E-mail and Privacy Issues

E-mail is neither private nor secure on the Internet. Most Internet users view their E-mail as they do their telephone conversations: private and secure. E-mail, by law, is not private. E-mail records are often kept both at the sending and the receiving servers and can be used in court as evidence. This happened in several high-visibility cases such as the Oliver North and Rodney King trials. Corporations that provide their employees with E-mail access to the Internet are not barred legally from accessing employees' E-mails. Several companies have used E-mail messages to prove sexual harassment and thus fire employees. In addition, deleted E-mails do not disappear from records. Backup tapes, which are often made at mail servers daily, keep both deleted and undeleted E-mail messages.

Another danger with E-mail that does not exist in voice communications is the ability to easily forward it to a large population. Voice-mail systems are often incompatible. The Internet mail formats, on the other hand, are standardized and can be sent to large mailing lists with the stroke of a few keys.

We encourage you, as a virtual store owner, to use E-mail to communicate with your customers and suppliers. Just be aware that E-mail that feels very private at the time of writing can become very public. Never put anything in E-mail that would embarrass you if you saw it later in print.

It is very important for you to communicate a clear E-mail policy to all your employees. Teach them to use E-mail constructively but to be very aware of its lack of privacy and security. Remember that, unlike the case with telephone calls or letters, the recipient of an E-mail is and can be held liable in court just like the sender.

Digital IDs and Signatures—What They Are and What They Mean to You

A *digital ID* is used to verify one's identity on-line, similar to the identification service provided by a driver's license or passport in the physical world. We value drivers' licenses and passports as identity cards because of the entities that have issued and stand behind them. The Departments of Motor Vehicles in different states and the international governments put a lot of effort behind ensuring that the IDs they issue are, in fact, bound to the physical individuals by using photographs, fingerprints, and other identifying features, such as height and weight. They also keep elaborate computer records and watch the underground markets of fake IDs, trying to eliminate these through prosecution.

On the Internet, all these functions surrounding digital IDs are even more necessary than in the physical world. As we saw in the discussion in Chapter 3, trust can be established in the virtual world, although you do not physically see and touch the entity with whom you are interacting, through trusted intermediaries. For example, a consumer would be a lot more willing to buy a watch from a virtual store at @cartier.com if a trusted third party verified that the store is the famous jeweler's virtual store by issuing a digital ID and then standing behind it.

Digital identification and authentication are possible today through the use of cryptography. (See Chapter 6 for a more detailed discussion on the technology of cryptography and public/private key pair generation technology.) *Digital identification* is the process of verifying that the entity on-line is, in fact, what it says it is through the digital cryptography keys that it holds. *Authentication* usually refers to the process of verifying that the information sent from the entity that had the digital ID was not tampered with. Authentication is achieved by the use of *digital signatures.* When one digitally signs a message, the recipient is ensured that the message was composed and sealed by the sender and was not tampered with.

Digital signatures employ a public/private key pair technology, as discussed in Chapter 6. These pairs of keys include a private key used to encode and sign messages and a public key used to decode them. Only a message signed by the private key can be decoded and verified using the public key. The public key is widely available, but the private key is kept private. So, in fact, the private key acts as the signature of the sender.

The consumer could be at the Cartier store on-line, see its digital ID, feel comfortable, and start checking out watches. During this process, the consumer wants to ensure that the information and prices he is downloading from Cartier are not altered by some mischievous hacker. On the Internet, this is achieved mostly by digital signatures.

Several companies have jumped in to offer these services. They have widely different approaches to digital IDs.

VeriSign of Mountain View, California, is the first company to issue digital IDs through its digital ID center. These digital IDs are based on the public/private key pair technology. Though a small company without much name recognition, VeriSign has very strong partnerships and an impressive list of investors. VeriSign is a spin-off of the RSA Technology, the holder of almost all of the encryption patents used on the Internet. VeriSign plans on gaining wide distribution of its IDs through having it integrated to Netscape's 3.0 browser. VeriSign's digital IDs are expected to have various classes, currently numbered at six, each requiring a different level of certification and, thus, trust. The first level of certification will be the certificates bundled with the Netscape browser and will be available free of charge to consumers. For further information on how to obtain a digital ID, visit the VeriSign home page at www.verisign.com.

Two other companies, Communications Intelligence Corporation and PenOp, have announced digital signature services. These two companies' implementations of digital signatures differ significantly from VeriSign's. Both these companies have been in the pen computing business and are looking at digital signatures, not based on cryptography, but on creating digital counterparts to hand signatures. Their software records the physical characteristics of the signature signing process and converts it to digital form so that it can be used at the bottom of electronic documents. These digital signatures can then be compared to recorded signatures in databases for verification. A disadvantage of this approach compared to the use of public/private key pair technology is that it requires an additional hardware device for inputting the signature into the electronic documents to be signed.

Both types of digital signatures require a certification authority to verify that the digital signatures actually belong to the person involved in the transaction. But before we continue the discussion of digital certificate authorities, we need to answer the question of what all this means to the virtual store owner.

One of the biggest deterrents to commerce on the Internet today is the lack of trust. Though consumers may find the Internet a convenient place to do Christmas shopping, not knowing the merchant at the other end makes them uneasy. As a virtual store owner, you should take advantage of digital IDs to verify your identity to your target market. In the future, you may also want to use digitally signed documents to communicate with your customers when sensitive information is involved. And finally, you may want to ask your merchant bank if you can publicize your relationship with it at your virtual store. Knowing that, as a merchant, you deal with a reputable bank will give your potential customers an increased level of comfort.

Digital ID and signature technologies are just beginning to evolve. Read up on these and visit the information sites of the vendors often. Being a leader in the use of digital tools for establishing trust will set you apart from your competitors.

Certificate Authorities and Key Escrows—What Will They Do for You?

A digital certificate is a digital ID that "notarizes" the connection between a particular electronic signature and the owner's identifying information. The electronic signature may be an RSA public key (as in the VeriSign system) or a digital representation of a hand signature. A certificate authority keeps a registry of digital signatures that others can use to verify that a signature actually belongs to a physical person. (The technology and methodology of certificate authorities are described in Chapter 6.

Without a digital certificate, there is no way to bind a digital signature to an actual person or a company. This binding process has to be done by an entity that commands a high degree of trust. These entities are referred to as *certificate authorities,* commonly called CAs.

Issuing a certificate means that the certifying authority attaches its own digital signature to a digital signature. This allows the holder of the digital signature to prove the legitimacy of the signature by producing its digital certificate, signed by the CA.

There has been a lot of discussion as to which entities are best positioned to become certificate authorities in the virtual worlds. Several banks, the U.S. Postal Service, and several technology companies are interested in this market. Because of the wide-reaching and international nature of the Internet, it is natural to assume that there will be multiple certifying authorities.

Someone living in the United States may be familiar with the name of a New York bank and therefore trust it as a CA, but there will be many other CAs in remote corners of the world that will be completely unfamiliar. A consumer in Ohio may never have heard of a CA in Singapore. This will create the need to certify certifying authorities, thus resulting in certification hierarchies.

What does all this mean to the virtual store owner? Because of the increased trust established through the certifying authority infrastructure, you will be able to indulge in businesses on the Internet that require increased levels of privacy and security. The legal and medical professions will be able to use the Internet to provide professional services. Doctors and lawyers will be able to verify their identities through certificate authorities. In addition, the virtual store owner will be able to use the networks to negotiate and execute contracts, resting assured that the documents are being sent and received by authorized entities and are not being tampered with along the way.

As the virtual store owner learns to trust digital IDs, signatures, and certificates, there will be an increased need for safekeeping for these items. *Key escrow* services are designed to provide this safekeeping. As more of the security and trust is based on public/private key pair technology, one needs to have a safe-deposit box to keep these keys. Key escrow services provide the insurance that if, for example, one loses the key to an encrypted file or an employee quits without sharing the keys with the employer, the keys can be recovered and the secured documents accessed.

Several companies are providing key escrow services. Trusted Information Systems, which has been in the business of providing firewall and security software, is probably the best-known service provider for key escrow. For more information, visit its site on the Internet at www.tis.com.

There is significant concern by Internet users that governments will get into the key escrow business. There are several countries, such as France, where governments do not allow individuals and corporations to have public/private key pairs without depositing the keys with the government. Others, such as Spain, do not allow their citizens and corporations to have access to public/private key pair technology at all.

The U.S. government attempted to restrict all methods of encryption to the Clipper method, which would be provided on a special chip called the Clipper chip. Then all of one's encrypted messages would use a unique key, in addition to the key the user chose, that would be housed in the chip and kept in escrow by the U.S. government. This would make the U.S. government the de facto key escrow agency and give it the ability to read any encrypted message. The immense negative publicity the Clipper chip has received has, for now, given Americans flexibility in choosing their encryption method.

Copyright Protection

It would not be exaggerating to say that everything on the Internet is intellectual property. After all, it is content that is created by someone and stored electronically. Furthermore, in electronic commerce, everything we define as soft goods, such as software, information, and books, is all intellectual property.

Several publishers of intellectual property have traditionally shied away from the Internet, based on the ease of copying and forwarding trademarked and copyrighted material. Other publishers have been very active on-line for several years, such as Ziff-Davis, which makes its material available from on-line services such as CompuServe and its own Ziffnet. As Internet users are educated in respecting copyrights, more and more publishers are moving on-line. Many magazines and daily newspapers, such as *The Wall Street Journal* are beginning to create on-line versions of their publications as their readers move on-line.

Publishers are also getting reassurances from the legal system. Court cases are setting precedents. Cases such as the one in which *Playboy* received $500,000 from the company that offered *Playboy* photos on-line are becoming commonplace.

Many on the Internet argue that copyrighting is not good for publishers. In addition to the radicals who believe that all information should be free, there are many who argue that trying to have stringent protection for your material will limit its distribution and, thus, will not allow you large market share coverage. Netscape Corporation is often cited as a company that decided not to openly and freely distribute its software in exchange for market share. Today, Netscape enjoys a high market valuation and increasing revenues because of its market leadership position.

In general, one should assume that the same copyright laws that hold true in the physical world also hold true in the virtual world. In addition, other digital content on-line is covered by copyright protection, including:

- All postings to Usenet news groups, mailing lists, forums, chat groups, bulletin boards, and the like
- All E-mail messages
- All Web site content such as frequently asked questions and product and service descriptions
- All computer software including Java applets
- All databases, listings, categorizations, compilations
- All multimedia files including graphics, video, sound, and animation files

If you plan on selling copyrighted material such as software at your virtual store, make sure that you post copyright notices at your site, even if you were not the creator of the software. If you are the original creator of copyrighted material, consider registering your material with the Copyright Office for further protection.

Import/Export Laws of Various Countries

The Internet makes exporters out of merchants overnight. There are several products that the United States does not allow for export, including several types of software and hardware. There are also several countries with which the United States does not conduct trade. In addition, there are several categories of products that require an export license before they can be sold outside the country.

If you do not have experience in the export field, take the time to study the Export Administration Act of 1979. Here you will find lists of products that require export licenses and lists of countries with which the United States has trade restrictions.

In addition to studying the export laws of the country from which you will be operating, you may need to study the import laws of several countries where you might want to market your products. For example, France does not allow the importation of products that have high levels of cryptography. Singapore does not allow the importation of *Playboy* and *Penthouse* pictures.

Though the laws of various countries that govern and affect your business can be quite confusing, the good news is that a lot of the information regarding these laws can be found on-line. The Internet has its origins in government support and this continues both within and outside the United States, with many government groups having on-line information sites. The Commerce Department, the U.S. Census Bureau, the General Agreement on Tariffs and Trade (GATT), and the NAFTA (North American Free Trade Agreement) sites offer significant information.

The International Trade Administration publishes a very useful document called the *Basic Guide to Exporting,* which walks the potential exporter through methods of exporting and channels of distribution. It gives a comprehensive description of the intermediaries involved in exporting, such as the commission and shipping agents, export management companies, and export trading companies. Though some of these entities are easily eliminated in the virtual world, it is still useful for the virtual store owner to become familiar with the functions they provide, since most of these functions now will be fulfilled by the virtual store owner.

On the Internet, most stores will be direct exporters. When a product is sold in such direct fashion, the exporter is responsible for shipping, payment collection, and product servicing unless other specific arrangements are made.

There are also vast differences between selling services and products (both hard and soft goods) internationally. Though they may involve shipping and title handling if they are hard goods, products are often more successfully sold internationally since they are easy to define and more tangible and samples may be provided to the potential purchaser. Therefore, communicating a service offer in the virtual world internationally is more difficult than communicating a product offer, unless one can enable the potential clients to experience the service at no cost to them.

As a virtual store owner, you should look into any export regulations regarding selling your products internationally. Export licensing is often overlooked by virtual store owners and is likely to effect those who are selling technical products through their virtual stores.

For reasons of national security or certain foreign policies, the United States controls the export of some technical goods and information through licenses. Two types of export licenses are granted: general and individual. For most virtual stores, general licenses will be the ones required. The U.S. Department of Commerce can tell you if you need an export license and if you do, the Bureau of Export Administration can issue it for you.

The Changing World of International Distribution

Traditionally, major hardware and software distributors such as IBM and Microsoft have defined relationships with their distributors in specific countries and ensured that no others will sell their products in those territories. The Internet upsets these relationships since it makes geographies disappear.

Several virtual stores that sell computer hardware and software on the Net do not have the rights to distribute, market, and sell these products internationally in the physical world but can easily do so through their virtual stores. This can result in conflicts with international distributors, which usually have exclusive product marketing and sales rights in their territories.

These problems become even more exaggerated when there are differences in the pricing structures, usually making the virtual store prices significantly more attractive than the prices of the local distributors.

Local distributors still have a leg up when it comes to customer service. We think that, over time, the sales and service functions for international product sales will be uncoupled, with local distributors making most of their money from installation and service.

International Money Movement and Currency Conversion

Going international ultimately means accepting payments from anywhere in the world. If you are hoping to sell your software to the Italians and the Greeks, but accept only U.S. dollars, your sales will be restricted in those countries to only those who have access to U.S. dollars, which is generally a very small percentage of the overall potential market for your product. You will need intermediaries to do the currency conversion for you so that you can accept payments from customers who hold multiple currencies yet receive the money in your currency of choice.

Accepting multiple currencies is not a new concept. There are international entities that do this today, such as VISA International and MasterCard International as well as American Express and Diner's Club. The infrastructure to convert from the payer's currency to the recipient's currency is in place already. When German tourists go shopping in Mexico and use their credit cards, they in essence, are paying in German marks and the merchants are receiving payment in Mexican pesos. In this scenario, the credit card association is the one setting the conversion rate, taking the currency risk, and making the conversion profit.

For example, VISA keeps a market in 25 currencies. At any given moment, it can convert from one currency to almost any other currency in the world. The same goes for MasterCard, Carte Blue, and American Express. This convenience that the card associations offer can also be expanded to purchases on the Internet. When one pays with a credit card on the Internet, a similar situation can occur.

Several merchants on the Internet who accept credit card payments already enjoy these benefits. Virtual Vineyards receives a significant number of orders from Japan, where the cost of California wines is very high. With some of the highest sales figures for electronics, 47 Street Photo also enjoys a high percentage of international sales, paid with credit cards. The Internet Shopping Network makes 30 percent of its sales to individuals who are outside the United States. This international traffic is equally divided between Asia and Europe.

The Internet to date has offered the same capabilities as the physical world in accepting international payments via the use of credit cards. In the future, we expect Internet merchants and banks to offer improved and increased services.

The traditional international payment options in the physical world for large sales have been:

◆ Cash in advance

◆ Letter of credit

◆ Draft payments

Though these payment services are not available for the Internet merchant today, we expect international banks that are technically well versed on the Internet to start offering these payment services for the international virtual merchant.

Currency Conversion in Real Time

Two of the natural advantages of computers are performing mathematical tasks and receiving up-to-the-second information. Combining these two capabilities, we expect virtual stores to display prices in currencies other than that of their home country. We eventually expect a merchant's virtual cash register to "sense" the currency of choice for the consumer's wallet and offer pricing information in that currency.

Let's return to our German shoppers in a Mexican store. They have to have good calculators and knowledge of the current exchange rate to figure out how much, for example, the pewter candleholders are in German marks. Now let's put our German shoppers and the Mexican pewter store on the Internet. Our German shoppers are at the pewter store's site and specify their currency of choice, German marks. Now as they click on different items, they see the prices, not in Mexican pesos, but in marks.

The challenge is that whoever performs the conversion needs to be able to take a position with the currency rates and guarantee the rate up to the time of collection. Thus, some potential risk is involved in international currency conversion.

Big banks, such as Chase Manhattan and Citicorp as well as several European and Far Eastern banks, currently participate in currency conversion already. They take the conversion risks and keep several currencies as a hedge against losses in any single type. Because these banks and credit entities already perform currency conversion on a daily basis, it's not a big step to connect these capabilities to suppliers of payment services. Service providers, such as CyberCash, are expected to work with international banks to extend such services to the Internet.

There is currently a currency conversion program available at the GNN site that will give you instant currency conversions from any major currency to any other. This can be found at gnn.com/cgi.bin/gnn/currency.

What does all this mean to the virtual store owner? Take advantage of the international market that the Internet offers you. If you are targeting a specific country, consider creating Web pages in the language of choice for that country and posting prices in that country's currency. Keep up with the currency conversion services large banks offer on the Internet through the payment service operators.

Taxation

How does the merchant collect taxes in a virtual store? The best rule of thumb for the virtual store owner when it comes to taxes is to think of the virtual store as a catalog. Just as the catalog operator is responsible for the collection of state taxes and the payment of state and federal taxes, so is the virtual store owner.

In whatever states you operate, you are responsible for collecting any taxes due. Therefore, you must educate yourself about the sales tax rates that apply in each state. If you do not abide by the state's tax laws, you can be told to cease and desist by those states and fined back sales taxes. If, as the store owner, you don't feel ready to handle this task of collecting taxes for multiple states, you may consider a hosting service that will do this for you. This is one of the big advantages in setting up your virtual store on a hosted site, rather than undertaking your own server.

If you do set up your own server and hire a Webmaster to maintain it, keep in mind that he or she is not likely to be informed about all the tax consequences of conducting business on-line. More likely, the Webmaster will be more of a technologist, interested in keeping the machines running and the software up to date.

TIP   *Associations, such as the Direct Marketing Association, which are directed toward the multibillion-dollar catalog industry, can provide you with very valuable information on how to collect local sales taxes. There are easily available software programs that check the shipping address and calculate the taxes to be collected by the virtual merchant based on the zip code of the shipping address. These software programs may also alert you to certain other laws such as restrictions regarding the shipment of certain goods by zip code.*

In fact, a potential market opportunity exists for someone to develop a software package that keeps track of similar tax and restriction issues for the international markets. There are a lot of unique taxes that differ from country to country, such as value-added taxes, which the virtual merchant needs to keep track of.

Global Economy

As the on-line economy develops, more and more merchants will begin to think in terms of a global economic network. Eventually, many intermediaries will be eliminated, as a village in Peru can just as easily sell its goods in the United States directly using the Internet.

Closing Thoughts

As we saw in this chapter, no single entity controls the Internet. Actually, the Internet is not a single entity itself, but a collection of many networks that are owned and operated, and thus controlled, by many different entities. Your contract and your relationship with your Internet access provider and or hosting service is of utmost importance, because many of the rules and regulations that govern your virtual store will be set by them. In addition, the importance of Netiquette cannot be stressed enough. As a virtual store owner, you need to educate all your employees on these important social and cultural behavior norms of the Internet.

Who has jurisdiction over your virtual store and in what ways is a constantly evolving topic, though it is safe to assume that the entities that have jurisdiction over your physical store also have jurisdiction over your virtual store. Eventually, you will be able to shop for favorable jurisdictions by locating your virtual store in another state or country.

You now have a basic understanding of binding electronic entities. Be ready for the legality that will evolve regarding digital IDs, certificates, and signatures. You also have a realistic view of what laws hold true in the virtual world in the areas of copyright protection, import and export restrictions, and taxation. Finally, you have a sense of what the future will bring to your Internet business in the area of international currency conversion and how you should prepare for it.

To summarize, do not think that laws do not exist in the virtual world. Always keep up with the changing legislature and technology and take advantage of the new capabilities that are offered through digital IDs and certification and international currency capabilities.

CHAPTER EIGHT

PREPARING FOR THE FUTURE

Topics presented in this chapter:

- Bringing the Internet to the Home
- The Changing Role of the Telephone and Cable Companies
- The Evolving Technologies
- Interactive TV versus the PC
- The Changing Demographics of On-line Consumers
- Welcome to the New Frontier

This chapter helps you understand the long-term directions that on-line commerce will be taking over the next few years. Your business will need to keep pace with new developments and structural changes that the on-line world will experience. Internet services to the home will become commonplace. Several new technological developments are just around the corner, and they will affect your virtual store. The goal of this chapter is to put these technical and social developments in perspective and to prepare you, the virtual store owner, for success in the new world.

The first section of this chapter discusses the current state of underlying technologies for the information superhighway and the status of interactive cable trials. It follows with a realistic discussion of these technologies and their impacts on both the virtual store and the expectations of on-line customers. It also discusses the evolving business of the underlying industries, which include cable companies, Internet access suppliers, telephone companies, and the interexchange carriers (AT&T, MCI, Sprint), and their plans for the information superhighway.

Later in the chapter, there is a discussion of the social issues regarding the on-line environment and their implications for the virtual store owner, encompassing topics such as parental guidance, rating of content, legislative limitations, and the social structure of the global village.

As the owner of a virtual store, you'll want to keep abreast of these developments, staying up to date on the developments of companies that are bringing interactive personal computer (PC) and Internet services to the home and increasing the speed of these connections. Each one of these developments will result in major changes to the demographics and psychographics of your potential customer base.

MYTH: *The internet is all hype; electronic commerce is a fad; it will blow over like interactive TV did.*

Interactive TV offered a solution to a problem that did not exist. Consumers were not clamoring for video on demand. It was the cable companies and the telecommunications companies that believed consumers should have the service. The Internet is very different. It offers a solution to an innate human need: the need to communicate. E-mail and Internet forums have been successful because they are highly efficient. The Internet is not a fad. It is the fastest-growing human communication technology ever known.

Bringing the Internet to the Home

Fast forward your mind a few years. Your teenage son comes home from school and flips on the TV. He searches through the channels until he finds The Internet Channel, a 24-hour Internet access station. On the remote control, he pushes the login button. Instantly, his favorite Web site appears on the screen: www.pizza.com. He orders a large pepperoni and a six-pack of Coca-Cola.

When the message appears on the screen asking for payment, he inserts his smart card, a credit card–sized cash-carrying device, into the slot on the remote control device in his hand. The money is instantly beamed over to an infrared sensor below the TV screen. A friendly young woman's voice says, "Thank you." When the doorbell rings 20 minutes later, his pizza is delivered. His friends have already arrived. They've downloaded the latest environment and characters to their favorite computer game from the local video server, and they've alerted another friend's house that they are ready for some interactive game play between the houses.

In the next room, your daughter is watching her favorite game show at the corner of her PC monitor while she is hooked into her school's server, downloading her homework for the day. When she is done downloading her science project, a voice message from her teacher comes on, asking you, the parent, to please help her with the project.

How Can This Be Possible?

There are several companies today, including some large ones such as Sony, that are working on making Internet access possible via your TV. Though this may sound revolutionary, it is not. After all, the television set is yet another monitor, though of lower resolution quality than the PC monitors sold today. But TVs have much greater penetration of households than PCs. This has motivated companies to develop hardware to make television sets into virtual PC terminals. I expect that by the year 1998, all TV sets will come equipped to function as "dumb" Internet access monitors. This does not mean that we will do away with the need for PCs or other less expensive Internet access devices, called Internet appliances. Large corporations such as Oracle and Sun have been promoting and developing such appliances.

The Changing Role of the Telephone and Cable Companies

In 1996, the on-line services, such as AOL, CompuServe, and Prodigy, are the main channels by which consumers are accessing the Internet. The second largest group is the Internet Service Providers, such as Netcom and PSI.

According to the published numbers of these companies, 12 million consumers today have access to the Internet from their homes. Several of the Regional Bell Operating Companies (RBOCs) are also entering this business. Pacific Bell, which has a higher percentage of PC penetration and on-line usage among its customers than any other regional telephone company, is rolling out a multitiered Internet strategy for its virtual store owner and customers.

Services the Telephone and Cable Companies Will Offer to Virtual Store Owners

Most of the telephone companies will launch their interactive PC services targeted at virtual store owners before the end of 1996. The approach that the telephone companies are using is to take advantage of their traditional telephone lines (twisted-pair copper plant) and roll out their interactive services based on this existing narrowband technology. The advantages of the telephone lines for interactive services is that, by definition, they are interactive, although they are limited in the amount of bandwidth they can carry.

Several other telephone companies have similar ventures in the works, which will offer virtual store owners the ability to advertise on-line in a yellow page–like, cost-effective manner. Nynex has a national yellow pages site named Big Yellow. Big Yellow is also advertising-supported, based on the yellow pages model that the telephone companies created. Both At Hand and Big Yellow will sell on-line space at a cost based on per-thousand page views. Monthly, quarterly, and yearly packages will be available to the store owners, with price points varying depending on the location of the site. The search engines and personalized agent technologies available on the Internet will make the traditional yellow page services a lot more useful for consumers.

The cable companies are in a different situation. Their current networks consist of coaxial cable, which, by definition, has a lot more bandwidth than the telephone lines, but in general they are one-directional, not interactive. To make a cable plant interactive, the cable company has to change its repeaters from one way to bidirectional. This is often accompanied by replacing part of the coaxial cable with fiber optics, at least to the neighborhood, for increased bandwidth. Several cable companies launched aggressive efforts in 1994 to lay fiber optic cable associated with their interactive TV trials. These interactive TV trials encountered many obstacles, such as difficult-to-solve technical problems, higher-than-projected costs, and lack of consumer demand, which have slowed down the plans of many of the cable operators.

At Hand—Pacific Bell

When Pacific Bell's proposed $23.8 billion merger with SBC Communications (formerly known as Southwestern Bell) goes through, PacBell's services will expand beyond California and its borders. In addition to providing access to the Internet and on-line services, PacBell will have a premier content site named At Hand—not to be confused with @Home (pronounced "at home"), a joint venture between TeleCommunications, Inc., and the venture capital firm Kleiner, Perkins, Caufield and Byers.

At Hand is an Internet service that is a cross between a premier content location and an interactive yellow pages service. This advertising-supported service will provide localized informational content, similar in scope to the Yellow Pages, but with a lot more depth of information.

At this time, PacBell is focusing on three content areas: house and home, entertainment and leisure, and sports and outdoors. By 1998, PacBell plans to offer 15 theme areas and a database of over one million business listings, each offering personalized information regarding the business and hot links to the home pages of the listed businesses. Each theme area will also have its own community, with editorial content that should create a reason for repeat visitors and result in higher traffic than a yellow page site warrants. At Hand will also have transaction capability, even though PacBell does not look at this as a revenue stream for itself. This will enable the merchants listed at the site to close sales while the consumer is still on-line and to have the financial transaction verified in real time.

Recently, mostly based on the popularity of the Internet, the "full-service" networks offering telephone, digital video, and Internet data services to the home have become an area of excitement for the cable companies. Of these three services, Internet and data access services such as telecommuting are the focal points for the cable companies. TCI, Cox Communications, and Time Warner are aggressively developing full-service networks. Cable operators view themselves as evolving into

@HOME

@Home was founded in 1994 by the cable giant TeleCommunications, Inc., and the legendary Silicon Valley venture firm, Kleiner, Perkins, Caufield and Byers. @Home's charter is to work with a variety of cable operators in offering high-speed Internet access to consumers' homes and value-added services to virtual store owners. @Home segments the virtual purchases world into three:

♦ Purchases as we know them in the real world, where a purchase is made and the buyer takes physical possession of the good. This book has referred to this category as *hard goods.*

♦ Purchases of things that can be delivered on-line, such as information or software. This book has referred to this category as *soft goods.*

♦ Purchases of ongoing services. This book has referred to this category as *subscription services.*

@Home views as its target market all three types of virtual stores. Based on the work done in understanding the difficulties of operating a virtual store and lost opportunities in customer handling, support, and add-on sales, @Home has identified and provides three distinct advantages to the virtual store owner:

♦ *Database tie-ins and transactional systems at the back end.* These enable the virtual store to tie in to the traditional inventory databases and bank payment processes. Creating the front end of the virtual store where a customer can shop in a pleasant setting and is encouraged to make a purchase is only half of the challenge. Equally important is the need for well-thought-out and -designed back-end operations that tie the inventory database in to the store in

Continued

real time and handle the purchase transactions tying them in to accounting databases. @Home provides these system and integration capabilities to the store owner.

◆ *Customer service with promotional and upselling services.* Another often overlooked area for the enthusiastic virtual store creator is customer service. According to Lee Stein, First Virtual's CEO, customer service costs are a very significant part of the overall cost structure of virtual stores. But he is also quick to point out that, in addition to being a cost center, each interaction with a customer is a sales opportunity. @Home, through the involvement of TeleCommunications, Inc., and its expertise in handling millions of customers, has devised a service that provides, in addition to customer service, the ability to upsell or create postsales opportunities. The following examples illustrate the point of upselling:

◆ A customer calls in and orders cable service. When the installer comes to the house, he notices that there are children in the home and convinces the customer that the household should also subscribe to a few of the premium channels, such as Disney.

◆ When the new customer calls in with a problem, the customer service rep answers the technical question and then sells a pay-per-view event.

◆ In addition to the customer service–oriented sales opportunities, the cable operator uses its own venue and advertises its premium cable services on the air.

◆ The cable operator is also ready to sell to its customers nontraditional services such as long distance access and digital services.

@Home plans on providing high-quality, 7-day-a-week, 24-hour-a-day customer service for virtual store owners.

Continued

In addition to answering questions, they can make add-on sales. @Home intends to provide plans for virtual store owners that will have multiple touchpoints for additional sales.

@Home identifies that the issues of who collects the usage data and who owns it are important and sensitive topics. Virtual store owners will have the ability to collect their own data from their customers and own it. @Home will also collect data from customers independently and use that to offer personalized services. In every case, the customers' privacy will be maintained.

♦ *Increased traffic to the virtual store.* One of the main advantages that @Home provides to virtual store owners is increased traffic to their stores resulting from being hot-linked to the high-traffic @Home site. @Home plans to be compensated for that by charging either a percentage of the gross or a percentage of the net revenues that the merchant generates from the buyers who were directed to the virtual store from @Home's home site. The percentage will depend on the economics of the virtual store and the business model and relationship the store has with @Home.

Consumers will buy the high-speed access and content services that @Home offers from their cable operators. At this time TCI is the main cable operator distributing these services. @Home services will be billed directly to the consumer, and @Home predicts they will cost around $35 a month, including a cable modem for high-speed data services.

full-service providers of telecommunications, entertainment, and digital data services. They believe that only through becoming the full providers for their residential customers will they be able to discourage their customers from switching to another company and thus losing their established customer bases.

Services Telephone Companies Will Offer to Consumers

In addition to providing services for virtual store owners, telephone companies are also entering the Internet access business. PacBell, Ameritech, Bell Atlantic, Bell South, and Nynex all have announced such services. In addition to telephone companies, the long distance carriers have identified Internet access as their domain. Early in 1996, AT&T announced its commitment to bringing low-priced Internet access to consumers, joining MCI and Sprint. AT&T is expected to start aggressively marketing this service to its millions of long distance customers in 1997, which will include a certain number of hours of access free of charge.

The regional telephone companies cannot carry Internet traffic beyond their own regions without the aid of an Internet carrier with its own national backbone, such as Uunet and PSI. As long as the telecommunications rulings impose this regional restriction on the RBOCs, they will incur an additional fee that they will have to pay to the Internet long distance carrier, preventing them from having full control over their costs.

Pacific Bell Internet Services

Pacific Bell Internet Services (PBIS) is offering Internet access to two distinct groups of customers: users of AOL, CompuServe, and Prodigy who want to move on to "real Internet access" and customers of the traditional Internet access providers such as Netcom and PSI who are looking for a higher-quality service experience. Pacific Bell feels that its name as well as its knowledge and ability to offer high-quality customer service will be the main reasons that consumers will switch. Currently, PBIS offers two basic plans, one for 10 hours of access and another for 20 hours, both priced more aggressively than those of the traditional Internet access providers. The access speeds can go up to 28.8Kbps and an ISDN option is also available. PBIS also offers its customers the ability to create personalized home pages, access to a user directory, an optional registration feature that will tailor on-line searches of its directories to individual tastes, and on-line support for billing and account information.

What This Means to the Virtual Store Owner

Pacific Bell alone estimates that there are close to two million potential consumers out there who are targets for its Internet services.

The Evolving Technologies

Contrary to the perception created by the World Wide Web, the Internet still is a text-based environment. Over 90 percent of the data traffic on the Net today is text-based. The reasons are quite simple. One second of full-color, full-screen, television-quality video equals about 27 mega-bytes (MB) of digital data. Most people are attached to the on-line services and the Internet today through 14,400 modems, which limits the size of the connecting pipe. So making your store graphics- and video-rich causes an unavoidable delay for your potential customers in reaching and communicating with you. Therefore, if your store is targeted toward users who are coming to your site to save time and money, you should honor their needs by making it as quick as possible to access your site.

On the other hand, if your users are coming to your site for a sensual experience, you need to satisfy several of their senses by using graphics, photos, art, sound, and video. Fortunately, recent developments in digital compression technology reduce the size of the video and sound files. Until recently, a user had to download these files first onto hard disks and then play them back. Today, this need has been eliminated by removing excess information during transmission—primarily the static material, such as backgrounds, talking heads, and so on, which doesn't change from frame to frame—allowing the user to view or listen to the files in real time. This new technology is called *streaming video* or *streaming audio* and enables virtual store owners to create more interesting settings for their customers.

Companies such as VocalTec and Progressive Networks offer technologies to enable streaming audio over the Internet. Others such as VDOnet and Xing Technologies offer streaming video that allows up to 10 frames per second over a 28.8Kbps modem. Vextreme, Inc., claims 20 frames per second over 28.8 modems. But these still compare poorly to the 30 frames per second that consumers are used to getting over televi-

Making the best of bandwidth

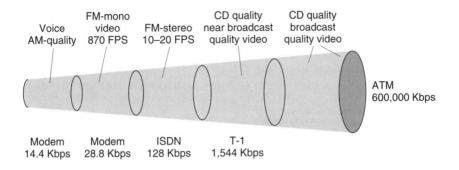

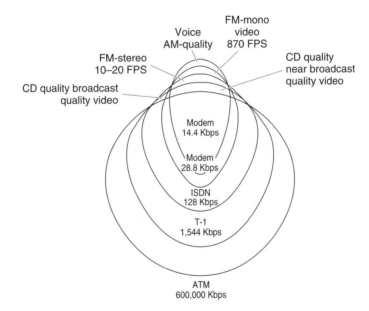

Figure 8.1 Making the best of bandwidth. (*Courtesy* Interactive Week, *April 8, 1996 by Joe McGarvey.*)

sion, which is the established yardstick for real broadcast video. Bandwidth is not always the bottleneck, though. Data congestion over the Internet, bad telephone lines, and inefficient routers often delay and distort the audio and video packets, even if there is sufficient bandwidth.

While all these companies are trying to deliver higher-quality audio and video on regular (analogue) telephone lines, their technologies will really leap forward when consumers start using digital lines to access on-line services and the Internet.

Several telephone companies are offering Integrated Services Digital Networks (ISDN) to their consumers at very attractive price points. These technologies jump the pipe speeds from 28,000bps of analogue modems to 350,000bps. Cable modems are expected to bring these numbers even higher. But it will be at least five years before people accessing the Internet via digital means outnumber the ones who access it via analogue lines.

The interactive TV movement started by the cable and telephone companies in 1993 has had a significant effect on the ability of consumers to attach their computers to the Internet and on-line services under the name of interactive PC services. The desire for these companies to use the cable infrastructure to connect PCs has resulted in the development of cable modems. These modems are similar to the 14.4- or 28.8Kbps modems used today, but they connect to the cable line, as opposed to the telephone line, in the house. Most of the cable infrastructure of the world today is for one-way communication—that is, for broadcast from one point to many. The interactive PC environment is inherently a two-way communication system, in which all points can both transmit and receive.

Several companies are working on developing cable modems, including General Instruments, Scientific Atlanta, Hybrid, Zenith, and LANCity. Table 8.1 summarizes the current status of the cable modem trials.

Why should the interactive data services from cable and telephone companies be successful now when interactive TV services that were heralded a few years ago failed? The interactive PC paradigm is very different.

First, there is a significant existing market for interactive data services today, with 12 million home users of on-line services and the Internet. These consumers have a well-defined appetite for services such as E-mail, chat and community groups, and information, compared to no identifiable desire for video on demand, the cornerstone offering of interactive TV.

Second, there is a secondary market, which is the business applications of these services. The majority of the Internet's use is for commer-

TABLE 8.1 Cable Modem Trials and Deployment, April 1996

Company/Location	Start Date	Vendors	Description	Long-term Plan
Cablevision Systems Corp., Yonkers, N.Y., and areas of Long Island	Mid-1995	Zenith Electronics	About 500 customers are on-line in the technical tests of symmetrical 500Kbps modems.	Expects to expand its deployment later this year.
Comcast Corp., Marion, Pa.	Late 1994	Intel Corp./ Hybrid Networks	Trial involves about 70 nonpaying customers.	In the third quarter Comcast will do its first commercial deployment of Comcast Online, which includes Internet access and local content, in Baltimore County, Md. Vendors have yet to be announced, but Comcast expects to use Motorola Inc. Hewlett-Packard Co. and General Instrument Corp. cable modems in the future.
Continental Cablevision	Summer 1995– March 1996	LANCity	Trials with Boston College, residential and business users in Boston. Running technical trial in Cambridge, Mass. Exeter Hospital in New Hampshire is doing telemedicine and medical data applications. The Jacksonville, Fla., residential technical trial is just beginning its rollout.	

TABLE 8.1 Cable Modem Trials and Deployment, April 1996 (Continued)

Company/Location	Start Date	Vendors	Description	Long-term Plan
Cox Communications	December 1993–	LANCity, Nortel, Zenith	Running Phoenix tele-commuting and Internet trials. Energy management tests are running in Hampton Roads, Va., and Orange County, Calif. Customers in San Diego are receiving Prodigy. Spokane, Wash., is a remote LAN trial. Providence, R.I., trials focus on residential Internet, and education distance learning and remote library access.	
Jones Intercable, Alexandria, Va.	January 1996	LANCity	Jones' Internet Channel offers two-way 10Mbps access to the Internet and to local information services for just under $30 a month.	The Internet Channel, an affiliate of Jones International, will market its services to other cable TV companies.

Company/Location	Date	Equipment	Service	Plans
Rogers Cablesystems, Newmarket, Ontario	December 1995	Zenith Electronics	Service called the Wave began commercially in early December at $39.95, plus $99 installation for 500Kbps access. Now has almost 400 customers.	Rogers will roll the service out further in Newmarket and other areas.
Tele-Communications, Inc., East Lansing, Mich.	Mid-1995	LANCity	Business customers pay $40 a month for symmetrical 10Mbps access.	In mid-1996 TCI plans to roll out its @Home on-line service including Internet access, browsers and specialized content, to residents in Sunnyvale, Calif. It will use equipment from Motorola Inc., among others. An earlier technical trial in Cupertino, Calif., has been terminated.
Time Warner Inc., Elmira, N.Y., San Diego, Calif.	July 1995, December 1995	Zenith and Hewlett-Packard Co. (Elmira); Toshiba (San Diego)	About 200 customers and local institutions now on-line.	Commercial service will be available in Akron and Canton, Ohio later this year. The Akron deployment will use Motorola equipment.
Viacom Cable, Castro Valley, Calif.	Early 1995	Intel/Hybrid Networks	Involves at least 200 customers who are paying $30 a month for unlimited usage.	Viacom is being acquired by TCI in a deal expected to close soon.

(Courtesy of *Interactive Week*, April 22, 1996.)

cial business services. The interactive data services such as full-service networks will also have as their customers small to medium-sized businesses as well as telecommuters.

Selling through the Use of New Technology

Technology for technology's sake serves no purpose at the virtual store. It all needs to be tied in to the ultimate goal of making a sale and making money. The biggest opportunity that increased bandwidth creates is the opportunity to sell in ways that were not possible before. Chapter 3 discussed the concept of infomercials as it relates to the Internet. Infomercials come alive with increased bandwidth and provide a great opportunity for upselling and merchandising. They transform the virtual storefront from a two-dimensional billboard throwing its message out there to a convincing, compelling, multisensual selling opportunity, where real information about the reasons to buy is being communicated instead of creating some HTML pages. Consider the following example.

Today's virtual flower shops have low-resolution pictures of predetermined floral and plant arrangements from which buyers can choose. In the near future, with the technologies being discussed here, potential customers will be able to download a high-resolution Java applet and start assembling the flowers of their choice as in a real-world flower shop, while viewing high-resolution flower buckets. The voice-over that the customer hears will talk about the freshness of the flowers and their wonderful smells, make comments on the customer's choices, and recommend flowers for this bouquet. The voice-over may also make suggestions for additional purchases, such as "Why not choose a second arrangement for yourself at 20 percent off?"

Figure 8.2 reviews the enabling technologies in the interactive multimedia and predicts when the impact of these technologies will be felt in a significant way.

To summarize, all new technologies, such as sound and video over the Internet, animation, and Java applets, need to be used to give potential customers a reason to buy and convince them to make the purchase right there. Bandwidth enables merchandising and promotion for the virtual store. A virtual store will not be successful if the store owner views the Web site as a virtual billboard.

Period	Enabling technology
Near term (less than two years)	CD-ROM-equipped PCs
	Multiplatform authoring
	CD-ROM and OLS integration
	Open Applications Programming Interfaces (APIs) in WWW browsers
Medium term (three to five years)	Faster PC modems
	Full-screen video
Long term (more than five years)	High-speed cable modems
	Portable multimedia playback devices
	Interactive television

Figure 8.2 When will the enabling technology impact the multimedia market? (*Courtesy of The Yankee Group*)

Scalability

One of the major issues that will face the Internet over the next few years is the problem of scalability. Businesses will want to move from 10- to 100MB Ethernet. Average homes will move from 14.4-Kbps and 28.8Kbps telephone line connections to higher-bandwidth technologies such as ISDN.

Telephone companies now forecast that it will be cost effective for them to install fiber optic cable to every curbside in America. Cable companies are looking to improve their image and deliver better customer service, chasing the almost mythical customer brand loyalty to AT&T.

Interactive TV versus PC

1993 was a very good year for the entertainment industry. During the summer of 1993, interactive TV was declared to be the next big wave in communications. Hollywood declared triumph over Silicon Valley, and the nerds who had been producing semiconductors, personal computers, networking devices, and software and felt that they dominated the

An annual Consumer On-line Services Report (April 1996) prepared by Jupiter Communications, a media research group, states that the consumer on-line services industry will grow to 35.2 million households by the year 2000. That's 34 percent of all households in the United States.

Jupiter said the popularity of on-line services is driven by growth in the number of subscribers to America Online (NASDAQ:AMER), as well as by heightened consumer interest in the World Wide Web.

The Jupiter report said that in 1995, America Online accounted for 66 percent of all new consumer on-line service subscriptions. It also said that other market competitors, such as CompuServe (NASDAQ:CSRV), Prodigy, and new market entrant, Microsoft Network (NASDAQ:MSFT), grew "steadily," but could not match pace with America Online.

Industry revenues totaled $2.2 billion in 1995. Jupiter's April 1996 report estimates that industry revenues are expected to reach $14.2 billion by the year 2000. The report's estimates were made using a base of 9.6 million on-line households in the United States during 1995.[1]

world were told "It's the Entertainment, Stupid!" and put in their places. Content was declared king, and technology did not even have prince status. Some others were kinder to these technologists, who had been making the world a nicer place in which to live by helping you do your accounting more efficiently, warm food faster, and win the Gulf War. Those kinder souls decided that the time had come for Silicon Valley to marry Hollywood and they even coined "Siliwood" as the new surname to this marriage. Several companies were formed with founding teams representing both the entertainment and the high-technology industries. But as in any ill-fated marriage, the wedding bells did not eliminate the innate differences and conflicts between technology's hacker types and Hollywood's creative types.

Even before these new hybrid companies could get themselves some T-shirts made with their new creative logos, the in-laws started fighting. The biggest fight centered around the final end-user devices that would access the wonderful content that the newly formed companies would create. Would it be the PC or the TV?

Hollywood argued that the TV was in the living room, prominently and respectfully displayed in the center of the entertainment consoles, while the PC was hidden in the den. It stressed that people thought of sitting in front of their TVs as fun, but they considered sitting in front of the PC as work. Then there were the wars about the final distance to maintain between user and end-user monitor. Should it be one to two feet as with the PC or eight to ten feet as with the TV? The PC contingency argued that, if you are going to be interactive, you should be close up and have a keyboard.

The computer game industry put itself in the center of these fights. It was, after all, part of the entertainment world but created its final product by employing a lot of software engineers. There the fights took place between the multimedia PC, enabled with a CD-ROM drive, and the dedicated game machines such as the SEA Saturn and the SONY Playstation, which were hooked up to a TV.

Three years hence, the PC has emerged as the clear winner of the end-user interface wars. The growth in end-user demand for the Internet and on-line services has powerfully surpassed any demonstrable demand for interactive TV's flagship offerings such as video on demand. It is useless to provide video on demand when there is no demand.

Some of the Siliwood marriages have predictably ended up in divorce.

The Future of Interactivity

Video on demand was the killer application that was going to make interactive television an indispensable entertainment tool for the '90s. Market research studies now show that video on demand gives consumers *too much choice* and does not compel them to buy because there is no urgency or scarcity associated with it. You can watch that video anytime, so you probably won't get around to it for a while. On the other hand, near video on demand, with which your options are limited in time, is showing itself to be more favored by consumers. The lesson to learn from this is that consumers need some sort of parameters that limit their choices. In the real world, people will often walk out of a store that has too many brands and styles of white shirts because they feel confused and overwhelmed. In the virtual world where shelf space is no longer an issue, it is even easier to throw a multitude of choices at the consumer without limiting and guiding them. Consumers prefer that some level of preselecting be done for them to increase their efficiency in shopping.

What Went Wrong with Interactive TV?

The biggest problem with interactive TV was that the revenue was too far in the future and the ongoing businesses could not justify spending money today for returns five to ten years out. There is a lesson to be learned for the interactive PC world from this exercise. Your business model should focus on real revenue in a realistic time frame and not search for gold at the end of the rainbow.

Interactive TV has not gone away. We predict that it will make a come-back—not with the arrogant personality it showed in 1993, but in a hybrid fashion, mixed in with interactive PC services. Consumer interest in interactive TV will vary from service to service, as shown in Figure 8.3 from the Yankee Group.

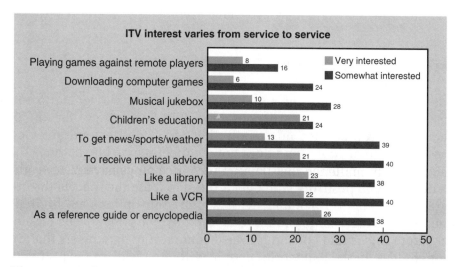

Figure 8.3   Interactive TV interest by service.

The Hybrid CD On-line Model

The multimedia CD revolution is said to be left behind by the Internet. However, there are a lot of reasons why the CD is still a very important medium in the world of interactivity. Ultimately, the offerings that married large storage capability to the immediacy of on-line information will be the winners.

- ◆ CDs can store a lot more multimedia information; therefore, they're the perfect medium for video-rich graphics and sound to create a highly sensual environment.
- ◆ CDs are the perfect medium for information that does not change on a regular basis. Such things as archival data from publishers and pictures of items from catalogers are very appropriate for storage on a CD.

The immediacy and updates of information that is stored on CDs can be provided by on-line downloading. An example is the catalog from 2 Market. While most of the content of the catalog remains on the CD, up-to-the-minute information, such as pricing and availability, are obtainable from the on-line companion.

Motorola has funded the Cyberseed project. The money allocated to this goes to content providers for retooling their content for broadband applications. Large corporations need to fund the building of the infrastructure for the interactive world. Companies such as AOL, with its Green House Project, and Intel, with its broadband initiatives, have made a big difference in enabling innovative companies to get off the ground.

The direct-response (mail-order) business in the United States attracts approximately 25 percent of the population. Direct-response shoppers have a high propensity to shop from catalogs on a regular basis. The most difficult challenge that the mail-order catalogs have is converting noncatalog shoppers into catalog shoppers. That is the reason that catalogers are willing to pay high fees to obtain each others' mailing lists. If you have shopped from a catalog once, you are a lot more likely to buy an item from a new catalog than someone who has never shopped through mail order. This self-selecting trait also holds true on the Internet. People who have shopped on the Internet are a lot more likely to shop there again. It is much more difficult to convert an individual who has never shopped on-line than to sell a new item to an on-line shopper. This may seem like a major obstacle for the virtual store owner since the number of on-line shoppers today is limited.

The on-line environment offers many advantages over catalog shopping:

- ◆ Ability to search for specific items
- ◆ Ability to do price-comparison shopping very conveniently
- ◆ Ability to link on-line stores together through hot links to keep those consumers with a high propensity to buy on-line within a select family of stores

The desire for speed is insatiable when it comes to computer technology. We have already discovered that with the PC industry and expect it to repeat itself with the appetite for bandwidth. Higher bandwidth will allow richer content which takes too much time to download on 28.8 Kbps modems. Tools such as Shockwave and Java will allow dynamic Web sites, making the content the user receives seem highly animated.

The analogue to video on demand in the interactive PC world might be browsing off-line and downloading at a "down" time such as when sleeping. Point Cast products have given consumers the ability to search for information without requiring that they be on line.

Johnny, Turn off the PC!

With the PC becoming the device of choice for interactive services, it faces some of the same problems that arise with the television set. According to the extensive market research study published by Management Forum of Palo Alto in the fall of 1994, the increased time that people are devoting to on-line services and the Internet is coming from reduced hours in television viewing. The updates to the study validate this point. Management Forum says that the average number of hours that a user spends on one of the on-line services or the Internet has *tripled* since 1993. In addition to the on-line environment, the proliferation of computer games for the PC platform has meant tough competition as an entertainment device for the TV with the under-25 age group. Affectionately referred to as "screenagers," this age group is becoming as comfortable with PCs as they are with their TVs.

Until 1994, the PC was regarded by parents as an educational device. During the Christmas season of 1994, PC sales hit record numbers as well-meaning parents rushed to stores to pay over $1,500 for multimedia-enabled computers. The goal was to offer their children another venue for education and make them more competitive in their schools. They bought educational CD-ROM titles and spent many hours trying to teach their four-year-olds to read or their twelve-year-olds to use *Compton's New Encyclopedia.* They subscribed to on-line services for the children's content and proudly told other parents that Johnny knew how to get onto the Internet and communicate with thirteen-year-olds in Russia. They encouraged their children to stop watching TV and play with the PC. The PC had replaced the TV as the acceptable interactive device.

Then something happened that parents had not foreseen. The children started using their PCs to play computer games instead of looking at the encyclopedia. Some children discovered the ".alt" groups on the Internet, of which their parents were not even aware. So instead of doing research for their geography homework on the Internet, they joined steamy chat groups, downloading sexually explicit content, dating on-line, and locking themselves up in the den, preventing Dad from entering the family budget into Quicken.

The worst effect of the PC for parents has been the shift in power and control in the family. Parents and children generally have equal abilities when it comes to television set operation. Parents know how to control TV set usage. But the PC has brought new complexities to these unsuspecting parents. Because of the technical nature of the PC and childrens' initiation to the PC through schools, friends, and computer game equipment, children have developed a power base around the PC. They have become the systems operators of the PC, having the ultimate say in its configuration and content.

Controlling What the Kids Watch on PC

Controlling the content of television viewing has been a constant challenge for parents. Now there is a new challenge for parents who willingly brought PCs into their homes: controlling the content their children access via on-line services and the Internet.

The courts, both in the United States and in other countries, are trying to decide where the responsibilities lie in controlling content. In Germany, CompuServe was held by the courts as the responsible party for the objectionable content in its discussion forums, which resulted in CompuServe discontinuing the availability of its forums in Europe. Singapore has outlawed the sexual and alternative content of the Internet and the on-line services. In the United States, Prodigy was held accountable for the content in its chat groups.

Ultimately, the courts both in the United States and abroad will realize that the Internet and the on-line services are not much different from communications pipes. And eventually, we will see a clear delineation between access to the networks and content on these networks. Most access providers, such as AOL, @Home, and Netcom, view themselves as offering a menu of content to their subscribers and expect the subscribers to control access to services. This puts the responsibility back in the parents' laps.

There are several companies that are providing technologies to aid parents in this content-filtering task. SurfWatch is the first entrant into this market, and is fully dedicated to Internet content filtering. Its software blocks sexually explicit and violent sites. NewView is the newest entrant and an advanced service provider targeted toward the consumer market of families with children. It rates and indexes Internet sites according to a wide range of criteria and markets a service called iscreen!.

There is an innate concern regarding where to draw the line on the inclusivity of content. This concern will eventually make these systems fail, unless they are continuously changed and adapted to the family. The hardest part about these systems is gauging the level of filtering. Systems that are too inclusive will be missing objectionable sites and letting through too much objectionable content. Systems that are too exclusive will be too limited in the content they provide. And since "objectionable" is very much a relative term that changes continually as the children grow up, these systems will likewise need to change and be customized on an ongoing basis.

As a virtual store owner, you need to keep in mind that the content of your store will eventually be rated by one of these companies. Your goal as the store owner is to make sure that the rating is in line with your desires. You should work with the rating companies to achieve that, just as the movie producers work with the rating authorities in Hollywood, re-editing movies until the desired rating is achieved.

The Changing Demographics of the On-line Consumer

The demographics of the on-line consumer are changing fast.

- In the fall of 1994, according to the demographics study conducted by Management Forum, less than 20 percent of people on the Internet were women at that time. Today, women constitute 35 percent of the Internet population.
- The percentage of Internet users accessing the Net from on-line services and corporations has also been climbing steadily.
- In 1994, the majority of Internet users were either in research and education or government jobs. Today, the number of users coming from commercial sites far exceeds that from nonprofit organizations.
- According to Management Forum, in 1994, people spent an average of 2.4 hours per week on-line. Today, it has climbed to 7.6 hours per week.
- The amount of money consumers are willing to spend for on-line service providers has also climbed. In 1994, it was just under $10. Today, the average on-line service or Internet customer pays $18 per month for on-line access and an additional $14/month for the second telephone line for this access.
- Shopping on the Internet was not a possibility in 1994. The on-line services, such as AOL and CompuServe did have stores, but this was not the big draw. According to a recent study released by IDC, one in three Web browsers shops while browsing the Net.
- The on-line services will continue to grow at a rate of around 35 percent per year, bringing new users to the Internet with more typical consumer demographics.
- IDC also reported that home shoppers on the Internet spend an average of $50 per month, and business shoppers spend an average of $500 per month.
- IDC expects Internet commerce in the year 2000 to surpass $150 billion, up from $300 million in 1995. (IDC's press

releases and additional results from its research studies can be found on the home page at http://www.idsresearch.com.)

- According to the market research firm INPUT, business-to-business commerce over the Internet is growing very quickly and is expected to surpass consumer-to-business activity by 1998.

With all these changes in the demographics of Internet users, they can still be categorized as technology heat seekers and early adopters. According to Management Forum in 1996:

- Over 73 percent of Internet users have two phone lines in their homes, compared to 16 percent of the general U.S. population.

- Sixty-eight percent of Internet users have PCs at home, compared to 35 percent of the overall U.S. population. (Those who do not have PCs at home have Internet access at their offices.) In comparison, 90 percent of the homes in the United States have TVs.

- The cost of the average PC is expected to go down, from around $1,600 today to under $1,000 by late 1998.

In the future, the PC is not going to be the only Internet access device for consumers. Throughout 1996, Oracle Corporation has led the technology companies in developing an "Internet appliance." Oracle claims the end-user price for this appliance will be under $500. Other firms joining Oracle in this area are Sun Microsystems, Olivetti, and IBM. These network computing devices are not expected to have hard disk drives to store application software such as Microsoft Word or Lotus 1-2-3. Instead, software will be stored on network computers and downloaded only on an as-needed basis.

As shown in Figure 8.4, according to the Yankee Group, the Internet will also change in the functionality it provides to its users. Internet phones will provide low-cost international calling capabilities for Internet users. Internet telephones will be in 24 percent of the households for Internet access.

The Internet will become a major banking channel for consumers. The home banking revolution in the early 1980s never took off because there

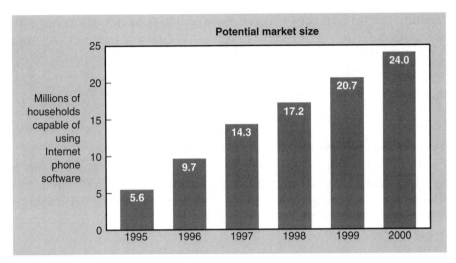

Figure 8.4 Potential market size for Internet phones.

were not enough home PCs equipped with modems. Access speeds were also very slow—around 1200bps. In the future, home banking via the PC will become a real competitor to home banking via the telephone. Companies such as Intuit, Microsoft, and the newly announced joint venture between IBM and ten major banks will be offering interactive personal finance and home banking services.

Welcome to the New Frontier

Frontiers have a way of changing the old established rules and creating new ones. They also tend to have far-reaching effects and change the lives of even those who live far from the frontier. This is happening with the Internet.

In this new virtual world, geography as we know it has disappeared. A virtual store in Madrid, Spain, or Dampasar, Indonesia, looks as close as the store of the merchant located down the street. So for soft goods and services, which are delivered directly on the network so that shipping is not an issue, the local store does not have a significant advantage over the one halfway around the world.

As frontiers appear, they create new industries and make other established ones obsolete. Following is a look at the winners and losers on this new frontier.

The Winners on the Virtual Frontier

The Consumer

Consumers are the ultimate winners in the on-line world. They can price-shop without having to buy every Sunday paper and rip out the pages. They can use the vast resources of data to collect information on products before making decisions to buy and they can take advantage of intelligent agents to update them on their areas of interest. They can also save time by doing gift shopping on-line.

The Soft Goods/Information Manufacturer

Software vendors, publishers, computer game manufacturers, information vendors, and all others that produce soft goods will be winners on the on-line frontier. Who needs to go to the corner computer store if you can download the latest version of Windows directly from Microsoft's home page? This new medium also allows soft goods manufacturers to sell their wares in new ways.

One of these new ways is selling a la carte, whereby consumers pay only for the specific items in which they are interested, such as a subset of Microsoft Word instead of the whole package. The additional features of Microsoft Word can be sold as added-on sales later. Another example of a new way of selling is renting the on-line delivered goods. The user may not be willing to pay $200 for that graphics package but may be willing to rent it for one day for $10.

The Manufacturer of Branded Hard Goods

The effects of selling on-line are especially magnified for branded hard goods. A 32-inch Sony TV is the same, regardless of who sells it to you. So if you are a manufacturer with an easily identifiable brand, you can use the virtual store to take your goods directly to your consumers and eliminate the costs you incur with distributors and retailers.

The key to your success is to assure your purchasers that you do indeed represent the genuine brand name, which gives the purchaser an incentive to buy on-line as opposed to your other distribution channels.

The Low-Cost Supplier of Habitual Commodity Goods

Commodity goods are defined as goods for which the consumer is not willing to pay a premium to get an identifiable brand. They are usually items for which the basic functionality of the goods is the key to the purchase, not the specific features that a manufacturer has decided to include. Most manufacturers try to move their products from the commodity category to the branded category. Crest and Colgate have done a very good job with toothpaste, which, in essence, is a commodity product.

There are still several product types that remain mostly in the commodity goods category, though manufacturers may have been able to create some brand awareness. These are household goods such as toilet paper and paper towels and office goods such as pencils, pens, and copier and printer papers.

Manufacturers of commodity items compete on shelf space and price. If you have the shelf space and a good price, you can move the products. The virtual store, especially for habitually purchased items such as office supplies, becomes a great time-saver for the consumer by fulfilling the need for habitual commodity items at a prearranged interval. So all I have to do as a buyer is fill out my monthly shopping list at my favorite virtual store and I receive my monthly shipment that automatically fills up my pantry or office cupboard.

In summary, the virtual store is going to succeed only if it is better than the other shopping experiences we have today. Taking the print versions of mail-order catalogs or moving the home shopping programs from television to the Internet will not result in success. The on-line environment is still cumbersome to access, compared to pressing a button to turn on the TV or flipping through the pages of a catalog dropped in your mailbox. The on-line environment is also still unfamiliar, uncomfortable, and untrustworthy for the average consumer. So virtual store owners must offer advantages to all the other shopping media to attract customers. They need to offer *better* goods and services cheaper and faster—just cheaper or faster is not sufficient.

The Losers on the Virtual Frontier

The Intermediaries That Do Not Add Real Value

The emergence of the virtual world is a big threat to all intermediaries that earn their livings by positioning themselves between the ultimate buyer and seller. These include the classic distributors that take the goods from the manufacturer and see them through to the retailer, as well as the retailers that put the products on the shelves, in front of the ultimate buyer.

This does not mean that every distributor will go out of business because of the Internet and on-line services. As long as distributors are adding real value, such as overseeing the shipment of goods in the most cost-effective way, they will continue to have a role to play and will make money. But intermediaries that rely on arbitrage opportunities and the imbalance of information on the price and availability of certain goods will be out of business because information about all items will be easily available.

For example, today when you buy a sweater for $100 at one of the high-fashion boutiques on Madison Avenue in New York, over 80 percent of the retail price is absorbed by the distribution channel, leaving only around $15 to the manufacturer in Hong Kong. This interactive medium, which diminishes the need for intermediaries, enables consumers to experience great savings while manufacturers get larger sums for their goods.

Arbitrage opportunities, which enable distributors to make money, will continue to exist in countries where imports are strictly controlled. In the Eastern Bloc countries, prior to the fall of the Berlin Wall, one paid very high sums for a pair of Levi's jeans or nylon stockings. These Eastern Bloc buyers lacked two things: information about the cost of these goods elsewhere and the sheer availability of the goods in their country. The Internet will make the first problem disappear. Someone in Turkmenistan can enter a chat group and ask how much Levi's 509 jeans sell for in London. But the information still cannot solve the availability problem if the government of Turkmenistan does not allow the import of Levi's jeans into the country or if it is strictly controlled via quotas.

The High-End Retailer of Branded Products

High-end retailers will continue to exist and thrive as long as they provide shopping experiences that cannot be provided elsewhere. Shoppers who go shopping as a social outlet and those who enjoy the sensual experiences of a high-end retail environment will continue to frequent these stores, since the high-end retailers know how to offer this better than anyone else. My mother spends every Saturday at the Stanford Shopping Center, a very high end shopping mall. She enjoys observing the well-dressed people, the flowers, the restaurants and cafes, the pleasant courtyards, and the lovely boutiques and stores. She makes a few purchases of things that catch her fancy, just for entertainment. I personally like spending a little time at my local electronics retailer, Fry's in Palo Alto. It is a social spot as much as a retailer, and I often run into people I have not seen for a while. But when it is time for both my mother and me to purchase a major item, we both shop for price and usually end up purchasing the item at another store or shopping center.

The virtual stores will extenuate this scenario. The high-end retailers that make most of their money on charging a premium for branded products will be threatened by the virtual world. For example, as long as Ralph Lauren sells its bedding only through Neiman Marcus, then the retailer can safely charge the premiums. But what if I can buy that bedding through other channels—especially through a Ralph Lauren virtual store—at a more attractive price? Or, if I can buy that Sony TV on-line after having searched for the most attractive price and have it delivered to my front door, why should I go to Macy's on my day off and have to carry it up my steep stairs? The alternative sales channels of branded goods have always been a threat to the high-end retailer, but with the high-end demographics of the virtual stores and the ability to price-shop through the search engines, this threat is intensified.

Those Afraid of Technology

Computers are here to stay; they are not going away. If you have the attitude that they are scary, difficult to understand, and a threat to mankind, it is time for you to revisit those premises. The Internet is the fastest-growing human communications tool we have ever experienced. It is spreading faster than the telephone, the telex, the facsimile, and the television. Now is the time to learn what the virtual world is all about and how you can take advantage of it and be one of the winners on this new frontier.

Those who say the Internet is the "fad-du-jour" are wrong. This is the new frontier and now is the time for you to stake out your virtual ground. Welcome to this most exciting new frontier!

Closing Thoughts

The Internet is here to stay. If you do nothing else after reading this book, start taking advantage of the communications capabilities that the

Internet offers. Send E-mails and files and see how much more efficient your business can become by using the Internet.

As discussed in this chapter, there is no need to argue what the interactive device of the future will be. Personal computers, televisions, Internet appliances, and various new devices that we have not even thought of will be used to access the world's fastest-growing communications and information infrastructure. How you get there will not matter; whether you are there *will*.

It will be imperative, however, for you as the virtual store owner to keep track of the different access technologies so that you can constantly update your virtual store to meet the capabilities and perceived needs of your customers. As access to the Internet moves from 14.4Kbps modems to T1 speeds, you will need to update your store's "decor" accordingly. Remember the term *Web years*. It communicates the concept of fast change on the Internet, where in one month as much change is accomplished as would take a year in the real world. In summary, always stay on top of the changing technologies and realize that you need to update your store and stay current.

In addition to the fast technological changes, the social issues regarding the on-line environment and their implications for the virtual store owner will be vastly different in the next few years. Topics such as parental guidance, rating of content, legislative limitations, and the social structure of the global village will affect your virtual store. The changing demographic and physiographic makeup of the on-line consumer will also create new markets for on-line merchants, such as homework helpers or dating services.

Finally, the emergence of any new frontier affects even those who live far from it. There will be many businesses that will be adversely affected by the Internet. Intermediaries who have made their money taking advantage of the information discrepancies due to widespread geographic locations will be the losers of the Internet revolution. The Internet will provide information regarding cost of goods and availability to flow freely across geographies, eliminating these arbitrage opportunities. Retailers of branded products will also lose part of their market share when manufacturers go directly to consumers over the Internet. We are already seeing some of this with the software industry. The biggest losers of the Internet revolution, though, will be those who do not take advantage of it.

On the winning side, consumers will come out way ahead. They will be able to purchase goods that were not available before. They will be able to price-shop and have access to lots of product and service information, and, ultimately, they'll have a virtual staff to shop for them.

Software vendors, publishers, computer game manufacturers, information vendors, and all others that produce soft goods will be the winners on the on-line frontier. They will be able to keep a larger percentage of the retail price by eliminating the distributor and retailers and still pass savings on to consumers. Manufacturers of branded hard goods will also be able to take their goods directly to consumers and eliminate the costs they incur with distributors and retailers, as long as their brands are well known and sought after by consumers. Suppliers of low-cost habitual commodity goods will also be able to take their products directly to consumers by fulfilling standing repeat orders efficiently and cost effectively.

EPILOGUE

Many people wonder why so much attention is being given to the Internet. After all, technologists have been producing new technologies for the last several decades—for example, the microprocessor, user-friendly operating systems, storage technology, and applications software—but none has received the same type of coverage in the media and this sort of valuation on Wall Street. Why is the Internet being singled out and treated with such high esteem?

In their early years of commercialization, technologies that came before the on-line revolution affected, at most, millions of people. A year into its commercialization, the Internet has affected tens of millions of people, and it will affect hundreds of millions before we know it. It is orders of magnitude more powerful than any other technical revolution.

Just think, if we could have provided telephone service to 100 million people around the world in a period of three years, what the social and business impact of that would have been. That is the magnitude of change the Internet is about to bring to all of us.

Major shifts in technology have a way of affecting things that are outside their immediate reach. Industries as we have known them, such as retail and distribution, will be very different by the twenty-first century, which is less than five years away. Banking, finance, and education will also undergo major changes. The Internet will touch all industries, no matter how low-tech they are today. We are all very lucky to be living through these times and to be here to experience one of the biggest revolutions in the history of mankind.

The virtual and real worlds are not disconnected; they are both part of the universe we will all exist in. All virtual E-mail messages have real people behind them, all virtual stores are run by real merchants, and all real merchants need to know about the opportunities presented in the virtual world.

Reading this book is a good step toward understanding this evolving virtual world and the effects on its physical counterpart. Now it is time for you to put this knowledge to good use.

APPENDICES

Certain material included in the following appendices has been adapted by the author from company literature. Its inclusion does not represent an endorsement by the author or the publisher.

Please consult the companies' Web sites for updated product and cost information.

WEB TRACKING PRODUCTS AND INFORMATION

This appendix provides details about companies and products discussed in Chapter 4.

Internet Profiles Corporation (I/PRO)

Products: I/Count, I/Code, I/Audit, JavaCount, I/Analysis

I/PRO has developed a broad product line of Web measurement systems, the primary components of which are Nielsen I/PRO I/Count, Nielsen I/PRO I/Audit, and the I/Code Universal Registration System. The I/PRO system enables organizations that own or manage Web sites to understand how and by whom their sites are being used. Advertisers and media buyers can use the I/PRO system to determine the optimal sites for delivering their messages. The I/PRO system is compatible with World Wide Web standards and respects Internet culture and users' privacy. I/PRO is a member of the CommerceNet consortium.

I/PRO and Nielsen Media Research, the premier television audience information service, announced the formation of a strategic partnership to develop and deliver a broad range of measurement and evaluation services for the Internet.

Partners collaborating on I/PRO Web development and technology deliverables include Poppe Tyson, CKS Group, W3.com, MediaSmith, Network Publishing, Vivid Studios, and Free Range Media.

I/PRO customers include Chrysler Corporation, CMP Publications' TechWeb, CompuServe, Hearst New Media Corporation, Individual,

Inc. Newspage, CyberCash, Netscape, Microsoft, *Playboy, Penthouse, USA Today,* Starwave, ESPNet Sportszone, Women's Wire, Yahoo!, and Ziff-Davis Publishing ZDnet.

I/PRO Products and Services

Nielsen I/PRO I/Count

The first product to market is I/Count. With the I/Count service, Web site owners can monitor aspects of site usage such as number of visits, most frequently accessed files, and origin of visitors (geographic or by organization). Service has been commercially available since May 1995.

With I/Count, a user can analyze visits and/or pages, not just hits, at a Web site. Primarily, the system enables a Web host to:

◆ Determine the geographic distribution of companies accessing the site.

◆ Determine the names of organizations accessing the server.

◆ Determine the most frequently accessed files and directories.

◆ Analyze site usage based on industry codes (SIC), number of employees, or corporate revenue.

◆ Limit reports based on time and date, geographic or organizational data, or specific files and directories.

A Web site can analyze a visitor's site usage or visitation anytime. Report selections include popular preformatted reports and custom reports. Once a report is created, I/Count allows a user to see it on-line or receive it via E-mail on a regularly scheduled basis. I/PRO archives and processes a Web site's data, so that the Web developers and hosts can concentrate on making the Web site as effective as possible.

When the I/Count system is combined with the I/Code system, a company can merge site usage information with detailed demographic information about its site visitors.

The I/Count system is installed on a host's Web server; however, no maintenance by the host is necessary. Each night, the usage data is securely transmitted from a Web site to I/PRO, where the data is processed, encoded, indexed for maximum performance, and loaded into a relational database. Since the data is stored in a fully relational structure, a Web site will be able to break down the information in many useful ways. I/Count is compatible with all major Web servers and platforms.

Nielsen I/PRO I/Code

The second product from I/PRO is the I/Code Universal Registration System. With the I/Code service, sites benefit by obtaining detailed demographic data, while avoiding redundant site-specific registration that negatively impacts traffic. This system offers the following:

◆ Raw demographic data on all I/Code members who sign on at your site, provided free of charge

◆ Insights into the depth of repeat visits to your site

◆ Access to aggregated audience demographics for all I/Code members (not just those who register at your site)

◆ Ability for visitors to share their demographics while maintaining respect for their privacy

◆ Understanding of audience preferences and their reactions to your site's content

With the I/Code System, end users register once and use the same I/Code at all I/Code-enabled sites. Internet users benefit by:

◆ Sharing their valuable demographic data in exchange for rewards and access to custom content.

◆ Staying in control of their personal contact information. Entering an I/Code releases only anonymous demographic information. I/PRO will never disclose any I/Code member's identity or personal contact information without the user's explicit authorization.

◆ Avoiding the hassle of registering at multiple sites and remembering multiple user IDs.

◆ Actively shaping the future of the Web through the sharing of demographic information in a safe, controlled manner.

When a user gets an I/Code at your custom registration page, you co-own that user's profile data with I/PRO. I/PRO will allow sites to include custom questions in the registration process. I/PRO is developing real-time demographic profile lookup and transmission, which makes possible:

- Customized page and site content
- Customized ad delivery

I/Code allows sites employing site-specific registration to enhance their existing databases by adding I/Code demographic profiles. Hybrid solutions are available to integrate I/Code into existing registration systems. I/Code is the only system that gives end users who are willing to share their demographics a means of doing so without revealing their identity or contact information.

The I/Code system, in its current form, represents a first step toward a secure and integrated universal registration system. I/PRO is currently developing and expanding I/Code in the areas of:

- Enhanced privacy and control of personal information for end users
- Encryption techniques to ensure the secure transmission of information
- Verification and certification of users and their demographic and contact information
- Integration of the I/Code system into browsers, cookies, and end user applications to speed and facilitate the flow of information

Nielsen I/PRO I/Audit

Provides a third-party audit of a Web site's advertising statistics. With I/Audit, a Web site can demonstrate its audience characteristics to advertisers and potential advertisers. Options include:

- Visits per month
- Number of pages
- Average visit length
- Visits by day of the week and by time of day

- Most frequently requested files accessed
- Visitors by state and country
- Visitors by organization name

The Nielsen I/PRO I/Audit Advertiser Insert provide a third-party audit of advertising banners on your site. With I/Audit Advertiser Insert, you can demonstrate:

- AdViews by day
- AdClicks by day
- AdClick rate by day
- Comparisons against other advertisers on the site, without compromising the confidentiality of each advertiser
- Summary statistics by page
- Based on your log files, an independent analysis, verification, and audit of your site usage, which provides you with a standard report that you can furnish to third parties

I/PRO works with NetGravity, an electronic advertising software company, to audit the statistical advertising traffic information, including impressions and click-throughs as generated by the NetGravity AdServer.

AdServer consists of a high-performance database and optimized scheduling software for placing, rotating, tracking, targeting, and reporting advertisements. AdServer is ultimately responsible for displaying the correct advertisement in the right ad space at the right time and for collecting statistics vital to ad planning. AdServer delivers practical, powerful, and reliable advertising and promotions management features, including:

- *Online interactive ad calendar:* Accessible from any Web browser, the on-line calendar automates ad placement, eliminating manual error and saving on administration costs.
- *Key reports:* Ad statistics are easily accessible by Web administrators and remotely by advertisers, allowing Web sites and their advertisers to work together to maximize the effectiveness of advertising campaigns. Statistics and reports are audited and approved by Nielsen/I/PRO.

- *Impression-based scheduling:* AdServer's scheduling system allows Web sites to deliver a guaranteed number of impressions to their advertisers and increase sales by selling unused impressions to other advertisers.
- *Grouped ad categories:* AdServer enables sites to simplify the process of selling ad blocks to advertisers by categorizing ad spaces within a Web site according to criteria such as popularity, subject matter, or viewer demographics.
- *Keyword-based ad targeting:* AdServer provides Web sites the means to sell targeted ad displays by delivering ads in the context of a search or a news feed.

Nielsen I/PRO Java Count

Java Count, a joint venture between I/PRO and Sun Microsystems3, measures Java Applets on the Web, providing a complete measurement and tracking solution and allowing the accurate and detailed analysis of user interaction with a Java Applet. This includes methods to track the time that the visit occurred, the duration of the visit, and a detailed recording of the interactions with the Applet during the visit.

The Need for Measurement   The acceptance of the I/PRO system for measurement, tracking, and independent auditing of activity on the Web has created exciting opportunities for sites and advertisers to expand their business with assurance. Advertisers can purchase ad space knowing they will be able to accurately track the impressions and usage of their ads. However, the use of new technologies such as Java has created demand for expanded measurement and tracking solutions. The Java Count System from I/PRO represents the natural extension of the I/Count and I/Audit services to include Java.

Existing Problems with Measuring Java Applets   Java Applets are dynamic objects existing on the Web, unlike the static HTML page or GIF file commonly used. Because of this dynamic nature, logging a Java Applet in the standard log file records only the begin time and the name of the Applet, not any information about what happens during user interaction with the Applet or when that interaction ends. Java Applets usually run completely on the client machine, providing no useful information back to the server.

Detailed Information Is Needed   Java Count from I/PRO provides the ability to track information at the level of detail required by the Applet developer. For example, in the case of an on-line tic-tac-toe game, the Web developer may be interested in how long a user spent playing the game, how many times the user won, and how many times the user choose to play X instead of O. Another example might be a Java Applet used to advertise a vegetarian cookbook. The developer may wish to know how many users requested the nutritional content of eggplants versus that of carrots. In either case, the flexible architecture of Java Count allows the Applet developer to choose the appropriate level and type of detail.

How Does Java Count Work?   There are three main steps needed for Java Applet measurement:

1. Data collection
2. Data recording
3. Data reporting

Java Count has been created to make each step easy and completely integrated into both Java Applet development and the overall I/PRO system.

Java Count sites will be able to work with I/PRO directly to specify the types of reports that they would like generated from any specific Java Applet. By providing I/PRO with the details on the type of information being recorded using Java Count, specific reports on user activity can be generated.

At a minimum, the I/PRO analysis of the usage data will allow a report that indicates the begin time and end time of the Java Applet. Additional reports on specific user actions can be requested through the I/PRO Account or Sales Executive.

Reports on Java activity will be included with the I/Count system for Web site measurement and tracking and with the I/Audit system for independent and authenticated third-party audits.

Nielsen I/PRO I/Analysis

The I/Analysis service is similar to the current I/Count system; however, I/Analysis does not enable Web sites the extensive data-tracking capabilities of I/Count. This installation requires local server memory and hard-disk space as well; the Webmaster must manage the software while I/Count is hosted and accessible within the within the I/PRO Web site.

I/PRO Summary

I/PRO services offer the following:

- Multiple product offerings for different client uses, with product and service upgrades on the way.
- No local server maintenance requirement. All log-file information is transferred and repurposed directly through the I/PRO Web site.
- Expanded reporting capabilities for I/Count Version 2.0 XL.
- No software purchase requirement; all fees are negotiated in service contracts based on traffic flow.
- Excellent customer account servicing.

For updated information, contact:

Internet Profiles Corp. (I/Pro)
785 Market St.
San Francisco, CA 94103

I/Pro's Web site is located at: www.ipro.com.

Intersé Corporation

Intersé Market Focus is an off-the-shelf solution that lets Web sites conduct analyses at the place of business, protecting the confidentiality and privacy of Web site data. Unlike Web-tracking service bureaus, Intersé enables companies to easily and cost-effectively integrate new Internet information into a business's existing customer data infrastructure.

Compatible with most Web server software, Intersé Market Focus software takes hit-based usage data and uses several inference-based algorithms to reconstruct the actual visits of users and organizations that interact with the Web site. Intersé Market Focus enables users to conduct in-depth analyses and produce a comprehensive suite of standard or customized analysis reports, providing valuable insights for making more informed Internet business decisions.

As an analysis tool, Intersé Market Focus enables you to determine how your customers are spending their time and money. Typical analysis questions that Intersé Market Focus answers include:

♦ Where did visitors spend the most time within the site?
♦ How many visits did it take each user to reach the order page?
♦ Which Web advertisements attracted the most visitors?
♦ For visitors that filled out the order page, what was the referring URL?
♦ For each of our Web advertisements, what percentage of the visitors were repeat visitors and what percentage were new?

For many analysis reports, Intersé Market Focus leverages the Intersé Internet Database, which contains U.S. and Canadian Internet domains indexed by state, city, and postal code. Intersé Market Focus supports personal and client-server relational databases, and is available in standard and developer's editions to meet your needs.

Intersé Market Focus 2 system requirements include:

♦ Windows 95 or Windows NT 3.51
♦ Pentium processor
♦ 32 MB of memory recommended (16 MB minimum)
♦ Disk space equal to 40 MB plus the size of your log files

The following are optional, but nice to have:

♦ Internet connection for looking up HTML titles and resolving IP addresses
♦ Microsoft Word v7 or higher to produce MS Word reports

Interse Summary

The Interse system offers:

- Simple and intuitive analysis interface
- Canned reports for analyzing complex data
- Reports, charts, and tables in HTML
- Fairly sophisticated query capabilities
- Ability to track the path (click-stream) that each visitor travels within the Web site
- Capacity to run on Windows 95 and NT
- Compatibility with Microsoft SQL server databases

For updated information contact:

Interse Corporation
111 W. Evelyn Ave., Suite 213
Sunnyvale, CA 94086
(408) 732-0932
Fax (408) 732-7038

The Interse Web site is located at: www.interse.com.

Cortex Group (SiteTrack)

The SiteTrack Tracking System is an add-on to the Netscape server, which allows it to track users as they move through the Web site. One important aspect of SiteTrack is that it can provide its tracking functionality completely transparently to both the client requesting pages and the Web site developer.

The core of SiteTrack is a Netscape API library, which the Netscape Web server loads at start-up. This library wraps a shell around the server in order to provide it with the ability to track users and dynamically alter pages.

With respect to server activities, SiteTrack performs functions at two distinct times. SiteTrack intercepts every request it receives at the beginning, before it reaches the normal functions of the Netscape Server to remove and store the session identification information in the request. In this fashion, SiteTrack is able to identify each user. At the end of every request, SiteTrack intercepts the output of the server to put session identification information into each page that is sent to the client. This way, the SiteTrack system can provide full tracking functionality without affecting any other functions that the server is running.

SiteTrack provides Webmasters with the first drop-in tool for tracking Web surfers as they enter, move through, and leave a Web site. SiteTrack is the perfect solution for building merchant storefronts, constructing E-zines and electronic news sites, and demonstrating Web site value to advertisers.

SiteTrack's high-performance engine comes complete with all of the tools needed to track user preferences, maintain a "shopping basket," construct sophisticated on-line games, and even build your own innovative tools and utilities for letting Web surfers interact with your Web site.

SiteTrack also performs the following data-gathering functions:

- Identifies who is visiting the site
- Records the actual number of people who visit
- Finds which links they follow and traces their complete paths
- Learns which sites users came from and which sites they depart to

Features and Benefits

SiteTrack offers the following features and benefits:

- *Session management:*   Track people as they enter your site, move through it, and eventually leave it. Find out which pages and sections most interest users and how users navigate your Web site. Determine exactly what visitors do as they move from point to point in your Web site.
- *Exterior tracking:*   Track how people leave your site and where they go. Determine how people arrived at your Web site and where they enter your Web site. Compare users from different entry points.

- *Support for Netscape API:* Unlike tracking systems managed via traditional CGI scripts, SiteTrack provides full support for NSAPI functionality. SiteTrack is the only way to take full advantage of the power and of a Netscape server.
- *On-the-fly interactivity:* Real-time manipulation of Web pages is provided by the SiteTrack API, a powerful tool for accessing SiteTrack's information about users and adapting your Web site to the user, based on this information. The SiteTrack API allows access to information via CGI, SHTML, and custom HTML elements.

SiteTrack Summary

The SiteTrack Tracking System provides:

- An off-the-shelf product that is easy to install
- An advertising/web-tracking application in one
- Assistance with building and maintaining merchant store-fronts
- An effective measurement tool for content providers
- Netscape Commerce and Communications server software support
- Hardware compatible with SGI and Sun boxes
- Log-file analysis and reporting capabilities

For updated information contact:

Group Cortex, Inc.
2300 Chestnut Street, Suite 230
Philadelphia, PA 19103
(215) 854-0646
Fax (215) 854-0665

Group Cortex's Web site is located at: www.cortex.net.

Digital Planet (NetCount)

NetCount's products include NetCount Basic, NetCount Plus, and Ad-Count. NetCount's tracking system provides detailed analysis and reporting of Web site usage. Through NetCount, Web site creators and advertisers can make use of a universally recognized ratings system (comparable to Nielsen) that provides precise traffic information, broken down by Web site, subject, page, day, and hour.

The NetCount service is designed not only to collect and interpret data, but to provide a standard for optimizing the effectiveness of on-line advertising as a medium. The NetCount tracking system, which is currently being tested by such major corporate advertisers as MCA, NutraSweet, MGM/UA, and Young & Rubicam, will provide independently verified, site-by-site, quantitative reports on Internet usage. For the first time, Web site managers and media buyers alike will be able to create universally recognized advertising rates—comparable to those employed in traditional media—based on the traffic generated by individual Web sites.

The NetCount service is thus able to accomplish what traditional services cannot: It monitors traffic both within a Web site and between specified Web sites. Using NetCount, advertisers can verify which advertisements—and which sites—are most effective in bringing targeted users to their own home pages.

AdCount is the authoritative way to determine if a specific Web ad is achieving, exceeding, or falling short of expectations and to find out whether a Web advertisement is cost efficient. For accurate evaluation, this exclusive advantage reveals both quantitative usage information and qualitative user information, such as:

◆ How many times a specific Web ad is clicked on
◆ How many users the ad actually pulls to the advertiser's Web site
◆ Weekly, monthly, and quarterly reports for the life of each AdCount subscription

For Web sites, AdCount also makes it possible to profitably offer advertising space on a per-inquiry or commission basis to advertisers.

Digital Planet's services provide:

- An advertising and Web site traffic analysis tool in one
- Ease of installment into host server
- Basic and advanced versions of the software
- An advertising measurement tool with some web-tracking reporting functions
- Log tracking and query capabilities
- Product that must be managed and maintained by the host and on the host's server

For updated information contact:

Digital Planet
310-287-3636
3555 Hayden Ave.
Culver City, CA 90232
http//.www@digiplanet.com

Becoming a CyberCash Merchant

CyberCash's Secure Internet Payment Service enables merchants to provide their customers with an on-line payment mechanism. It does this by extending the point-of-sale (POS) paradigm to on-line transactions, with fees that are competitive with those of existing in-store electronic payment systems.

Like today's automated POS systems, the CyberCash system represents a front end to the existing infrastructure of financial networks, banks, and payment processors. Unlike physical POS systems, Cyber-Cash substitutes an on-line payment mechanism for an in-store payment (e.g., card-swipe) terminal. Thus, to meet the needs of Internet merchants and their customers, the CyberCash system is:

- *Universal*—Any consumer with a valid credit card can take advantage of the CyberCash system to make payments via that card to any certified CyberCash merchant *without any prior relationship.* In addition, the consumer can pay for low-value transactions using the electronic coin payment option.

- *Convenient*—Consumer/merchant transactions are performed on-line and are typically concluded in less than 20 seconds.

- *Automated*—Hands-off, lights-out operations are supported to meet the needs of continuous around-the-clock commerce.

- *Secure*—Credit card information is automatically encrypted using highly secure 1,024-bit public-key encryption technology.

◆ *Exportable*—The CyberCash system is usable around the world and approved for export by the U.S. government.

How the CyberCash System Works

The CyberCash system maintains the metaphors of physical payment: consumer wallets, merchant cash registers, and gateways to private payment networks. The main components are:

◆ The CyberCash Wallet, which is distributed free to consumers
◆ The Secure CyberCash CashRegister for cybermerchants
◆ CyberCash Gateway Servers linking to existing financial networks

CyberCash Wallet: Universal Payment in Cyberspace

The CyberCash Wallet is software that resides on the consumer's personal computer (Microsoft Windows or Macintosh-based) to enable secure Internet payment. It's universally available—the software can be downloaded *free of charge* at any time from the CyberCash Web site or from merchant sites at the time of a purchase. Anyone can download the Wallet. It is also distributed on a private-label basis by such companies as CompuServe and Checkfree, bundled with many popular Web browsers, and included on CD-ROMs that are often packaged with popular Internet books or given away at major trade shows.

Once the software is installed, the CyberCash Wallet will work with all leading Web browsers to connect to merchant Web sites. During the brief installation process, the consumer establishes a CyberCash Wallet ID and links or "binds" existing (and new) credit cards to this ID for authentication purposes. A consumer's credit card numbers are stored only in the Wallet, not at the merchant's server and not by CyberCash.

Then, just like a customer opening a real wallet in a physical store, the CyberCash Wallet presents a choice of payment instruments—credit cards and coins today, debit cards/electronic checks by mid-1997. To make a payment, the consumer simply clicks on the CyberCash **Pay** button displayed on a merchant's Web page. This automatically "opens" the CyberCash Wallet.

Secure Merchant CashRegister: Automated POS in Cyberspace

The Secure Merchant CashRegister is a software package distributed by CyberCash to merchants, either via their banks or by downloading the software from CyberCash's Web site: www.cybercash.com. The Cyber-Cash CashRegister (CCCR) resides on the merchant's Web server, interfacing with a customer's CyberCash Wallet on the front end (once the **Pay** button is clicked) and with CyberCash Gateway Servers on the back end.

In effect, the CashRegister assumes the familiar role of a merchant's electronic cash register/POS system for Internet transactions by:

- Authorizing transactions
- Providing electronic receipts
- Handling voids and returns

Besides enabling secure credit card processing, the CCCR provides merchants with important administrative functions, including manual card processing, transaction status checking, and database functions to support balancing, accounting, and inventory.

The CashRegister also allows merchants to process credit card payments for toll-free-number telephone orders as well as faxed and E-mailed orders. This means that a single program can handle all of a merchant's "card-not-present" transactions. The CashRegister software is designed to:

- Handle multiple concurrent payment transactions as a merchant's business expands
- Easily integrate with merchant Web sites, meaning that merchants' applications don't have to be shoehorned into an inflexible framework
- Support multiple on-line stores

CyberCash Gateway Server: Bridging the Internet and the Banking World

CyberCash Gateway Servers are the software and hardware platforms operated today by CyberCash to provide the secure link between merchants and (1) their customers residing on the Internet and (2) their banks, which use existing financial payment networks. From a bank's point of view, CyberCash transactions arrive looking and behaving exactly like traditional POS terminal transactions.

CyberCash Gateway Servers provide: firewall protection, message translation between Internet and financial network protocols, the maintenance and authentication of CyberCash Wallet IDs, merchant-originated charges (toll-free-number, fax, or E-mail orders), and comprehensive message tracking.

Credit Transactions

Following a Credit Transaction

The following tracks the customer and merchant flow through a typical credit card transaction, automated from end to end, and taking 15 to 20 seconds to complete.

Shopping on the Internet

1. A customer visits your Web site using standard Web browser software and fills a shopping cart.
2. You exchange details on addresses, delivery, and final price, all on-line.
3. Your Web server then displays the CyberCash **Pay** button to the customer.

Initiating a Transaction

1. The customer clicks on the **Pay** button, prompting your Web server to send an electronic invoice.
2. The customer's CyberCash Wallet automatically opens, allowing the customer to select a payment instrument.
3. An encrypted charge payment message is then sent to your Web server.
4. When your CashRegister software receives the payment message, it adds your merchant identification information.
5. The payment request is then forwarded to the CyberCash Gateway Server.

Through the Gateway to the Bank

1. The CyberCash Gateway Server decrypts the message and authenticates (a) your customer's CyberCash Wallet and (b) you as a valid merchant.
2. A message is then sent (using secure, private financial networks) to your bank or its authorized processing center to request charge approval.

Your Bank Responds

1. Once the request is processed, a positive or negative response is sent back to your server and on to your customer.
2. If positive, your server receives a digital receipt. If negative, your customer can select an alternative payment option so you don't necessarily lose the sale.

Transaction Complete and Captured

To complete the transaction, your server sends your customer a digital receipt. A transaction can be captured and posted to your account while your customer is still on-line or later if you cannot ship the purchased product immediately (mail-order regulations state that charges cannot be posted until merchandise is shipped). The CyberCash system supports host- and/or terminal-based capture (along with a full complement of exception-handling capabilities for either method), depending on your individual bank's systems.

Just as in the physical world, once a transaction has been captured, your CashRegister software allows it to be voided on the same day. Returns are supported at any time.

Housekeeping

On the customer end, all CyberCash transactions are automatically added to a log contained within his or her CyberCash Wallet. On the merchant end, all transactions are added along with all system actions into a transaction log (a series of databases) within the merchant's CashRegister. Transactions can be searched for and displayed individually or grouped by card types (MasterCard, VISA, AMEX, and so on). The ability to query the bank for additional information is also provided.

The transaction records in this database are kept encrypted and only made available under password control in the event of a chargeback or some other exception item event. This further protects the merchant, its consumers, and its bank from a merchant server being compromised.

Security Details

CyberCash transactions use protected encryption, combining DES private-key and RSA public-key encryption technologies. In fact, Cyber-Cash's 1,024-bit RSA key encryption capability is unique in that it is the most powerful encryption technology currently licensed by the U.S. government for export. The greater the number of bits used by an encryption algorithm, the more difficult it is to unscramble or crack.

SET and New Security Initiatives

In addition, CyberCash is committed to complying with standardized security initiatives for Internet commerce as they evolve and are deployed. This includes the Secure Electronic Transaction (SET) specification defined by VISA and MasterCard.

Combining DES and RSA Encryption

Messages between the Wallet, the merchant, and the CyberCash Gateway Server are all encrypted by industry-standard 56-bit DES technology. The DES key itself is encrypted by RSA technology and appended to the DES-encrypted message.

RSA encryption uses a key pair, one private and one public. One is for coding; the other is for decoding. Only the public key is transmitted over the Internet, thus making an RSA-encrypted message much more difficult to compromise.

RSA encryption supports the use of digital signatures. A digital signature is simply an electronic identifier that can be created and encrypted only by the sender's private key, but which can be read by any receiver's public key. The CyberCash system uses these digital signatures to verify the senders of messages to support the all-important authentication process as well as nonrepudiation of charges.

Additional Payment Options

In addition to credit cards, the CyberCash system supports micropayments in the form of electronic coin and electronic checks. These options will be downloadable to the CyberCash Wallet.

Merchants can avail themselves of these alternatives for payment of goods, services, or information in situations where a credit card is not feasible or cost effective. For example, pages of information or digital images can be sold in 25¢ to $5 increments and paid for by electronic cash. This kind of low-value but high-volume sale is expected to proliferate widely on the Internet once such a viable payment medium is available.

Additionally, because these types of payment will be secured by real money residing in a customer's bank (as opposed to an extension of credit), consumers with insufficient credit can still be sold goods and services without risk to the merchant. In fact, electronic checks will present less risk to merchants than paper checks (like a debit transaction—if there are no funds present, there is no transaction), and electronic cash will be more difficult to counterfeit than paper currency.

Getting Started with CyberCash

To begin benefiting from secure Internet payment transactions, merchants need to progress along two parallel paths that will quickly converge:

- ◆ Setting up a Web or other commercial on-line presence
- ◆ Working with a bank to become a certified CyberCash merchant

All leading credit card processors (sometimes referred to by banks as *service bureaus*) have certified the CyberCash system for use by their bank clientele and their bank's merchants. These include Global Payment Systems (MAPP/NDC), VISA/Vital, American Express, Wells Fargo Bank, Checkfree, First Data Corporation (Envoy, CES, NaBANCO, and FDR), and NOVA.

As these processors service the vast majority of banks in North America, a merchant's existing bank is usually its leading candidate to help implement and support the CyberCash payment solution. A list of banks that have certified the CyberCash system can be found at the CyberCash Web site.

Getting on the Web

If a merchant does not already have a Web storefront, the first steps revolve around creating one. While CyberCash does not actively involve itself in this process, the company has partnered with leading third-party Web integrators that can help a merchant implement the CyberCash system, as well get up on the Internet in the first place, with applications for product display and ordering.

The CyberCash system is designed to easily integrate with these applications—either new or existing—so merchants do not have to shoehorn their operations into an inflexible payment infrastructure. CyberCash is also compatible with all leading Web server operating systems, including BSDI, SunOS, Solaris, Windows NT, HP-UX, SGI Indy, and LINUX. The system also works with all major firewalls.

All the Way to the Bank

Concurrently with building or modifying a Web site, a merchant needs to contact his or her bank to become an authorized CyberCash merchant.

The types of products being sold in cyberspace are diverse, ranging from physical goods to on-line deliverable information and services. What a merchant delivers, and how and when it is done, has a large bearing on the type of payment instruments that customers will most often employ, as well as on how payments are captured and settled. For example, sellers of information will likely find their customers using electronic cash, while larger-ticket items will probably continue to be paid for by credit cards in most cases. Also, if you are dealing with goods that will not ship immediately, then you cannot by law post the charge to your account until the shipment is made.

Banks can help merchants sort through these and other issues and deploy appropriate processing and settlement solutions in concert with CyberCash.

Typical Setup Procedure

Once a bank certifies a merchant for on-line commerce, the bank will typically:

- ◆ Issue a merchant TID (a terminal ID of the same type issued to a physical merchant's POS terminals).
- ◆ Establish the TID with its credit card processor or service bureau.
- ◆ Communicate the TID to the merchant.

The merchant meanwhile integrates the CyberCash CashRegister module into a new or existing Web server application. The bank communicates the TID to CyberCash so the merchant can begin accepting secure credit card payments via the CyberCash system.

Promoting Secure On-line Payments

The commercial on-line sites that provide a convenient and trusted payment environment to as wide a portion of this audience as possible obviously possess a competitive advantage—an advantage akin to that enjoyed by retail stores, restaurants, and so on that display MasterCard, VISA, and AMEX stickers in their shop windows. The advantage is actually greater in cyberspace because there are so few viable payment options.

The CyberCash system is designed to be as universal as possible:

- ◆ The Wallet software is free and works with any Web browser.
- ◆ Anyone surfing the Web can download it at anytime from the CyberCash Web site, merchant Web sites at the time of sale, CompuServe, and more.
- ◆ No prior relationship with either a merchant or CyberCash is necessary to use the Wallet.
- ◆ Electronic check and electronic cash will soon be added to the credit card payment option.

♦ CyberCash's powerful encryption techniques are unique in having been licensed by the U.S. government for export.

The result is the Internet's largest ready-made pool of customers. Authorized merchants typically place the CyberCash logo in their sites' shopping pages, the same way physical sites do credit card stickers—to assure customers that their payments will be fast, easy, and secure.

APPENDIX C

BECOMING A FIRST VIRTUAL MERCHANT

The First Virtual Internet payment service was introduced on October 15, 1994. Since then, First Virtual has signed on over 2,000 merchants operating in various countries and has over 100,000 consumers who have registered with the system.

First Virtual's system differs in many ways from all other proposed approaches to Internet commerce, most notably in the fact that it does not rely on encryption or any other form of cryptography to ensure the safety of its commercial transactions. Instead, safety is ensured by enforcing a dichotomy between nonsensitive information (which may travel over the Internet) and sensitive information (which never does travel over the Internet), and by a buyer feedback mechanism built atop existing protocols.

First Virtual's payment system is built on top of the preexisting Internet protocols, notably the SMTP/RFC822/MIME (E-mail), telnet, finger, ftp (file transfer), and HTTP (Web) protocols. Because those protocols are insecure in the sense that they carry no strong proofs of identity, First Virtual has found it necessary to design a payment system based on E-mail callbacks.

How the First Virtual System Works

In the First Virtual system, a buyer and seller may meet and decide to transact business in any manner they desire. While this often occurs when a buyer browses a seller's Web page, it also frequently happens by E-mail, ftp, Internet Relay Chat, or even off-net entirely, and it could easily happen in the future via protocols that do not exist today. Once the buyer and the seller have an intent to do business, they submit a transaction to First Virtual. That transaction can be submitted via standard E-mail or via a new protocol, SMXP, designed by First Virtual for real-time exchange of MIME (E-mail) objects.

When First Virtual is asked to process a financial transaction, it looks up the buyer's account identifier in its database and finds the buyer's electronic mail address of record. An E-mail message is dispatched to the buyer, asking the buyer to confirm the validity of the transaction and a commitment to pay, to which the buyer can respond with a simple answer of "yes," "no," or "fraud." Only when the buyer says "yes" is a real-world financial transaction actually initiated. Simple attacks based on Internet "sniffing" are rendered unappealing because their value is sharply limited by the fact that First Virtual IDs are not useful off the net and require E-mail confirmation for use on the net. More sophisticated attacks require criminals to break into the victim's computer account and monitor the victim's incoming mail, a crime that is much more easily traced. It is also worth noting that such a break-in would also probably yield access to the victim's encryption keys in any commerce schemes that make use of public-key cryptography for encryption.

In First Virtual's system, the valuable financial tokens that underlie commerce—notably credit card numbers and bank account information—never appear on the Internet at all. Instead, they are obtained by First Virtual when the customer enrolls as a First Virtual buyer, a procedure that involves an off-Internet step for the most sensitive information. Currently, the sensitive information is provided by either an automated telephone call (for buyers to provide their credit card numbers) or by postal mail (for sellers to provide their bank account information). However, it would also be possible to provide the VirtualPINs automatically en masse to buyers, for example, by direct mailing from the credit card issuers, as is done with traditional ATM PINs.

The exclusion of the most valuable (to criminals) information from the Internet data stream eliminates any need for encryption, which in turn eliminates the need for any nonstandard software on the buyer's end. Ordinary E-mail, which effectively represents the lowest common denominator of Internet connectivity, is all that anyone needs in order to participate. The simplicity of this approach gained First Virtual more than a year's head start in the marketplace over the encryption-based approaches and greatly lowered the entry barrier to anyone wishing to become a First Virtual user.

Buying and Selling Information with First Virtual

First Virtual transfers products and payment between information buyers and sellers. There are several parties that are involved in a First Virtual transaction:

First Virtual

- A financial service that transfers payments from buyers to sellers, and keeps track of accounts
- An archive service that stores information products for potential buyers to browse and review
- A delivery service that transfers information products from sellers to buyers

InfoMerchant

- A person or entity making an information product available for sale over the Internet, and/or advertising or promoting it
- A large corporation or organization, small business, individual, or family
- The bearer of payment risk associated with First Virtual transactions

InfoConsumer

- A person or entity purchasing information over the Internet
- A large corporation or organization, small business, individual, or family
- A consumer entitled to evaluate information before deciding whether to buy it
- A party responsible for paying for information that is found to be valuable

VirtualPIN Security

The FV Internet Payment System uses a VirtualPIN to provide the first safe link to the world of credit cards, banks, processing agents, and the Internet. The system features a secure line that separates buy-sell transactions on the Internet from secure banking transactions and financial operations done off the net. Customers simply register with FV and make on-line purchases from participating merchants using their VirtualPIN above the line. All transactions are confirmed with the buyers via E-mail before being posted below the line to the credit card networks over separate, secure, dedicated lines that are not accessible from the Internet.

Using FV PINcryption, credit card numbers are never sent over the Internet or typed into a computer connected to the Internet, thereby eliminating the need for encryption and significantly reducing the potential for fraud.

Accepting First Virtual Payments at Your Virtual Store

In order to become a seller, you need:

◆ A private E-mail account
◆ A bank account that accepts direct deposit via the U.S. Automated Clearinghouse (ACH) system

Getting Your VirtualPIN (Account ID) as a Seller

In order to sell with First Virtual, you need a Seller's VirtualPIN (account ID), which will identify you within transactions. Follow these steps:

1. Complete an application.
2. Send a check to First Virtual. The address will be included in the E-mail confirmation message sent to you after you complete your application. The check must be from the account you want your proceeds deposited into. The routing/transit

numbers and account information on this check should tell First Virtual where to deposit the funds.

3. First Virtual will send you an E-mail message when your seller's account has been activated (this generally takes 10 business days). The message will contain your seller's VirtualPIN (account ID), which you will need to build a storefront on the InfoHaus or to submit transactions to First Virtual for settlement if you make sales on your own server.

A seller may have as many VirtualPINs as desired. You can activate a VirtualPIN for selling, buying, or both, depending on your planned use. To operate a store on the First Virtual InfoHaus (our on-line mall for information products), you must either activate your VirtualPIN for both buying and selling or get two separate buying and selling VirtualPINs. This is because, while you sell, you are also buying your space on the InfoHaus.

If you operate your own server, you can set up your store there. If not, you can sell information products on the InfoHaus, First Virtual's on-line mall.

Setting Up a Storefront on Your Own Server

If you already operate your own Internet servers, you can make them compatible with First Virtual. FV's protocols are specified and integrated into almost any existing Internet application, including the World Wide Web and ftp.

A wide variety of free software for sellers is available from First Virtual, including Web CGI scripts that make it easy to collect donations and membership fees and charge for documents. This software is sufficiently customizable that it will meet the needs of most sellers. It is located at ftp://ftp.fv.com/pub/code.

If you require additional customization, you may wish to install the First Virtual API, a library of C utilities that handle tasks such as checking VirtualPINs for validity and submitting transactions. The First Virtual API is compatible with E-mail, ftp, and Web sales.

For more technical information, visit First Virtual's Web site and consult the technical index at http://www.fv.com/tech/, or download the technical documentation available at ftp://ftp.fv.com/pub/docs.

Becoming an InfoHaus Merchant

Information sellers who don't wish to go to the trouble and expense of maintaining their own Internet servers can open a store on First Virtual's InfoHaus, the on-line mall for information products.

Any First Virtual seller may become an InfoHaus information seller by activating a VirtualPIN for buying and selling and then sending a new seller request to the InfoHaus by E-mail or telnet.

Using simple procedures, your information products are uploaded into the InfoHaus, along with a description of each product and a price. The InfoHaus automatically delivers products to any buyer who requests them and provides a VirtualPIN, and InfoHaus does the billing for the merchant.

Note: You need either a seller's VirtualPIN and a separate buyer's VirtualPIN (recommended), or a VirtualPIN activated for both buying and selling. This is because, unlike your First Virtual fees, which are deducted from your sales revenue, InfoHaus fees are billed to your credit card through your buyer-activated VirtualPIN.

Differences between HardGoods and Information Merchants in the First Virtual System

A seller of GOODS must ship all goods within 24 hours of receiving confirmation from First Virtual that the buyer said "yes" to the sale. Sellers who do otherwise face the very real risk that the buyer will chargeback the purchase.

A seller of SERVICES must complete all services to be paid for before sending an E-mail query notifying First Virtual of the transaction. Sellers who do otherwise face the very real risk that the buyer will chargeback the purchase.

Getting Paid by First Virtual

You will be paid by direct deposit into the bank account you registered with First Virtual at the time you signed up for your VirtualPIN. FV will inform you of such deposits by electronic mail at the time they happen.

(For your own protection, the mail won't mention your bank account number.)

First Virtual waits to bill a buyer's credit card until either a certain dollar threshold (for example, $10) has been reached or a certain amount of time (for example, ten days) has elapsed. If the buyer makes frequent purchases or makes purchases in large dollar amounts, the time until the buyer is billed will be relatively short.

The second factor you must understand is that your First Virtual account is not a credit card merchant account. This means that First Virtual cannot advance money to you; it will pay you for your sales only after the buyer has paid FV *and* after FV is reasonably sure that the transaction will not be subject to a chargeback. As described in the "Seller's Terms and Conditions," First Virtual will wait at least 91 days from the date it charges the buyer's credit card until it deposits the funds into your account. This 91-day hold is required so that First Virtual can protect itself against a buyer refusing to pay after First Virtual has paid you.

For more information regarding this holding period, refer to FV's "Seller's Terms and Conditions" document, which is available by sending mail to fineprint-seller@fv.com.

Chargebacks

The term *chargeback* refers to the debiting of a credit card merchant's account or the withholding of settlement funds for all or part of a particular sale. Chargebacks occur when a buyer disputes a credit card charge and refuses to pay a bill.

A buyer can request a chargeback for a variety of reasons outlined by the credit card company. These include everything from a dispute with a seller to a mistake in the arithmetic of a charge. Several examples of chargeback rules are included in the "Seller Terms and Conditions." It is important to note, however, that the chargeback rules may vary between credit card companies. Even though current credit card procedures allow sellers to dispute a chargebacks, it is important to understand that you waive that right when you become a First Virtual seller.

You must take into account your inability to contest a chargeback when selling goods and services. This is one reason that it is very important to follow the rules about shipping goods or performing services within 24 hours of sending E-mail to First Virtual that the transaction has occurred.

Checking Up on the Consumer

To do a quick manual check on a single VirtualPIN, use the FINGER command—for example, finger foobar@inquiry.card.com. The response will tell you if "foobar" is an active or invalid VirtualPIN. (inquiry.card.com ignores all spaces and punctuation in a VirtualPIN. For example, "foobar," "foo-bar," and "foo bar!!" are considered equal.)

A second way to manually validate a VirtualPIN is to send an E-mail message to inquiry@card.com and place the VirtualPIN in the Subject line of your message. The E-mail reply will tell you the state of the VirtualPIN.

For automated validation of VirtualPINs, consult the technical document, "The Simple Mime Exchange Protocol (SMXP)" (http://fv.com/pubdocs/smxp-spec.txt). This document will explain how to do an inquiry request without the delay of E-mail.

International Merchants

The First Virtual Internet Payment System is designed to be used the same way from anywhere in the world. If you have the necessary Internet access, a VISA or MasterCard credit card (for buying), and a bank account that accepts direct deposits through the U.S. ACH system, it doesn't matter what country you're in.

Currently, all prices for products are set in U.S. dollars. Also, all credit card charges, First Virtual fees, and InfoHaus fees will be calculated in U.S. dollars. This will change in the future—the First Virtual system includes support for multiple currencies and rates of exchange.

Virtual Stores That Use the First Virtual System

Merchants using the First Virtual system include Apple's QuickTime software, Reuters New Media, National Public Radio, The Washington

Weekly, Dave Farber, MacChat, Kagi Shareware, Code Bleu Jeans, and companies and individuals selling sophisticated developer software, books and marketing information, Internet navigational tips, and a variety of other digital products. First Virtual enables new, more valuable information to appear on the Internet for small amounts of money. For more information, visit www.fv.com.

BECOMING A DIGICASH MERCHANT

DigiCash

Founded in 1990, DigiCash has developed a system of electronic payment mechanisms for open, closed, and network systems that provides security and privacy. DigiCash's technology is based on patent advances in public-key cryptography developed by the company's founder and managing director, David Chaum. Leading organizations with which DigiCash has worked in technology development include MasterCard, VISA, IBM, and Siemens, as well as various European telecoms.

E-cash

E-cash is designed for secure payments from any personal computer to any other workstation, over E-mail or Internet. E-cash has the privacy of paper cash, while achieving the high security required for electronic network environments exclusively through innovations in public-key cryptography. In the past, DigiCash has pioneered such cash for chip cards and electronic wallets, always with a tamper-resistant chip for storing the value.

With E-cash, you can pay for access to a database, buy software or a newsletter by E-mail, play a computer game over the net, receive $5 owed to you by a friend, or just order a pizza.

Adapted with permission from the DigiCash Web Site, 1996.

The E-cash Concept

With the E-cash client software a customer withdraws E-cash (a form of digital money) from a bank and stores it on his or her local computer. The user can spend the digital money at any shop that accepts E-cash, without the trouble of having to open an account there first or transmit credit card numbers. Because the amount of received E-cash is equal to the value involved in the transaction, shops can instantly provide the goods or services requested. Person-to-person payments can also be performed with E-cash.

To demonstrate the ease of using E-cash, various actual transactions involving two customers, Alice and Bob, are described as follows.

Start-up and Background Operation

Once Alice starts E-cash, it runs on her PC in the background, much like a memory monitor or clock program. While E-cash is running, a small window is displayed that shows her the amount of E-cash available to spend, along with an optional toolbar that allows her to initiate various functions (see Figure D.1).

Withdrawing E-cash from the Bank

In order to use E-cash to purchase goods or services, it must first be available on the payer's hard drive, just as cash is needed in a wallet to pay for goods or services in the physical world. Withdrawing E-cash is as simple as withdrawing regular cash from an ATM. Alice simply enters the amount to be withdrawn from the bank and clicks the OK button. This amount of E-cash is then transferred to her hard drive. Figure D.2 shows the actual dialog box (version 2.1 of the actual MS Windows E-cash client is shown throughout) used to withdraw E-cash that appears when the bank icon has been clicked on the toolbar.

Figure D.1 E-cash status window.

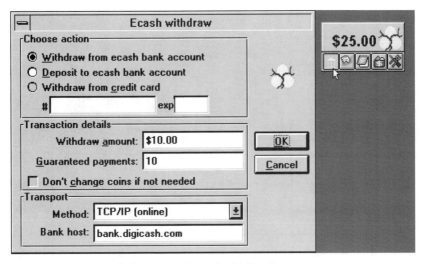

Figure D.2   Withdrawing E-cash (Alice).

Making a Payment

There are two ways to make a payment using E-cash. Alice can respond to a payment request issued by someone else or she can initiate a payment herself.

Responding to a Payment Request

Bob may send a payment request to Alice, who has asked to buy something. (Merchants' software will send such requests automatically.) For example, in the dialog box in Figure D.3, Alice is asked to make a payment of $0.02 to start a tic-tac-toe game. If she wants to make the payment, the YES button is clicked; similarly, clicking the NO button refuses the payment.

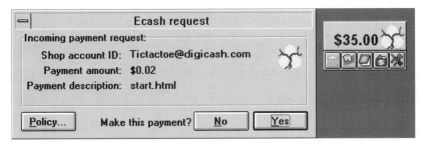

Figure D.3   Incoming payment request (Alice).

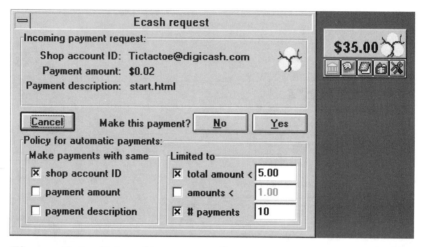

Figure D.4   Set policy to perform payment automatically (Alice).

As an ease-of-use aid, Alice may also instruct her system to respond automatically to payment requests. When the POLICY button is clicked in the window (see Figure D.3), the dialog box is extended downward, as shown in Figure D.4, and she may set the policy under which payments are to be made automatically. This simplifies certain repetitive payments.

Initiating a Payment
To make an unsolicited payment directly, Alice brings up the payment dialog box from the toolbar and fills in the blanks, much like writing a check (see Figure D.5).

Receiving E-cash
When Alice pays Bob, he has the option of depositing E-cash into the bank or retaining it on his hard drive for future use. The dialog box shown in Figure D.6 will appear on Bob's screen.

Just as Alice could set a policy for automatic response to payment requests, Bob can also set a simple policy for automatic handling of incoming payments, as shown in Figure D.7.

Depositing E-cash in the Bank
E-cash can, of course, be deposited in the bank. Again, a simple dialog box is used. (See Figure D.8. Actually this is the same box shown in Figure D.2 for withdrawals.)

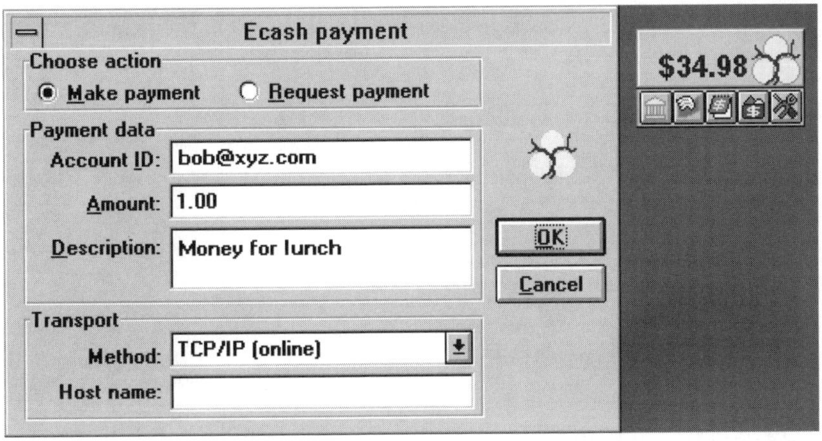

Figure D.5   Outgoing payment request (Alice).

Receipts and Records

E-cash automatically tracks withdrawals, payments, receipts, and deposits, creating various electronic statements (see Figure D.9).

How E-cash Works Inside

Overview

Like banknotes, E-cash can be withdrawn from and deposited to transaction demand deposit accounts. And like banknotes, one person can transfer possession of a given amount of E-cash to another person. But

Figure D.6   Incoming payment (Bob).

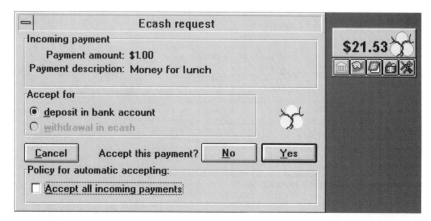

Figure D.7   Set policy to accept payment automatically (Bob).

unlike cash, during customer-to-customer transfers, banks will have an unobtrusive but essential role to play.

The following examples explain how a withdrawal works, followed by a payment to a retailer. Combining these two transactions, it is then illustrated how the system can be configured so that the customer perceives that E-cash is paid from person to person without involving any accounts.

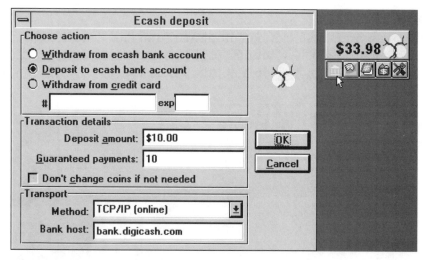

Figure D.8   Depositing E-cash (Alice).

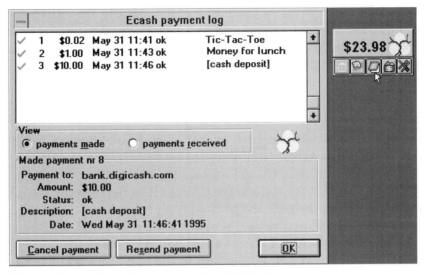

Figure D.9 E-cash payment log (Alice).

Finally, the withdrawal is explained in greater detail to illustrate the *blind signature* concept, which is the foundation of the privacy feature.

Simple Withdrawal of E-cash

Figure D.10 shows the two participants in the withdrawal transaction: the bank and customer Alice. Also shown are the digital coins that have been withdrawn from Alice's account at the bank and are on their way to her PC. When they arrive, they will be stored along with the few coins left over on her hard disk.

Although no physical coins are involved in the actual system, the messages sent include strings of digits, each string corresponding to a different digital coin. Each coin has a denomination, or value, so that a

Figure D.10 E-cash withdrawal.

portfolio of digital coins is managed automatically by Alice's E-cash software. It decides which denominations to withdraw and which to use to make particular payments. (The E-cash software contacts the bank in the rare event that change is needed before a next withdrawal, to let it restructure its portfolio of coin denominations.)

An E-cash Purchase

Now that Alice has some E-cash on her hard drive, she can buy things from Bob's shop, as shown in Figure D.11.

Once Alice has agreed, by clicking on the Payment Request dialog box shown in Figure D.3, to pay a certain amount to Bob's shop, her E-cash software chooses coins with the desired total value from the portfolio on her hard disk. Then it removes these coins from her disk and transmits them over the network to Bob's shop. When it receives the coins, Bob's software automatically sends them on to the bank and waits for acceptance before sending the electronic goods to Alice.

To assure that each coin is used only once, the bank uses the serial number of each coin to point to where it should be stored in the spent-coin database it maintains. If the coin serial number is already stored at that position, the bank has detected someone trying to spend the coin more than once and informs Bob that it is worthless. If, as is the usual case, no serial number has been recorded at that position, the bank stores it at that position and informs Bob that the coin is valid and the deposit is accepted.

Person-to-Person Cash

When a consumer receives a payment, the process could be the same. But some people may prefer that, when they receive money, it be made available on their hard disk immediately, ready for spending—just like

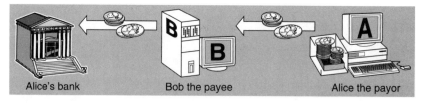

Alice's bank   Bob the payee   Alice the payor

Figure D.11   E-cash purchase.

when someone hands them a five dollar bill. This user preference can be realized as depicted in Figure D.12.

The only difference between this payment from Alice to another consumer (Cindy) and the one Alice paid to Bob's shop in Figure D.11 is what happens after the bank accepts the cash. In Figure D.12, Cindy has configured her software to request the bank to withdraw the E-cash and send it to her PC as soon as the coins are accepted. (Actually, Cindy's bank will check with Alice's bank to make sure that the coins deposited are good.) When Alice sends Cindy five dollars, that money is immediately available to spend from Cindy's PC.

How Privacy Is Protected

In the simple withdrawal shown in Figure D.10, the bank created unique blank digital coins, validated them with its special digital stamp, and supplied them to Alice. This would normally allow the bank, at least in principle, to recognize the particular coins when they are later accepted in a payment. And this would tell the bank exactly which payments were made by Alice.

However, by using blind signatures, a feature unique to E-cash, the bank can be prevented from recognizing the coins as having come from a particular account. The idea is shown in Figure D.13. Instead of the bank creating a blank coin, Alice's computer itself creates the coin at random. Then it hides the coin in a special digital envelope and sends it off to the bank. The bank withdraws the requested dollar from Alice's account and makes its special "worth one dollar" digital validating stamp on the outside of the envelope before returning it to Alice's computer.

When Alice's computer removes the envelope, it has obtained a coin of its own choice, validated by the bank's stamp. When she spends the coin, the bank must honor it and accept it as a valid payment because of the stamp. But because the bank is unable to recognize the coin, since it

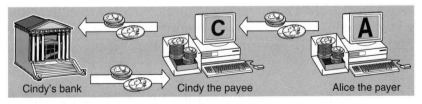

Figure D.12   Person-to-person payment.

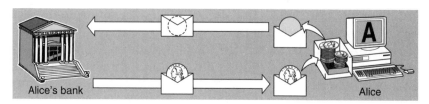

Figure D.13   Blinded withdrawal.

was hidden in the envelope when it was stamped, the bank cannot tell who made the payment. Thus the blind signature mechanism lets the validating signature be applied through the envelope. The signer can verify that it must have made the signature, but it cannot link it to a particular object signed.

How It All Works with Numbers

The coin system is a close analogy to the way the E-cash software actually works. When Alice's computer creates a blank coin, it chooses a random number. The bank's validating stamp on the coin is a public-key digital signature formed by the bank, with the random coin number serving as the message signed. Checking the validity of a coin involves the verification of the digital signature using the bank's corresponding public key. The blinding operation is a special kind of encryption that can be removed only by the party who placed it there. It commutes with the public-key digital signature process and can thus be removed without disturbing the signature.

How Funds Flow

While for the consumer E-cash is functionally equivalent to cash, to a bank its properties are somewhat different. As can be seen in the top of Figure D.14, the first step in each case occurs when an amount is removed from a customer's account. In an ATM transaction, the currency given to the consumer is a reduction in vault cash; in an E-cash withdrawal, however, the amount is moved within the bank and becomes an E-cash liability that will be reversed when the E-cash is presented for deposit.

The second step is the spending of the amount, in which respect cash and E-cash are very similar. In each case, the merchant (or other party

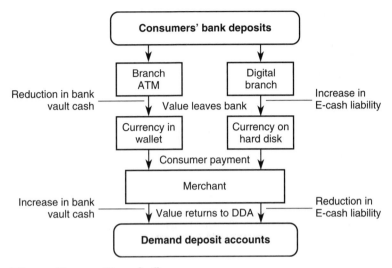

Figure D.14   E-cash flow.

receiving it) has the option of accumulating or depositing it, as detailed later with reference to Figure D.15.

When the merchant takes the final step and deposits the cash, it results in an increase in vault cash. A deposit of E-cash reduces the E-cash liability and increases deposit liability.

Figure D.15 shows in more detail the difference in the actual transaction path for a cash payment and an E-cash payment, particularly when they are made from customer to customer. While the main difference is invisible to the consumer, it is necessary to protect the integrity of E-cash.

The left side of the chart in Figure D.15 shows a cash payment from Customer X, who may have originally withdrawn it, to Customer Y. The payment goes directly from X to Y's wallet, and at some later time Y has the option of either depositing the cash in the bank or using the cash to pay Customer Z. The process continues indefinitely until the cash is deposited.

The right side of the chart in Figure D.15 shows an E-cash payment from X to Y. Before the payment is accepted, Y verifies the validity of the E-cash with the issuing bank, the main step that is not necessary with cash. Customer Y chooses at this time whether to store the E-cash

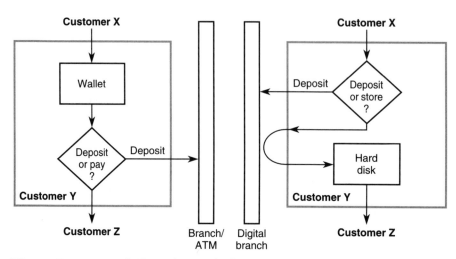

Figure D.15 Cash flow / E-cash flow.

or deposit it immediately in the bank. If Y chooses to store the E-cash, it may later be used to pay Z, and so on.

E-cash Security and Privacy

RSA (public-key) cryptography is the basis of E-cash security. It is beyond the scope of this appendix to describe all the aspects of public-key cryptography, but the following properties reflect the value of this technology:

◆ Conventional cryptographic systems use one and the same key for both encoding and decoding a message. The RSA system uses a pair of keys.

◆ A message that has been encoded with one key can be decoded only with the other key of that pair, and vice versa.

◆ From just one key, the related key can't be computed.

When executed for the first time, the E-cash software automatically generates a pair of RSA encryption keys. Every person or entity using E-cash has a unique pair of keys. One key will be kept secret (the secret key) and the other key will be made public (the public key). A party that wants to authenticate a message encrypts it with his or her own secret key; everyone can verify that that party signed this message by decoding it with the party's public key. A party that wants to send a confidential message encrypts the message with the public key of the receiver; the receiver is the only one who will be able to decode the message.

The DigiCash blinding technology introduces the privacy aspects.

How E-cash Works Inside

Every person using E-cash has an account at a digital bank on the Internet with which they can withdraw and deposit E-cash. E-cash is a coin-based system, which means that digital money is implemented by digital signatures that represent a certain fixed amount of money. We call such a digital signature a coin.

When an E-cash withdrawal is made, the PC of the user calculates how many digital coins of what denominations are needed to withdraw the requested amount. Next, random serial numbers for those coins are generated and the blinding factor is included. The result of these calculations is sent to the digital bank.

The bank encodes the blinded numbers with its secret key (digital signature) and at the same time debits the account of the client for the same amount. The authenticated coins are sent back to the user, and, finally, the user takes out the blinding factor introduced earlier. The serial numbers plus their signatures are now digital coins; their value is guaranteed by the bank.

The coins can be stored locally on the PC of the user. As soon as the user wants to make a payment, his or her PC collects the coins needed to reach the requested total value. These coins are sent to the receiver, then the receiver sends them directly to the digital bank. The bank verifies both the validity of these coins and that they have not been spent before. The account of the receiver is credited. Every coin is used only once. Another withdrawal is needed if the receiver wishes to have new coins to spend.

NETSCAPE LIVE PAYMENT: SECURE COMMERCE SERVER

Netscape LivePayment extends the Netscape development platform by providing Web sites with a point-of-sale terminal.

LivePayment makes it possible to integrate financial transactions with Web page content, enabling a whole new class of commercial Web sites. The LivePayment system provides a convenient, simple, low-cost solution for developers who want to create a Web site that executes financial transactions over the Internet, using high-grade encryption technology.

The LivePayment system allows a developer to include payment instructions directly within static or dynamic World Wide Web pages. The developer can build a Web page that prompts for a credit card account number, verifies the account, and then sends the transaction to the bank over the Internet, in much the same way that a bank card authorization system ("the little gray box") verifies and charges a bank card in a manual transaction through a conventional retailer.

Figure E.1 shows the model for electronic commerce over the Internet. Using Netscape LivePayment, on-line merchants can display their wares using Web pages that consumers access over the Internet with a standard Web browser. Consumers select goods or services to purchase and provide payment information to merchants. The merchants transmit the payment information over the Internet to their banking institutions, which in turn process the charges.

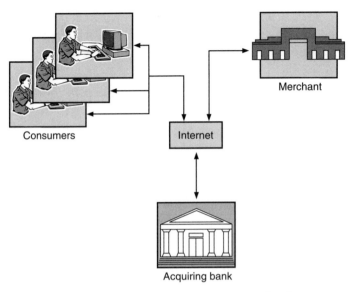

Figure E.1   Electronic commerce over the Internet.

The LivePayment product consists of a payment processor, a set of LiveWire commands, a set of utility commands, and an administrative interface. The product works in concert with the Netscape Enterprise Server and the LiveWire development environment. These tools make it simple to set up a Web site that accepts credit card payments.

LiveWire is an on-line development environment that lets an application developer build interactive Web pages. LiveWire provides extensions to the Netscape HTTP server that executes JavaScript statements embedded in HTML documents. LivePayment provides a set of additional LiveWire objects specifically for handling on-line electronic payments from Web pages. LivePayment also provides utility commands that perform the same transactions as do the LiveWire objects, but can be used from other development environments.

LivePayment Benefits

LivePayment provides a number of benefits for a business planning to build an on-line commerce system:

♦ *Low-cost solution.* LivePayment provides a low-cost solution for Internet commerce applications. Not only is the Live-Payment product itself very economical, but it eliminates many of the barriers to entry for electronic commerce.

> Sample applications reduce time and costs in developing on-line applications.

> Netscape's established relationships with financial institutions simplify setting up a banking relationship with an institution that can support electronic commerce.

> LivePayment's support for standard client interfaces means applications can be available to a large number of potential customers while allowing a wide choice of browsers.

♦ *Instant payments.* LivePayment features immediate payment. An application can verify a customer's ability to pay and transmit charges to the bank (known as *capturing payment*) as soon as the service is performed or the product is shipped.

♦ *Internet-based communication to banking network.* Communication with the merchant's credit card processing institution (known as an *Acquirer*) is done over the Internet, providing a flexible and low-cost method for transmitting transactions. This eliminates the need for dial-up modems or leased lines.

♦ *Simple development.* Writing an electronic commerce application using LivePayment is simple. A developer embeds JavaScript statements in HTML Web pages to send requests to the LivePayment Card Processor, which then handles all the communications with the acquiring bank (the card processing institution).

> Figure E.2 shows a simple Web page used for store checkout and the associated JavaScript code that executes the checkout process transaction logic. The line that begins with "processor.authorize . . ." is the request to the LivePayment card processor to authorize the transaction with the Acquirer.

♦ *Portability and platform independence.* LivePayment runs on Unix platforms and Windows NT, so the developer can implement an application on a variety of server types. The use

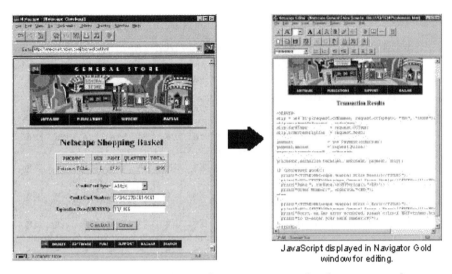

Figure E.2 LivePayment application example showing Web page and associated JavaScript code. The JavaScript is displayed in a Netscape Navigator Gold window on the right for editing.

of Java and JavaScript means the application is portable across a wide set of servers and is highly extensible.

◆ *Security.* LivePayment information travels over the Internet using a secure transfer protocol: Secure Sockets Layer (SSL). SSL uses public-private-key encryption, which in turn relies on authenticated security certificates. For the merchant, one step in setting up a commerce system is to obtain an authenticated security certificate that enables mutual authentication between merchant and Acquirer. The SET protocol provides a higher level of security between merchant and Acquirer, and between merchant and consumer.

Uses of LivePayment

LivePayment is extremely versatile. It can be used in a variety of innovative ways by businesses of all types and sizes.

Hard Goods

Small retailers can quickly set up Web sites to display their goods and to accept and process orders. Using LivePayment's sample application, they can easily set up small databases for their goods and build Web sites that include on-line catalogs as well as interfaces that allow consumers to order products. The benefit of Web sites for small retailers is that they provide national or even international reach at a fraction of the cost of a traditional mail-order operation.

For large retailers, LivePayment can integrate into merchants' existing order processing or inventory databases. It also allows developers to have a great deal of control over the content—the look and feel of the Web site—to provide an interactive, dynamic, and unique appearance.

Soft Goods

LivePayment provides significant benefits for merchants who deliver their goods and services on-line—such as distribution of software or on-line information services that charge for content.

Online Publishing

LivePayment enables an on-line publisher to collect fees for electronic content using a variety of payment models. For example, an application might levy a subscription fee and then aggregate usage fees. It could also charge by time (by the minute or hour) or by the item accessed. In the future, LivePayment will also allow microtransactions—charges of very small amounts.

Software Publishing

LivePayment makes it possible to verify a consumer's credit, deliver the products, and collect the payment, all on-line over the Internet. This reduces the risk for the merchant, while allowing customers to receive the products they've ordered immediately, rather than having to wait for an off-line process to verify and process payments.

Services

For service providers, on-line systems can supply a high level of responsiveness to customers while reducing overhead costs.

Food Services

A food delivery service, such as for a grocery chain or restaurant, could provide an on-line system for placing orders and scheduling delivery. LivePayment lets the merchant receive payment immediately, before the product is prepared and delivered.

Reservation Services

For airlines and hotels, a system that lets consumers make reservations directly can yield significant customer service cost savings. The ability to verify and charge the consumer immediately saves processing time and helps reduce losses.

Credit Card Processing Overview

Making purchases over the Internet involves three parties: the consumer or credit card holder, the merchant who is offering products or services for sale, and the financial institution that processes credit card payments and is known as the Acquirer. Indirectly, there are two other parties involved: the bank that has issued the consumer's bank card and the merchant bank where the merchant's account resides.

The consumer interacts with the merchant's Web site using a Web browser, such as Netscape Navigator. In order to make credit card purchases, the consumer must obtain a bank card from an Issuer bank and provide bank card information to the merchant applications when he or she decides to make a purchase.

The merchant develops the commerce application that makes goods and services available for sale. In order to accept credit card payments, the merchant must have an established relationship with a Merchant bank and an Acquirer.

The Acquirer is the financial institution that operates the payment gateway used to accept transactions from merchants on the Internet on behalf of Merchant banks. The Acquirer and the Merchant bank can be the same institution or they can be separate institutions.

The Issuer bank is the bank that issued the bank card to the consumer. The Merchant bank is the bank at which the merchant's account is established. The Merchant bank may also function as the Acquirer, or it may designate another financial institution to function as Acquirer on its behalf.

The process of handling a transaction using LivePayment is shown in Figure E.3, and proceeds as follows:

1. When the consumer decides to buy something, the Web application prompts the consumer for credit card information, usually along with other information such as shipping address.

2. The consumer may enter payment information into either an SSL-secured form or an SET-compliant application, such as Netscape Navigator. If using the secured form, the payment information is sent to the merchant protected using SSL. Under SET, credit card information is enclosed in a *slip*. A slip is an encrypted, electronic analogy to a paper credit card slip. The slip is then sent to the merchant.

3. The merchant sends the slip to the credit card Acquirer for authorization (first creating a slip, if necessary) via the Live-Payment card processor.

4. The Acquirer responds either with an authorization for a certain amount of money or a refusal of the transaction.

5. Assuming the transaction is authorized, a *capture* takes the information from the successful authorization and charges the authorized amount of money to the credit card. Because the merchant should not capture until the ordered goods can be shipped, there may be a time lag between the authorization and the capture.

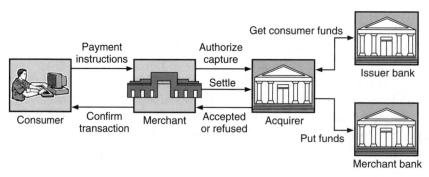

Figure E.3   Netscape payment process overview.

6. If a customer returns goods or cancels an order, the merchant generates a *credit* for the customer.

7. The final step is to *settle* the transactions between the merchant and the Acquirer. Captures and credits usually accumulate into a *batch* and are settled as a group. This step effectively confirms all the transactions.

8. At settlement, the Acquirer begins the transfer of money from the consumer accounts at various Issuer banks, to the merchant's account at Merchant banks.

LivePayment Architecture

LivePayment provides a Card Processor module that routes financial information to the Acquirer over the Internet using a secure transport protocol and receives replies from the Acquirer. It also provides a set of JavaScript objects for use in a LiveWire application.

A LiveWire/LivePayment application is a Web page with embedded LiveWire JavaScript code. The JavaScript code is processed and interpreted by LiveWire, which generates Web page content based on the JavaScript. Figure E.4 shows the components of a LivePayment application.

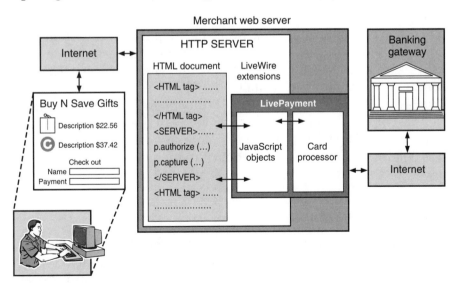

Figure E.4   Netscape LivePayment architecture.

The application designer typically designs a Web page, using Java-Script and LiveWire, that presents goods or services to the consumer and lets the consumer select items for purchase. The consumer interacts with the application using a Web browser. When he or she is ready to complete the purchase, the Web page prompts for the transaction information: name, shipping address, and credit card account information.

The consumer provides his or her payment information directly in response to the Web page prompts. The information is then transferred via SSL or within an encrypted and signed slip using the SET protocol. The Netscape HTTP server receives the information from the browser and passes it to the LiveWire server extensions. If the consumer's payment information is not already contained in a slip, the LiveWire JavaScript code puts it into one. The slip is one of the LivePayment JavaScript objects, and is used to communicate payment information to the Card Processor.

When the LiveWire application has set up the consumer's payment information, it sends it to the Card Processor as part of a request for an authorization, capture, or credit action. The Card Processor handles the actual transactions with the acquiring bank. It transparently maintains the Internet link to the banking network. The Card Processor communicates with the Acquirer's gateway using the SSL protocols and also uses certificates for mutual authentication between the merchant and the Acquirer.

When it receives results back from the Acquirer (transaction authorized or refused, capture succeeded, etc.), it communicates these back to the LiveWire application through the LivePayment objects. The application, in turn, can communicate the results back to the consumer.

LivePayment also provides a set of utility commands that can be used from a CGI or shell script to communicate with the Card Processor. The utility commands perform the same functions as the LivePayment Java-Script objects and allow LivePayment functions to be used from other types of code modules.

Administration Modules

LivePayment includes an administrative interface that is used to set up and administer the LivePayment environment. This includes configuration and administration of the merchant, terminal, and Card Processor parameters, as well as administration of the LiveWire applications running on the Web server.

Developing Applications with LivePayment

To create an application with LivePayment, the developer uses the LiveWire development environment to build a Web page that includes embedded, server-executed JavaScript code. Server-executed JavaScript code is embedded in an HTML document using the HTML <SERVER> and </SERVER> tags.

The Web page typically will provide a way for consumers to select the items they wish to purchase. For example, the developer may use LiveWire embedded-SQL capabilities to get information from a database that contains product information and then dynamically create a Web page to display those items.

The application may also need to keep information about consumers and their behavior and preferences. The developer can use LiveWire state management features to track the state of the consumer's shopping cart and remember what items the consumer is purchasing. The developer may also want to track the consumer's shopping flow and, based on this information, customize pages the shopper sees. For example, the application could display other items related to those the shopper has already chosen or present special promotions based on the consumer's choices.

The developer also needs to design or extend a database to keep slip and payment information and information received from the Acquirer about the consumer transactions.

LivePayment includes a set of sample applications that the developer can use or modify to quickly implement the payment portions of an application. The key steps that the LivePayment portion of the application performs are:

- It creates the appropriate LivePayment objects needed to communicate to the Card Processor and manage the transactions.
- It obtains payment information from the consumer.
- It creates a Slip object for the consumer's payment information and encode it for security.

- It authorizes the payment. This is done using the *authorize* method on the Processor object and causes the Card Processor to ask the Acquirer to authorize the transaction.

  Depending on the circumstances, the authorization step can authorize the actual payment amount or just verify the validity of the credit card account and authorize for the payment amount at a later time.

- When the authorization has been completed, the application can capture the payment. For soft goods such as software or information that is delivered online, the capture can be done immediately, along with the authorization. For hard goods, the capture must be done later, after the goods have been shipped.

- If customers return products or change their minds after payments have been captured, the application can request credits to the accounts.

- Payments are settled in batches. The batch settlement operation reconciles the transactions between the merchant and the Acquirer and requests that the Acquirer actually transfer money from consumers' accounts to the merchant's account. It also performs a verification to make sure the merchant and the Acquirer agree on the number and value of the transactions that have occurred.

Testing the Application

Initial development of a LivePayment application can be done without actually communicating with the Acquirer. The LivePayment system has three modes:

- *LoopBack Mode.* This mode uses default values for the merchant and terminal IDs, security certificates, gateway host, and port. This mode allows the developer to debug and test the Web pages without engaging in any actual transactions.

- *Test Mode.* This mode is used to test the link to the Acquirer. This mode uses temporary IDs and a test gateway. It does require a security certificate. In this mode, the developer can

LiveWire Pro Development Environment

Netscape LiveWire provides an integrated, visual environment that enables content providers to easily build and manage next-generation live applications and content for enterprise networks and the Internet. The LiveWire environment and the JavaScript language together enable the features needed for on-line applications.

♦ LiveWire server extensions include a run-time/interpreter for executing scripts, and the ability to add and update Web pages either locally or remotely. LiveWire extensions are designed to snap into the Netscape Server Application Programming Interface (API).

♦ JavaScript is an easy-to-use object scripting language designed for creating live, on-line applications that link objects and resources on both clients and servers. JavaScript is designed for use by HTML page authors and enterprise applications developers to dynamically script the behavior of objects running on either the client or the server.

♦ LiveWire allows dynamic and personal customized page generation through server execution of JavaScript embedded in HTML pages. Pages can be generated on the fly based on information retrieved from a database. Information can also be manipulated whenever a new page is requested, based on the results of specific calculations.

♦ LiveWire state management makes it easy to maintain state information, such as session information, user information, and application information. This information persists across multiple user Web accesses and can be used to personalize and customize the user's on-line experience.

Continued

- LiveWire Pro provides powerful features for database integration. LiveWire allows in-line SQL statements embedded in HTML pages for retrieving or storing information. This makes it possible for a LiveWire application to access and record information in an existing database.
- LiveWire Pro comes with a full-blown Relational Data Base Management System (RDBMS). LiveWire also supports most popular databases, including Oracle, Sybase, Informix, and ODBC drivers.

The LiveWire Development Environment also includes the following components:

- *Netscape Navigator Gold.* A WYSIWYG editor that enables easy navigation, creation, and editing of live, on-line documents and LiveWire applications.
- *LiveWire Site Manager.* A visual site management tool allowing Web sites to be modified with drag-and-drop ease, while automatically maintaining links and identifying invalid links.

test the application's ability to send and receive information through the gateway and perform transactions. However, no actual transactions are performed. Once the application is certified by the Acquirer, the system can be run in production mode.

- *Production Mode.* This is the fully functional mode, using permanent merchant and terminal IDs and the production gateway to the Acquirer.

Security Features

The Netscape LivePayment system uses high-grade encryption technology.

Consumer-to-Merchant Link

The customer uses a Web browser, such as Netscape Navigator, that supports the Secure Sockets Layer (SSL) transport protocol to connect to the merchant's Web site. SSL protects the information being transferred from consumer to merchant using channel encryption technology. Additionally, the upcoming SET protocol will allow the consumer to create an encrypted and signed slip that contains sensitive payment information and that is only transferred through the merchant.

Merchant-to-Acquirer Link

The LivePayment processor and the Acquirer gateway use SSL's channel encryption. They also use mutual authentication features to interrogate each other's security certificates to assure that they are communicating to the correct entity. The SET consumer-generated slip information is passed through for decryption at the Acquirer gateway.

Netscape is actively involved in the definition of the Secure Electronic Transaction (SET) specification being developed by VISA and MasterCard. Once the SET protocol is implemented, Netscape will use SET throughout the payment system to provide a higher grade of security. This will include enabling the client (the consumer interface) to encrypt the payment slip using the Acquirer's security certificate and allowing the consumer to "sign" the slip using a certificate-based digital signature.

Developing a Complete On-line Store with LiveWire and LivePayment

Many small retail businesses want to expand their reach beyond their immediate geographic area but do not have the resources to undertake a full-blown mail-order catalog operation. An on-line store application allows businesses like these to reach and service a wider audience without the expense of a mail-order operation.

The LiveWire/LivePayment application (Web pages) will need to perform the following functions to implement an on-line commercial application for a small business—in this case, a small manufacturer of

MasterCard and VISA's SET Efforts

In response to the demand for electronic commerce, MasterCard, VISA, and a small group of key technology partners, including Netscape, are jointly developing the Secure Electronic Transaction (SET) protocol as a method to secure credit card transactions over open networks.

SET is being published as an open specification for the industry. The specification is currently in a public comment review phase. The specifications are available to be applied to any credit card payment service, and may be used by software vendors to develop applications.

SET will support electronic payment systems that:

◆ Provide for confidential transmissions.

◆ Authenticate the parties involved.

◆ Ensure the integrity of payment instructions.

◆ Authenticate the identity of the cardholder and merchant to each other.

In an application environment, such as LivePayment, the SET specification will allow payment instructions to be encoded into a secure payment slip by the consumer/client, rather than by the merchant. This means that the consumer will not need to give credit card information to the merchant. Instead, account information will be encoded in the slip that the merchant will forward to the banking institution but will not need to access as part of the payment process.

The SET specification addresses the following requirements:

◆ *Confidentiality of information*—ensure that cardholder information is accessible only by the intended recipient. The SET specification uses message encryption to ensure confidentiality.

Continued

♦ *Integrity of data*—guarantee that message content is not altered during transmission. SET ensures data integrity with the use of digital signatures.

♦ *Cardholder account authentication*—verify that the cardholder is the legitimate user of the account. SET ensures account authentication by using digital signatures and cardholder certificates.

♦ *Merchant authentication*—confirm to cardholder that a merchant can accept bank card payments. SET uses digital signatures and merchant certificates to provide merchant authentication.

♦ *Interoperability*—ensure that any cardholder with compliant software can communicate with any merchant running compliant software. SET provides specific protocols and message formats to ensure interoperability on a variety of hardware and software platforms.

organic pet products. The business has been operating a local pet store, selling pet food products, toys, and accessories such as bedding and flea protection products.

The Web page needs to let customers select a category of product (pet food, accessories, flea products, toys) and then view product descriptions, pictures, and prices. This can be done with embedded JavaScript code that accesses the product database using a looping Select statement, also known as a *database cursor*. To implement this, the developer designs the HTML page, possibly using Netscape Navigator Gold. The developer then inserts JavaScript in-line SQL statements to select items out of the relational database.

The application also needs to implement a shopping cart capability. The shopping cart is used to remember customer selections through a series of pages all the way to a checkout page. This is necessary due to the Web's stateless environment. To implement this, the developer writes JavaScript code that creates or modifies a named object. LiveWire automatically maintains the object's state through multiple user accesses (hits). The site administrator selects whether URL arguments or cookies are used to remember the state. The developer need not be concerned with coding URL extensions or cookie-parsing routines. The LiveWire environment handles all this transparently.

The Web page needs to prompt for payment information and then perform the LivePayment functions needed to authorize the payment. The developer implements this by embedding JavaScript code to prompt for payment and to perform the LivePayment functions. Netscape provides sample applications, which can be readily used or modified to quickly implement this function.

Once the purchase is approved, the application will need to record the customer information into the customer/order processing database to generate shipping instructions. The developer implements this by embedding JavaScript SQL commands to insert or modify the appropriate information. The LiveWire environment can access a database dedicated to the Web site or an existing corporate database.

The application will also need to interrogate the order-processing database to determine what orders have been shipped. Once orders are shipped, the application can access the customer's payment information and use the LivePayment features to capture the payment. To implement this, the developer creates a Web page that interrogates the shipment database, executes a capture transaction, and records the appropriate payment results.

The LiveWire development environment provides a great deal of flexibility to implement advanced features that can make the commerce application more dynamic, interactive, and personalized for individual customers. For example, the application can provide the customer with more focused or selective sets of product displays. The pet product business might create subcategories by type of pet, price range, or type of use for the product. The developer can also create more selective product categories by developing a more sophisticated database schema and then using corresponding SQL statements in the Web page.

The application can be designed to allow instantaneous access to specific products, rather than forcing the customer to go through a product category structure. By allowing the customer to enter keywords and by using SQL keyword searches on the database, the developer can design the application to retrieve specific information on individual products.

LiveWire state management provides features that support real-time click-stream and selection analysis on the consumer's progress through the application. The application can use this information to dynamically suggest product specials, complementary products, or additional areas of interest. For example, if the customer has viewed a number of items in the "dog chew toy" category, the application could offer a special on rawhide chew bones when the customer moves to the checkout page.

LiveWire eliminates much of the complexity of implementing this type of feature by facilitating the tracking and analysis of additional state information. As these examples show, the LiveWire/LivePayment development environment provides a great deal of functionality for implementing sophisticated electronic commerce applications. The environment provides ample flexibility for implementing very disparate commerce models such as electronic publishing, retailing, or service applications.

Setting Up a Commerce System

There are a few additional steps to enabling an on-line commerce application beyond developing the application.

Establishing a Relationship with an Acquirer

In order to accept credit card transactions, the merchant needs a business relationship and an account with a bank. Additionally, the merchant needs to establish a relationship with an Acquirer that will work with the merchant's bank and the Netscape payment system.

Netscape simplifies the process of server sign-up around the world. For example, strategic alliances with major acquiring and card processing institutions such as FDC, NaBanCo, and CIS make Netscape's payment system available to the majority of merchant banks in the United States.

When the Acquirer relationship is in place, the Acquirer will provide the merchant with ID information, the host name of the bank card gateway, and port numbers for test and production gateways.

Establishing a Security Identity

To be able to activate the security features of LivePayment, merchants must obtain a certificate that uniquely identifies them to on-line consumers and banks. The LivePayment package includes the necessary administration screens to apply for this certificate from an approved Certificate Authority and to install it into the LivePayment system.

Future Directions

Future directions for LivePayment include enhanced security features based on the ongoing SET effort. LivePayment will also support additional electronic payment methods in the future such as credit cards, debit cards, electronic checks, microtransactions, and electronic cash.
    If you have any questions, please visit Customer Service.

Corporate Sales (415) 937-2555
Personal Sales (415) 937-3777
Federal Sales (415) 937-3678
Web site: www.netscape.com

APPENDIX F

THE NETSCAPE
MERCHANT SYSTEM

The Netscape Merchant System

The Netscape Merchant System provides a suite of merchandise management capabilities that facilitates on-line shopping and allows merchants to manage inventory and sales in the rapidly changing marketplace of the 1990s. It enables merchants to create new businesses or extend existing businesses without compromising manageability, scalability, or the ability to customize. Netscape Merchant System capabilities include the following:

- Product loading
- Product display
- Merchandising
- Shopping
- Transaction processing, including shipping and taxes
- Secure order delivery

As shown in Figure F.1, the Netscape Merchant System leverages the security capabilities of the Netscape Commerce Server and the ease of use of Netscape Navigator.

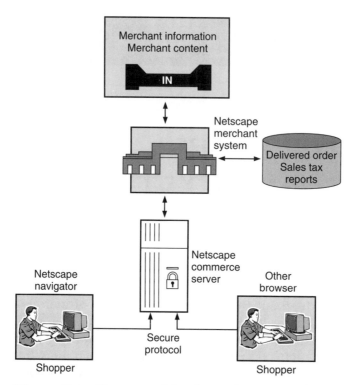

Figure F.1 Netscape Merchant System architecture.

What Is the Architecture?

Because the retail business—and the Internet—are changing so rapidly, the Netscape Merchant System has been designed to accommodate growth and changing requirements. It can be operated as a stand-alone system or integrated with existing software systems—for example, sales and order-processing systems.

An Open, Extensible System

To facilitate integration with other systems and software, the Netscape Merchant System is based on widely accepted industry standards, such as Structured Query Language (SQL) relational databases, HyperText Markup Language (HTML), HTTP, and RSA data encryption. The

Netscape Merchant System can be distributed on multiple servers, resulting in high availability, scalability to accommodate growth in volume, and security.

There are three primary components of the Netscape Merchant System: Merchant Server, Transaction Server, and Staging Server.

Merchant Server

The Merchant Server is the front-office component of the Netscape Merchant System. It offers the following features.

Automatic Product Loading

Merchandisers use the Merchant Server software to create, deliver, and update product display content. Using the automated loading program, merchandisers can load hundreds of products in a single batch. When the site administrator invokes the program, it loads the information the merchant has created into the database and places the files (HTML templates, graphics, video and sound files, and so on) into the correct locations in the Merchant Server's directory structure. The batch program loads a structured text file that contains the product data.

The Netscape Merchant System gives merchants the ability to update pages remotely for real-time display—a key benefit for mall operators and online service providers. Individual merchants maintain complete control over their product displays and the timing of updates. Merchants can transmit new files to the mall operator via file transfer protocol (ftp), E-mail, or by delivering physical media such as tape.

Automatic Content Generation

The Netscape Merchant System database program creates product pages automatically using templates. The templates are standard HTML pages with Meta Language Extensions, or MLE. MLE is a robust HTML extension that provides dynamic update capabilities, which is critical for successful on-line selling. For example, MLE can be used for price displays and price updates.

The HTML product-display templates that the merchant creates with MLE are automatically updated whenever the underlying database values are updated. For example, if the merchant updates the product price, then the HTML pages that refer to the product are automatically regenerated, reflecting the new price.

For the convenience of shoppers, the Netscape Merchant System generates two types of product pages. A *leaf* page contains summary information about multiple related products; a *bud* page contains more
detailed information about a single product.

Flexible Product Display

Merchants can also use MLE to create conditions for featuring particular
products—for example, IF walking shoes are in stock, THEN display
information on them; or IF walking shoes are not in stock, THEN display
information on running shoes. The result is that merchants can tailor
their product displays to maximize sales.

Robust Search Capabilities

Time-conscious shoppers are unwilling to navigate through thousands
of products in an on-line store or mall to find the one they want. The
Netscape Merchant System features a robust commercial search engine
that shoppers can use to quickly find individual items within any single
storefront or mall. They simply type key words—for example, "printer"
AND "high-resolution." In response, the Netscape Merchant System
generates a page with hyperlinks to all products or storefronts that meet
the conditions. The shopper simply clicks a link to view the page where
the product or storefront appears.

To enable customers to narrow their searches, the search engine supports use of Boolean operators such as AND, OR, NOT, and less than (<)
and greater than (>), and an expert mode using special commands.

The product search module consists of the following components:

◆ Interface to the text engine loader to index product pages
◆ A meta file used to index the products into the text engine
◆ Product Search Common Gateway Interface (CGI), which performs the search by retrieving product information and building the search results page

Merchants can stimulate cross-selling by defining related queries that
the search engine recognizes. For example, a shopper who searches for
entertainment centers might also be provided links to video and CD title
pages.

Shopping Basket Services

The Netscape Merchant System shopping basket service includes a mall- or storewide shopping cart that holds purchased items, allowing consumers to review or update their purchases at any time. This basket retains the unique SKUs, quantity, and attributes of each selected product. (See Figure F.2.)

The shopping basket resides locally on the shopper's browser software and is updated by the Netscape Merchant System as the

Continued

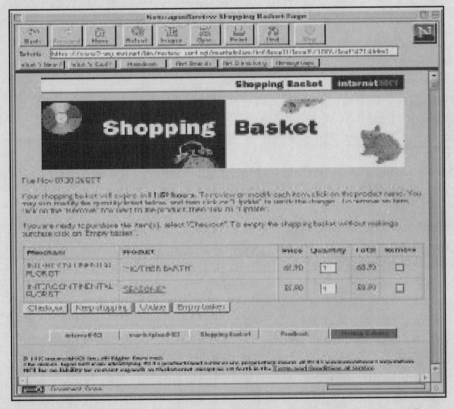

Figure F.2   The shopping basket holds information on products selected for purchase.

shopper purchases items or changes selections. Therefore, users may select products from different stores, browse elsewhere on the Internet, and resume shopping at any time without losing information on prior purchase selections stored in the shopping basket. The shopping basket supports all browsers that comply with Secure Sockets Layer (SSL) encryption standards and cookie specifications for capturing data.

When the shopper initiates checkout, the shopping basket passes all of the purchased-item information securely via HTTP to the Transaction Server module of the Netscape Merchant System. The Transaction Server then processes purchases, initiates the fulfillment process, and provides a detailed transaction receipt to the shopper.

Promotional Support

The ability to offer specials is critical to merchants who want to stimulate sales and move merchandise. With the Netscape Merchant System, merchants can assign special pricing to selected products, either as a reduction in dollar amount or a percentage of purchase price. The Netscape Merchant System automatically deducts the discount from the order subtotal amount.

Instant Buy Option

Merchants also can provide shoppers with an Instant Buy button for some or all items, enabling them to skip checkout review. This provides added appeal for customers who already know the single item they want to purchase during their shopping excursion.

Unlimited Text, Audio, and Video

To create an engaging shopping experience for shoppers, merchants can integrate audio and video data into their product display pages using MLE templates. In addition to text and graphics, the Netscape Merchant System supports audio and video files that users can interact with, using external players.

Support for Fixed Attributes

Merchants can assign each product multiple attributes, such as color and size. Shoppers can select the attributes for products they wish to purchase (see Figure F.3).

Figure F.3   Shoppers select attributes such as color on the product page.

Sales and SKU-Level Pricing

Merchants can assign specific prices to SKUs as well as sales prices for products and SKUs. With this capability, merchants can price more effectively, turn over inventory more quickly, maximize revenues, and provide better service to their customers.

Integrated Relational Database

The Merchant Server stores all merchandise information in an integrated relational database, including products, prices, SKUs, and other attributes.

Support for Free-Form Attributes

Merchants can allow shoppers to specify free-form attributes for personalization, such as greeting card inscriptions or shirt monograms. The Netscape Merchant System operator defines an entry form template that shoppers fill out to supply these attributes for the selected product.

Selective Product Display

Merchants can opt to suppress generation of certain product pages to enhance Netscape Merchant System performance. For example, a bookstore might choose not to display product pages for textbooks, about which prospective buyers need little promotional information. Shoppers can still select items for purchase that don't appear on product pages by choosing them from a text-only list.

Transaction Server

The Transaction Server provides a full suite of services for transaction processing, including checkout, real-time credit card processing, order fulfillment, automated shipping and order delivery, and collection of information used for archiving and audit reporting. The Transaction Server comprises the following components.

Credit Card Processor

The Netscape Merchant System provides an Internet credit card processor. This module encrypts the shopper's credit card number using public-key encryption. Even if the transaction is intercepted in transit to or from

First Data Corporation (FDC), the card number cannot be read. The Transaction Server also supports the use of X.25 Package Assemble Disassembler (PAD) and leased lines for credit card authorization with FDC (see sidebar).

Credit Card Payment Support

The Netscape Credit Card Processor enables rapid deployment of open electronic commerce applications. It uses industry standards for networking and security to create a secure and reliable platform for Internet credit card processing. Because the Netscape Merchant System supports the Credit Card Processor, merchants need not incur costs associated with leased lines for credit card payment processing.

One side of the Credit Card Processor connects to a credit card Acquirer's internal systems, using the proprietary protocols. The other side connects to the Internet using ASN.1 and DER message formats. As a result of this innovative design, bank card Acquirers can gain an Internet presence with little or no impact on their existing process or strategy. The Acquirer's legacy investment is protected while its applications are made available over the Internet.

The credit card processing system in the Netscape Merchant System supports two types of credit card verification: by leased line or

Continued

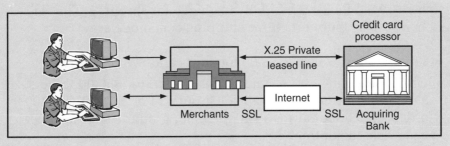

Figure F.4   Merchants communicate securely with Acquirers over the Internet instead of expensive leased lines.

over the Internet (see Figure F.4). The Internet connection option eventually will include built-in support for SET protocols, which provide a high degree of security for credit card transactions. SET prevents anyone other than the cardholder and acquiring bank from seeing the credit card number. Some credit card processors may reduce credit card processing fees for merchants who use SET because use of this protocol lowers risk.

The Credit Card Processor offers the following features:

- Point-of-sale (POS) terminal functions typically found at physical stores
- Support for transactions from multiple merchants—for example, in online malls
- Support for credit card number capture, authorization, sales, and card validity checks
- Automation of credit card batch and reconciliation processing

Secure communication is crucial for credit card payment transactions. Currently, the Netscape Merchant System uses Netscape's Secure Sockets Layer (SSL) to support secure communications.

Customizable Shipping Cost Calculations

Merchants need flexibility in how to charge for shipping. The Netscape Merchant System supports three shipping cost models:

- *Product*—for example, $5.00 for shirts and $7.00 for suits
- *Order subtotal*—for example, for $1.00 to $50.00 orders, $10.99 for airmail or $4.99 for ground. For $51.00 to $100 orders, $12.00 for airmail and $6.99 for ground. The customer can select the option.
- *Weight range*—for example, for 0- to 10-lb. orders, $10.00 for airmail and $4.99 for ground. For 11- to 20-lb. orders, $13.00 for airmail and $6.99 for ground.

Customizable Order Form

The Netscape Merchant System includes a highly flexible order form that merchants can customize to satisfy their branding and order-processing requirements. This form enables merchants to capture critical billing, shipping, and credit card information, and personalized messages for orders (see Figure F.5).

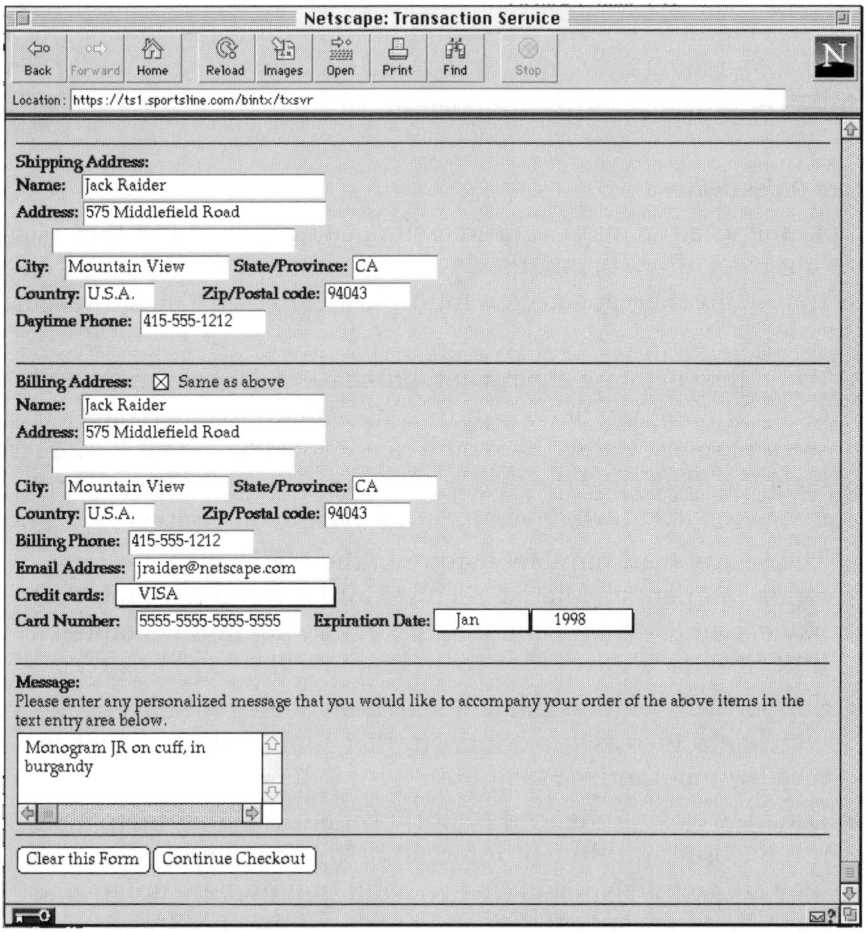

Figure F.5   Providing payment and shipping information.

Integrated Sales Tax Engine

Using TaxWare's Sales/Use Tax System engine, the Netscape Merchant System performs real-time sales tax calculations based on product codes, the merchant's business nexus (point of origin), and the zip code of the shopper's shipping address.

The engine also generates sales tax audit reports that the Netscape Merchant System delivers to merchants via secure E-mail. The site administrator can specify the auditing frequency for individual merchants that subscribe to receive sales tax audit reports, as well as for the state, city, and local jurisdictions where the merchant conducts business (see Figure F.6). TaxWare supplies monthly tax updates to the Netscape Merchant System sites so that merchants use the most current sales tax rates.

Secure Order Delivery

Storekeepers on the Internet need assurance that the orders they receive have not been altered maliciously or as a result of transmission errors. The Transaction Server employs multiple techniques to ensure security:

- When the customer checks out, purchase orders are encrypted at the Transaction Server for transmission to the merchant via secure E-mail. Using the secure mail program, the merchant's machine decrypts the order, creates an order report, and returns an acknowledgement to the Transaction Server.

- The secure mail implementation in the Merchant Server conforms to open standards: Secure Multipurpose Internet Mail Extensions (S/MIME) and Public Key Cryptography Standards (PKCS).

- Support for vendor-independent E-mail encryption enables merchants to reassure shoppers that their orders cannot be read by unauthorized people.

- Use of Privacy Enhanced Mail (PEM) ensures that merchants receive order fulfillment information for purchases as soon as they are completed, and that an audit trail of these orders and their delivery status is maintained within the Transaction Server.

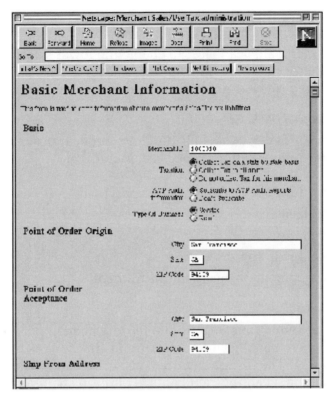

Figure F.6   Providing sales tax information.

◆ Use of digital envelope, digital signature, and certificate operations enables secure transmission of purchase order data between the Transaction Server and merchants. Digital certificates give each party assurance that the other party is who it claims to be and not an imposter.

◆ The use of digital signatures also ensures that messages are not altered in transit to and from the Netscape Merchant System host and merchant fulfillment houses.

Price Validation

When the shopper checks out, the Transaction Server validates the price stored in the shopping basket against the merchant's most current data.

The prices might differ—for example, if a special price goes into effect after the shopper deposits an item in the shopping basket. In the case of discrepancy, merchants can elect to charge the lower sales price.

Price validation also provides an extra level of security because it ensures that the price has not been altered in an unauthorized fashion.

Integrated Relational Database

The Transaction Server stores all purchase order transaction information in an integrated relational database, including:

- Credit card number, which can be encrypted
- Item purchased
- Item attributes
- Billing and ship-to information
- Acknowledgment of successful fulfillment

Sales Analysis

To maintain a competitive edge in the rapidly changing marketplace of the mid-90s, merchants need to detect trends in purchasing habits and respond quickly. The Transaction Server acts as a repository for purchase information, enabling merchants to perform analyses and respond rapidly by changing product mix or pricing.

Staging Server

The optional Staging Server software enables merchants to load and update product displays, pricing, and special offers for review before consumers see them. Like the Merchant Server, the Staging Server uses MLE for dynamic updates, generates new pages automatically, and supports store- or mallwide navigation and shopping basket capabilities.

The Staging Server is especially useful for on-line mall operators who want to allow merchants to remotely load, review, update, and approve product displays in a preproduction environment. When the merchant is satisfied with displays as they appear on the Staging Server, the merchant submits an approval form to the Netscape Merchant System operator, authorizing the transfer of the pages to the Merchant Server. The operator then invokes the Staging Server extraction utility program, which extracts the data, creates the product file, and securely delivers the approved product information via Privacy Enhanced Mail (PEM) to the Merchant Server production environment.

The system operator can create a script to run the extractor program automatically on a regular basis or invoke it manually.

Selecting a Hardware Configuration

The Merchant Server, Transaction Server, and Staging Server applications each require a dedicated machine (see Figure F.7). The Staging Server is optional, but provides a valuable preproduction environment for reviewing and updating store and product displays.

The hardware configuration required for the Merchant Server application depends on the expected number of hits. The configuration for the Transaction Server module depends on the expected number of users who will actually complete purchases. In general, the Merchant Server requires more memory and disk space because shoppers browse more than they buy.

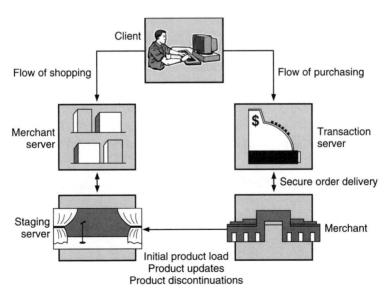

Figure F.7   Netscape Merchant System architecture.

For example, a merchant who sells high-priced items might expect many hits but just a few purchases. This merchant might deploy the Merchant Server application on a Sun SPARC-20 and the Transaction Server on a Sun SPARC-5.

In contrast, a merchant who sells commodity items might expect 250,000 hits a day on the Merchant Server and 8,000 hits a day on the Transaction Server, with 1,000 orders actually completed. This merchant might deploy the Merchant Server application on a Sun SPARC 1000-2 with 256MB of memory and 4GB of disk space and the Transaction Server on a Sun SPARC 20-2 with 64MB of memory and 2GB of disk space.

The Netscape Merchant System Staging Server is never accessed by users; it is used solely by merchants to review their storefront and product displays before shoppers see them. Therefore, this application can run on a system with less memory than the Merchant Server. However, the Staging Server must have as much disk space as the Merchant Server because it stores all storefront and product display content before it is transferred into the Merchant Server production environment.

Required Hardware

The following hardware is required:

- Sun SPARC workstation/SGI IRIX
- 64MB RAM per server; 128MB RAM recommended
- 500MB hard disk to accommodate Netscape Merchant System install, Transaction Server, Commerce Servers, SQL, and other components
- 200MB for Staging Server (optional)

Required Software

The following software is required:

- Solaris 2.4 operating system
- IRIX 5.3

CPU, Memory, and Disk Space Considerations

More powerful CPUs and more system memory are required in the following circumstances:

- Shoppers performing full-text searches for desired products
- Frequent use of CGI scripts for selecting attributes and items for purchase
- Frequent database access—for example, frequent updates to large product inventories

The total amount of required disk space depends on the number and size of the products in the Netscape Merchant System and the merchant's content update strategy. In general, 1.5GB of disk space on each Netscape Merchant System server should be adequate. Less disk space may be required if the merchant continually updates the same set of products rather than adding new ones with multiple SKUs and attributes.

If you have any questions, please visit Customer Service.

Corporate Sales (415) 937-2555
Personal Sales (415) 937-3777
Federal Sales (415) 937-3678
Web site: www.netscape.com.

THE MICROSOFT MERCHANT SYSTEM

The Microsoft Merchant technology includes an integrated set of components that facilitate a comprehensive on-line merchandising environment. The architecture allows merchants to leverage their existing investments in information technology and to extend these systems to the Internet. Retailers can also use the capabilities provided with Microsoft Merchant to develop a distinct Internet selling presence. Merchant technology is designed to address the needs of electronic retailers. Specifically, merchants have compelling security and selling requirements for conducting commerce across the Internet. Secure Internet retailing requires a platform that:

- Provides robust transactional and channel security
- Supports multiple forms of payment and makes the entire payment process easy to use for consumers
- Integrates with the emerging Internet commerce infrastructure of certificate authorities and payment gateways

Marketing over the Internet requires technology that:

- Makes setup of stores easy
- Provides rich merchandising and store management functionality

♦ Enables both customization and integration with existing systems

♦ Enables a rich consumer shopping experience

Microsoft Merchant is a set of technologies designed to provide these key ingredients.

Microsoft's Electronic Retailing Solution

The mission of Microsoft Merchant is to offer an easy-to-use, flexible, and cost-effective Internet retailing solution for merchants. As components of this solution, Merchant provides:

♦ Applications for setting up, managing, and stocking an on-line store

♦ Tools for tracking and managing consumer profile data, to facilitate creation of a custom shopping environment for the consumer

♦ Services for retailing functions such as product location, inventory checking, and order management

♦ A shopping application that is integrated with popular browsers such as Microsoft Internet Explorer and that provides a fast, easy, and secure shopping experience

♦ A flexible, standards-based architecture that can be integrated with alternative technologies

♦ Support for a single merchant or for multiple merchants (for example, when hosted by a public network operator, an Internet service provider (ISP), or an on-line mall)

Microsoft Merchant consists of three major components: the Merchant Workbench, the Merchant Server, and the shopping client (see Figure G.1):

♦ *Merchant Workbench.* This component provides a set of tools and applications that are designed to assist merchants in

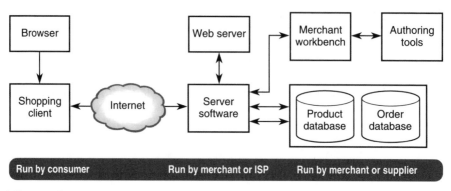

Figure G.1

setting up and managing on-line stores, in viewing and report-ing order data, and in administering the core services of the Merchant Server. The Merchant Workbench operates over HTTP for presenting information to the Merchant Server.

◆ *Merchant Server.* This component provides a high-performance, scalable server architecture supporting the core and supple-mental services that run on server computers at the merchant's (or other host's) location. Administered through the Merchant Workbench interface, functionality on the Merchant Server connects consumers to the merchant's product information, receives orders, and optionally provides a point of integration with other merchant-specific systems such as payment and order processing systems.

◆ *Shopping Client.* This component, designed to work with industry-leading browsers, manages product gathering across shopping sessions on the consumer's computer and provides secure local storage of credit card information as well as storage of the consumer's shopping history. Although in an ideal configuration (for example, when used with Internet Explorer), the shopping application runs on a consumer's computer, in an alternate configuration, a shopping applica-tion called the Proxy Basket can be hosted by the Merchant Server.

Using the Merchant Workbench

For a better understanding of how the Merchant Workbench component makes it quick and easy to establish an on-line store, consider the following scenario. Assume that a merchant has just purchased Microsoft Merchant and has installed it on the computer running the merchant's Web server, the Microsoft Internet Information Server. The following diagram illustrates how each member of the merchant's organization might use the tools of the Merchant Workbench.

Store Designers	Buyers	Stock Managers	Merchandisers
Use the authoring tools to design page templates and product categories (such as departments within the store).	Load data including images and descriptions for all products that will be offered for sale in the on-line store.	Enter inventory levels for each product.	Set prices for products, including discounts, promotions, and cross-selling activities.

Merchant staff members test the store site by placing it in a staging area where they can simulate shopping and identify and correct problems before "going live."

Shopping Cycle at a Glance

The following figure shows the end-to-end electronic retail-interaction platform provided by Microsoft Merchant. Notice that the flow of processes (indicated by arrows numbered 1, 2, and so on) corresponds to the sequence of steps in the following list.

1. Using the Merchant Workbench, the merchant sets up an on-line store on the merchant's Web server. (If the merchant uses a third-party aggregator such as an ISP to host the merchant's site in an on-line mall, the aggregator handles store setup.)

2. The merchant registers with the acquiring bank and gets a Secure Electronic Transactions (SET) certificate for each payment method that is accepted (for example, VISA and American Express cards).

3. The customer downloads the client-side shopper. This can be done from the merchant Web site or, as illustrated in Figure G.2, from the Microsoft World Wide Web site.

4. The customer registers each credit card and gets an SET certificate for each card that is accepted with the issuing bank's server.

5. Using a Web browser, the customer views the merchant's Web pages and places items in the shopping basket. If the consumer's connection to the merchant Web site is lost prior to placing the order, the shopping client retains the state of shop-

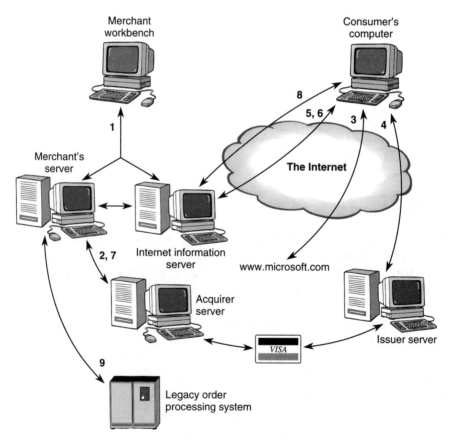

Figure G.2

ping—that is, keeps a record of items collected in the basket and stores related data, making it easy for the consumer to complete the purchase transaction when the connection is restored.

6. The customer clicks the Ready to Pay button. This creates a combined order description/payment instruction that is sent to the merchant's server.

7. The payment instruction is sent to the acquirer for authorization and approval via the existing card brand network.

8. The Merchant Server sends to the shopping application a confirmation of the order (with a tracking number assigned to the order).

9. The Merchant Server also forwards the order description to the appropriate legacy systems for payment and order processing.

Merchant Workbench Features

The Merchant Workbench is a set of tools for establishing and maintaining an effective merchandising presence on the World Wide Web and for managing the Merchant Server functionality that supports a merchant's on-line business. The tools of the Merchant Workbench support loading data, installing and administering the modules that run on the Merchant Server, and dynamically managing the Merchant Server environment. The extensible architecture of the Merchant Workbench also offers merchants flexibility in their choice of tools, enabling them to "plug in" alternate tools as needed. The following is a summary of the Merchant Workbench functions to be shipped with Microsoft Merchant:

- ◆ *Service configuration and management.* Tools for configuring and administering the software that supports tax calculation, shipping and handling, and address verification for orders. This software runs on the Merchant Server and can support one or more merchants.

- ◆ *On-line catalog management.* Tools for laying out the products and categories (shelves, departments, and so on) of an on-line store. With these tools, store designers can create product pages on the fly from information in a product database, with search capabilities and support for varied product attributes such as sizes, colors, styles, and so on. A staging capability is also provided, to enable merchants to test a new store configuration without altering operations of the production store.

◆ *Order management.* Tools for viewing orders and editing the status of orders as the orders pass through the merchant's processing channels.

◆ *Merchant information management.* Tools for setting up merchant-specific information (such as logos or accepted payment methods) and establishing security that limits user access to order data (for example, based on the user's job responsibility).

◆ *Traffic analysis.* Tools for reporting on consumer browsing and buying behavior on the merchant Web site. Merchants can obtain immediate information about sales, traffic, and consumers, such as the most visited departments or product pages.

Merchant Server Features

The Merchant Server is a comprehensive set of services used throughout the Merchant system for conducting electronic retailing. Designed for high performance and scalability, the Merchant Server runs on the robust Windows NT Server operating system. Its services, usable either right out of the box or in conjunction with third-party solutions, support end-to-end retailing operations ranging from product browsing on the client side, to order processing and financial transactions on the server side, and store or catalog management through the Merchant Workbench.

The Merchant Server may be operated by a single merchant or by a third-party host, such as an Internet service provider (ISP). In this case, the host aggregator can integrate the Merchant Server to back-end and existing systems such as payment processing and billing systems or order processing systems operated by the aggregator. Figure G.3 shows the core services and other server components.

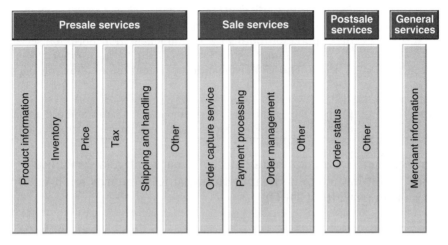

Figure G.3

For simplicity, think of the services supplied by the Merchant Server as relating to three different sequences of retailing events: presale, sale, and postsale. Presale services focus on content publishing and creation of orders. Sale services constitute much of the work of the Merchant Server: order processing (with taxing, shipping and handling, and pricing calculations), order routing, and so on. Postsale services include confirming orders and responding to client-generated requests for order status. General services consist of a merchant information service that provides merchant names and addresses, logos, the merchant's accepted payment types, and so on. The following table lists services running on the Merchant Server:

Summary of Merchant Server Functionality

Presale services	Supplies descriptive and cross-reference product information on products offered for sale, which is used for presenting products in the shopping basket. Checks the availability of the items ordered and reports whether they are in stock, backordered, and so on. Determines prices for the items ordered, as applicable for the consumer making the purchase, applying member discounts or other factors as appropriate. Calculates the tax due on items ordered. Calculates the cost of shipping and handling for the items ordered.

Sale services	Separates incoming customer orders received from the shopping client into a payment instruction and an order (includes description for routing by its component Transportation service, the Transaction Routing Service) (TRS), to the appropriate services. The TRS also handles payment information routing and tracking.
Postal services	Enables the consumer to check on account status and order status after a purchase. Provides support for other customer service.

The Merchant Server communicates with back end and systems already in place in the merchant's organization, using standards such as Open Database Connectivity (ODBC).

Shopping from a Consumer's Perspective

To understand how consumers might use the Merchant shopping client, consider the following Internet shopping scenario. A consumer named Joe, an occasional "net surfer" and die-hard baseball fan, decides to buy a baseball glove on the Internet so he doesn't miss an inning of tonight's televised game. After starting his computer and downloading the Merchant shopping client from the Microsoft Web page, Joe uses his browser to connect to the Clocktower Sporting Goods Web site.

In Clocktower's store "lobby" Joe clicks the Go Shopping button and browses the store by the type of sport ("Baseball," of course) until he reaches the baseball glove "shelf." Joe views the images and descriptions of the gloves on the shelf and picks the one he wants by clicking the Add to Basket button on the Web page. (The basket is a component of the shopping client that stores items that Joe has collected for purchase.) The next page displayed (a cross-sell message and a link to the shoe "aisle") reminds Joe that he needs a new pair of cleats, so he clicks the displayed link to the shoe aisle. If Joe finds a pair he likes, he can add it to the shopping basket that contains the glove; if not, Joe can shop at a different merchant before placing another item in the basket.

When he has finished shopping, Joe clicks the View Basket button on the toolbar of the Web page to view the goods he has selected and their line-item details, such as description, picture, quantity selected, unit price, and total price (according to whatever attributes the merchant has defined for the display).

Joe likes what he sees, so he clicks Pay Now on the toolbar of the Web page. An Invoice/Payment page is displayed, showing a detailed break-down of quantity, price, order-level tax, shipping and handling charges, and total order charge. The page looks similar to the checkout receipt from a retail store. Joe reviews this page as a final step before making payment on his order.

Near the bottom of the Invoice/Payment page, Joe's credit cards and payment types are displayed, stacked in a three-dimensional layout with his favorite card (the default card) at the front. Joe has already entered his credit card information (this information is stored securely on his computer), so unless he wants to pick a different card from the stack, all Joe has to do to finish his order is enter the password for the credit card and click the Submit Order button.

The shopping client then bundles the order information, gathers and encrypts the payment information, and sends the order to the mer-chant. When the credit card payment is authorized and the order is pro-cessed on the merchant end, Joe receives an order confirmation that is put into his Order History, stored on his computer. If Joe's credit card is rejected, the shopping client presents a page for submitting the order again using a different card. All data, such as addresses, payment methods, and order history, is stored by the shopping client and easily edited by Joe.

Overview of Shopping Client Features

The Merchant shopping client provides a rich, easy-to-use, and secure shopping experience that allows consumers to customize future shop-ping based on past activity, to search the merchant's on-line store for products based on any criteria, and to ensure the privacy of their confi-dential payment information through encryption technology.

To deliver automated customized shopping, the shopping client uses a unique scripting language. Running interactive scripts developed in this language and drawing on the consumer's purchasing history and demographics (accessed through the Merchant Workbench), the shop-ping client simulates a personal shopping assistant who leads the con-sumer to items of possible interest.

In addition, for fast and easy location of products from the merchant's on-line store, the shopping client enables consumers to search a high-performance database management system on the Merchant Server for items they couldn't find while browsing. Figure G.4 shows the architectural elements of the Merchant shopping client.

The following are descriptions of shopping client features.

- *Browser.* Although not built into the client, a browser is required to invoke the client components. The shopping client is browser-independent and can be integrated with advanced Web technologies such as ActiveX and Java.

- *Basket.* The Basket manages and displays the items selected for purchase, and provides the View Basket, Add to Basket, Delete from Basket, and Pay Now functions.

- *Storage.* The shopping client's persistent storage enables consumers to interrupt the shopping process and store items in the Basket storage for an extended amount of time without having to reselect the items when they resume shopping.

- *Address and payment information management.* With these features, consumers can use default shipping addresses and address "nicknames," as well as default payment types, payment type "nicknames," and merchant-specific payment types, eliminating the need to enter repetitive information for each transaction.

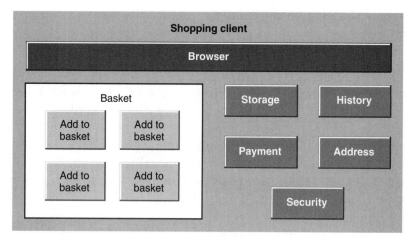

Figure G.4

◆ *History.* The Order History feature shows the consumer all purchases made with the shopping client. Consumers can sort and view information such as merchant, item description, amount, and order status.

◆ *Security.* The shopping client supports Secure Electronic Transactions (SET) and clear-text encryption. The SET protocol, developed jointly by Microsoft, VISA International, and other industry leaders, provides a comprehensive, universal, and secure bank card payment protocol for use by card members, merchants, and banks. Microsoft's implementation of SET will allow card issuers to enable all parties in the transaction to authenticate buyers and sellers of goods and services, and will ensure that merchants conducting Internet commerce can route information directly to the card issuer.

Operating Environments

The Merchant Workbench has the same platform requirements as the Shopping Client, with the additional requirement of Internet Explorer version 3.0 or later. The Merchant Workbench can run on its own computer, or on the Merchant Server. Remote administration is supported via an HTTP connection.

The Merchant Server runs on one or more Windows NT–based servers and can run in conjunction with, and on the same computer as the Merchant Workbench, the Microsoft Internet InformationServer, and other Microsoft BackOffice servers. With support for SQL and ODBC, the Merchant Server is database-independent.

The shopping client supports customers who choose to shop from various platforms, as described in the following list:

◆ Windows 95 operating system

◆ Windows NT Workstation operating system, version 4.0 and later

◆ Windows operating system version 3.1

◆ Apple Macintosh

◆ UNIX

For computers running Windows 95 and Windows NT, the shopping client runs with the shell browser update (currently code-named "Nashville") and takes advantage of ActiveX technology.

For computers running Windows 3.1 and for other Win16-based platforms, the Shopping Basket is hosted on the Merchant Server; there is no shopping client resident on the consumer's computer. This is also true for Apple Macintosh and UNIX installations.

BackOffice and Merchant: An Integrated Solution

Businesses of all types need a comprehensive set of system services that work together, including:

◆ Robust and scalable databases to manage information

◆ A reliable messaging system for communication, collaboration, and information sharing

◆ A powerful platform for publishing on the Internet and intranets

◆ Secure tools for access to host applications and data

◆ A complete solution for managing network systems

◆ A network foundation that provides easy and fast access to files and printers

Instead of a mix-and-match approach to meet these needs, the BackOffice family of products provides an integrated suite of server products. And, although designed from the ground up to work together, the BackOffice server suite supports the desire for choice by allowing integration with alternate or existing technologies.

For features and function, Merchant relies on several components of the BackOffice server suite including the following:

◆ Microsoft Windows NT Server, a multipurpose operating system that provides connectivity, reliability, fast file and print services, as well as superior application and communication services and administrative tools.

- ◆ Microsoft Internet Information Server, a fast, powerful, easy-to-manage platform for publishing on the Internet and intranets and the only World Wide Web server that is integrated with Windows NT Server.
- ◆ Microsoft SQL Server, a scalable, high-performance database management system for managing and storing data, designed specifically for distributed client/server computing. Although optimized for use with Microsoft Merchant and the BackOffice server suite, an alternative database management system can be substituted, according to the merchant's preference.

The BackOffice server suite also includes Microsoft Exchange Server for electronic-mail messaging and group scheduling, Microsoft Systems Management Server for managing networked PCs, and Microsoft SNA Server for reliably connecting personal computers and servers with IBM mainframes and AS/400 computers.

Support Services and a network of authorized support partners offer 24-hour, 7-day product support plus on-site multivendor systems integration with expertise in the operations of businesses in specific industries or professions.

Conclusion

Integrated with Microsoft core technologies such as Windows NT Server, SQL Server, and ActiveX, Microsoft Merchant provides a cost-effective, state-of-the-art electronic retailing solution for merchants. In addition, because Merchant is based on Microsoft technologies, merchants can be assured that there will be trained Microsoft Solution Providers available to support the product.

Merchant technology is scheduled to be commercially available by the end of 1996. For additional information regarding Merchant and other Microsoft Internet technologies, visit the Microsoft Web page at: http://www.microsoft.com. To contact the Microsoft Merchant team, send e-mail to: merchsvr@microsoft.com.

OR IMPLIED, INCLUDING WITHOUT LIMITATION ANY IMPLIED WARRANTIES OF MERCHANTABILITY, FITNESS FOR A PARTICULAR PURPOSE OR NON-INFRINGEMENT. SOME JURISDICTIONS DO NOT ALLOW THE EXCLUSION OF IMPLIED WARRANTIES, SO THE ABOVE EXCLUSION MAY NOT APPLY TO YOU.

LIMITATION OF LIABILITY.   IN NO EVENT SHALL MICROSOFT CORPORATION BE LIABLE FOR ANY SPECIAL, INDIRECT OR CONSEQUENTIAL DAMAGES, WHETHER IN AN ACTION OF CONTRACT, NEGLIGENCE OR OTHER TORTIOUS ACTION, ARISING OUT OF OR IN CONNECTION WITH THE USE OF OR INABILITY TO USE THE MATERIAL CONTAINED HEREIN.

ERRORS/UPDATES.   THE MATERIAL CONTAINED HEREIN MAY INCLUDE TECHNICAL INACCURACIES OR TYPOGRAPHICAL ERRORS. MICROSOFT CORPORATION MAY MAKE IMPROVEMENTS AND/OR CHANGES TO THE MATERIAL WHERE PUBLICLY AVAILABLE, AT ANY TIME, WHICH IMPROVEMENTS AND/OR CHANGES MAY NOT BE REFLECTED HEREIN, FOR THE MOST CURRENT EDITION OF THIS ARTICLE GO TO http://www.microsoft.com

NOTES

Chapter 1

1. *The New York Times,* Cyber Times, May 4, 1996.
2. Ibid., Philip Wolf, based in Sherman, Conn.

Chapter 2

1. "E-Commerce Emerges," *Interactive Week,* June 17, 1996.

Chapter 3

1. Peter Drucker says that new technologies are adopted when they increase a customer-pleasing feature tenfold. Examples would be to reduce the cost of an item to ¹⁄₁₀ of the original cost or increase speed of service ten times.

Chapter 5

1. Quoted in Vince Emery, op. cit., p. 244.
2. *Report on Electronic Commerce,* April 30, 1996. You can contact Interactive Imaginations at (212) 598-9455.
3. *Report on Electronic Commerce,* April 30, 1996. You can contact Freeloader at (202) 686-0600.
4. *Report on Electronic Commerce,* April 30, 1996. You can contact Juno at (212) 478-0800.
5. *Report on Electronic Commerce,* April 30, 1996. You can contact FreeMark at (617) 492-6600.
6. *The Wall Street Journal,* May 16, 1996, p. 1.

7. *Report on Electronic Commerce,* April 30, 1996. You can contact Greet Street at (415) 536-1870.

Chapter 6

1. Example used by permission from Leslie Lundquist and Dan Lynch, *Digital Money: The New Era of Internet Commerce* (New York: John Wiley and Sons, 1996).

Chapter 8

1. Reuters, April 29, 1996.

REFERENCES

Research References and Sources

Alex Brown & Associates. 1995.

America Online Subscriber Study. 1995.

CyberPulse Research and Citicorp. *On-line Shopping Behavioral Study.* 1994–1996.

Find/SVP American Internet User Survey. 1995.

Forrester Research On-line Report. 1995–1996.

GVU4/Nielsen Internet Survey (Georgia Tech Valuance Study #4). 1995.

Hambrecht & Quist Research. 1995, 1996.

International Data Corp. 1995.

I-Traffic, Inc., *Traffic Research.com.* 1996.

Jupiter Communications. *Jupiter/Yahoo! User Profile Study.* 1995–1996.

Killen & Associates Research. 1995.

MasterCard/National Retail Federation Web Survey. 1995.

Mecklermedia. *Internet World Subscriber Study.* December 1995.

Morgan Stanley Intrenet Research Report. 1995.

NewsLink Research. 1996.

Nielsen New Media. *CommerceNet/Nielsen Internet Research Report.* 1995.

O'Reilly & Associates Research, 1994, 1995.

SIMBA Research. *Electronic Marketplace Report.* December 1995.

Survey.Net. *Internet Shopping Habits Survey.* July 1995.

WebTrack Advertising Report. 1995.

Yankee Group Research. 1995.

Recommended Reading

The following articles and books contain additional background material. Readers are encouraged to consult these references for more information.

Bellare, M., and P. Rogaway. *Optimal Assymmetric Encryption.* San Diego: Eurocrypt 94, 1994. (http://www.cse.ucsd.edu/users/mihir/papers/oae.ps.gz)

BSAFE 2.1. RSA Data Security, Inc., 1994. (http://www.rsa.com/rsa/prodspec/bsafe/rsa_bsaf.htm)

Data Encryption Standard. Federal Information Processing Standards Publication 46, 1977.

Emery, Vince. *How to Grow Your Business on the Internet.* Coriolis Group Books, 1995.

Fahn, Paul. *Answers to Frequently Asked Questions about Today's Cryptography.* RSA Laboratories, Redwood City, CA: 1993. (http://www.rsa.com/rsalabs/faq/)

Graham, Ian S. *HTML Sourcebook.* New York: John Wiley & Sons, 1995.

ITU Rec. X.509 (1993) / ISO/IEC 9594-8: 1995, including Draft Amendment 1: Certificate Extensions (Version 3 certificate).

Kaliski, Jr., Burton S. *An Overview of the PKCS Standards.* RSA Laboratories, 1993. (http://www.rsa.com/pub/pkcs/doc/ or http://www.rsa.com/pub/pkcs/ps/)

Public-Key Cryptography Standards (PKCS). RSA Data Security, Inc., Version 1.5, revised Nov. 1, 1993.

Schneier, Bruce. *Applied Cryptography,* 2d ed., New York: John Wiley & Sons, 1996.

Wiggins, Richard W. *The Internet for Everyone: A Guide for Users and Providers.* New York: McGraw-Hill, 1995.

INDEX